Marina Carr

Brought up in County Offaly, a graduate of University College Dublin, Marina Carr has written extensively for the theatre. She has taught at Villanova, Princeton and currently at Trinity College. Awards include the Susan Smith Blackburn Prize, the Macaulay Fellowship and the E. M. Forster Prize from the American Academy of Arts and Letters. She lives in Kerry with her husband and four children.

MARINA CARR

Plays Two

On Raftery's Hill
Ariel
Woman and Scarecrow
The Cordelia Dream
Marble

Introduced by
the author

faber and faber

This collection first published in 2009
by Faber and Faber Ltd
74–77 Great Russell Street, London WC1B 3DA

Typeset by Country Setting, Kingsdown, Kent CT14 8ES
Printed in England by CPI Bookmarque, Croyon, Surrey

A CIP record for this book is available from the British Library

ISBN 978-0-571-24803-2

For Dermot, William,
Daniel, Rosa, Juliette

Contents

Introduction

Who knows what goes on in a writer's addled head when they sit down to write a play? I certainly don't. Or if I did, I've forgotten. What I remember most about these plays was I was either pregnant, breastfeeding or about to be pregnant again.

On Raftery's Hill was completed as I was expecting my second child. I remember sitting on the floor of a room in Trinity College with four drafts of the play in four unwieldy piles around me and wondering how in the name of God can I put shape on this thing. I had been working on it for a couple of years alongside other plays, but the final version was eluding me. And then gradually it dawned on me that the problem was one of location. If I cut back the three locations of the play to just one, maybe it might work. I did and it did.

Ariel was a mountain to climb. It was a fourteen-draft monster. At one point it was over two hundred pages. At another it was down to twenty. It was loosely based on the *Oresteia*, but I wanted to squash Aeschylus' three plays into one. The astounding cheek of me, which was of course pointed out. The writing of *Ariel* went to the wire, the rehearsal process was fraught, the director and I could not agree, the set designer went AWOL, the actors could not be heard. Nevertheless I learnt a lot and nevertheless would probably do the same again.

The Cordelia Dream was written in five days in a cottage in Connemara. Yes, of course I was pregnant. I lit a fire, turned on Lyric FM, locked the doors and wrote into the night. I had five days before my husband arrived with our sons, five days with no one screaming for marshmallows. I had to have something to show for it. It came quickly and for better or worse I have not tampered with it since. Its form is taken from Act Three of *Lear*, one of the greatest acts ever written.

The first draft of *Woman and Scarecrow* was written in Paris, at the old Irish College, now the Centre Culturel Irlandais. I had escaped my children again, this time for two weeks. One night in the courtyard, as I wrote, an owl watched me from under a tree. She was so curious as to what I was doing. Eventually I told her 'I'm writing a play.' Then I smiled at her. I may be assuming too much but I think she was happy for me. She was great company anyway.

Marble was a pure gift. I got the story from Fiona Shaw one hot summer's night in London over a mackerel dinner. Fiona Shaw got the story from Ted Hughes, who got it from an Icelandic poet, who probably got it from an Eskimo, who got it from a seal, who got it from a wandering meteorite . . .

My fourth child had come safely into the world. I was hungry to get back to work and this gift of a play comes from nowhere, everywhere. Sometimes it is a great privilege to write.

Marina Carr
June 2009

ON RAFTERY'S HILL

On **Raftery's Hill** was first performed as a Druid Theatre
Company/Royal Court Theatre co-production at the
Town Hall Theatre, Galway on 9 May 2000, and
subsequently at the Royal Court Jerwood Theatre
Downstairs, London, on 29 June 2000. The cast was
as follows:

Sorrel Raftery Mary Murray
Ded Raftery Michael Tierney
Dinah Raftery Cara Kelly
Shalome Raftery Valerie Lilley
Red Raftery Tom Hickey
Isaac Dunn Kieran Ahern
Dara Mood Keith McErlean

Director Garry Hynes
Designer Tony Walton
Lighting Designer Richard Pilbrow
Sound Designer Rich Walsh
Composer Paddy Cuneen

Characters

Red Raftery

Dinah Raftery

Sorrel Raftery

Ded Raftery

Shalome Raftery

Dara Mood

Isaac Dunn

Setting

The kitchen of the Raftery household:
table, chairs, stairs, landing

Door stage right leads to the yard

Door stage left leads to the pantry

Act One

*Lights up on Sorrel, standing at door to the yard,
listening to Ded's fiddle playing.*

Sorrel That's beauhiful Ded, ya make thah up yourself?

Ded (*music stops, off*) Aye, came to me in the cornfield
last nigh.

Sorrel Dinah wants to know will ya have your dinner in
the cowshed or will ya come in?

Ded Where's Daddy?

Sorrel Ya know righ well he's gone huntin.

Ded Just checkin he didn't slide back in like a geenie.

Sorrel Come on in Ded, c'mon.

Ded Ya sure there's ne'er a sign of him?

Sorrel Tould ya.

Ded Alrigh I'm comin so.

Sorrel A' ya?

Ded I'm near at the duur.

Sorrel Would ya come if ya're comin, swear ya were a
debutante in the high season.

*Enter Ded, a man in his mid-thirties, big-shouldered,
long-haired, bearded, filthy; cowdung all over his
clothes.*

Ded Quick give us the dinner and give us a buh (*a cigarette*). G'wan, give us three.

Sorrel lights one for him. He stands there shaking, smoking nervously, shuffling in his wellingtons. He teeters, he blinks, he starts, a huge man, beaten to the scut.

Sorrel Dinah bring in hees dinner before he runs off again. There's all straw in your hair, Ded. (*Begins picking it out.*)

Ded (*flailing wildly*) Would ya lave me head alone. Can't abide anywan pawin me head.

Enter Dinah, puts the dinner on the table.

Missus, if you think I'm atin me dinner off a the table. (*Voice rising in panic.*) Supposin he came clackin the yard, I'd choke wud the frigh.

Dinah Humans ates their dinner off of a table, Ded. Animals ates ud off a the fluur and slapes in sheds. (*Handing the dinner to him.*) A' ya an animal a' ya?

Ded Thanks.

Shoves the dinner into his mouth, with an eye on the door and an ear cocked like a frightened bird. He manages to smoke at the same time. Dinah watches him.

Dinah God gimme patience.

Sorrel Dinah lave him, ya'll frighten him.

Dinah And whah abouh him frightenin us? You're like somewan ouha the Stone Age, Ded.

Ded Am I?

Dinah I mane when's the last time ya looked in a mirror?

8

Ded You're no oil paintin yourself.

A groan from upstairs. Ded jumps, terrified.

What's thah? Is thah him?

Sorrel Only Granny moanin in her slape.

Dinah D'ya want some a' Daddy's whiskey? Calm ya down.

Ded D'yees have any swates? I've enough a thah (*dinner*).

He holds out the plate for one of them to take, edges towards the door.

I'll have me bag a swates now . . . when yees have a minuhe.

Sorrel (*gives him sweets and cigarettes*) Dara brung ya them yesterday and there's ten Woodbine and matches.

Ded But Daddy says no smokin in the shed.

Sorrel Daddy doesn't have to know everythin.

Ded Rules is rules. (*Leaves cigarettes.*) I'll go back to the shed now.

Dinah (*coming towards him with a dishcloth*) Here, wipe your face and hands.

He does.

(*Watching him.*) I allas knew wan of us wouldn't make ud, Ded, allas knew thah. Lots thought ud'd be me. Who'd a' ever thought ud'd be you, Daddy's golden biy and Mother's darlin . . . what d'ya want for your dinner tomorra?

Ded Jelly and custard.

Dinah Christ. (*And exit Dinah to the pantry.*)

9

Ded What's wrong a' her apart from everythin?

Sorrel She's only barkin, don't mind her.

Ded Ya want a calf nuh?

Sorrel Alrigh. (*Takes a few.*)

Ded Lovely aren't they?

Sorrel When're ya goin to come back and live in the house?

Ded When Daddy dies. I behher get back to the cattle.

And exit Ded as Shalome enters across the landing and down the stairs. She wears a nightdress, a straw hat and struggles with a suitcase and an armful of flowers. She is well spoken and a bit gone in her mind but with flashes of accidental lucidity.

Shalome Goodbye Raftery's Hill. I shall not miss you. (*Strews flowers grandly over landing, stairs, kitchen below.*) Goodbye disgusting old kitchen and filthy old stairs. I shall never climb you again. Never. Goodbye Slieve Blooms, goodbye Mohia Lane, Black Lion, Ruedeskank, Croggan, Mucklagh. How could anyone be happy in a place called Mucklagh? Sorrel my darling, goodbye.

Sorrel On your travels, Granny?

Shalome I'm going back to Kinnegar and to Daddy. Goodbye.

Sorrel Bye, Granny, safe journey.

Shalome (*struggles with suitcase*) Sorrel, could you help me please?

Sorrel I'll walk ya to the end a' the lane and then I'm bringin ya back to bed alrigh?

Shalome Wasn't it an awful pity your mother had to die?

Sorrel Never knew her granny and so never missed her.

Shalome She was a lady. When she first came to the Hill we had musical evenings, card parties, dancing, always dancing, sandwiches and port wine and fruitcake all laid out in the parlour. But your father put a stop to all of that. I don't know why it is, Sorrel, but he never liked to see people enjoy themselves, a big smuth on him when everyone else was happy. Daddy was the same. (*Going out the door.*) I'll be away now. Wish me luck.

Dinah (*entering*) Get back up them stairs, you.

Shalome I'm never sleeping in this house again.

Dinah That's three times I'm after puttin ya down tonigh.

Shalome And I want you all to know I never loved Old Raftery. It was all just one terrible mistake.

Dinah A' ya hungry, Granny? Ya allas go wanderin when you're hungry.

Shalome And do you know what Daddy said when he heard I'd married Brian Raftery?

Dinah 'I'd liefer see your white body floatin down the Shannon than for you to marry Brian Raftery.'

Shalome Oh he was master of the vicious barb, Daddy. Even his compliments had a sting. And he never came to see me after, or spoke to me, returned all my letters, don't you think that was a little? . . . a little?

Sorrel I do, Granny, I do.

Shalome No matter, I'll seek him out tonight in Kinnegar and make him account for his actions. Goodbye all. (*Strews the last of the flowers grandly.*

Nearly out the door.) I shall send you a postcard from
Kinnegar and a long letter full of news and a bar of soap
for Ded so one of these days he can wash himself.

Dinah (*bars her way*) Bed! Where's the time for me, hah?

Shalome You manage time a plenty for your sly pursuits.
Now, young lady, out of my way before I give you an
ass's bite. I'm going home to Kinnegar, Lord shall I ever
get there?

Dinah Kinnegar, Kinnegar. Thah thick fah kip of a town.
Even the dogs apologise for comin from there. Come on,
Granny, till I warm the blue ouh a' them feeh or I'll have
to take a chainsaw to them. (*Puts her sitting, kneads her
legs.*) Sorrel, geh her a jammy scone. Jam soothers her.

Sorrel does.

Shalome I was going to Kinnegar, Dinah, and I forgot
something.

Dinah Did ya now, ya daft auld yoke ya.

Shalome When I lived in India and Mother was still
alive . . .

Dinah (*softly*) India, India. Kinnegar, Kinnegar. You're
like an auld record that's stuck in the groove.

Shalome Oh but the flowers, the colours and the cool air
that came down from the mountain at night. Once a
man with a gorilla came to our house and the gorilla
licked me all over as if I were its baby and the old man
told me about the language of gorillas, how they
encompassed the poetry of the sea . . . I didn't know
what he meant . . . still don't. Girls! Sorrel! Dinah! Do
you know what he meant?

Dinah We don't now, Granny.

Shalome And Mother came and saw me in the arms of
the gorilla and was terrified it would harm me and
shouts at the man and the gorilla runs down the
verandah with me gripped tightly in its armpit. Next
thing myself and the gorilla are looking down at Mother
and the old man, we're up an orange tree. We pick
orange blossom, and throw them down on Mother and
the old man. Nothing will make us come out of that
orange tree . . . it was a wonderful wonderful time.
I couldn't have been more than three, for Mother died
at the end of that summer and we left India and came
back to Kinnegar.

Dinah (*to Sorrel*) How d'ya think Ded is?

Sorrel Same as ever.

Dinah Ah ya blind young wan. He should be puh away.
Why should I be the wan has to watch him splinter into
a thousand pieces? You'll go off and marry Dara Mood
and I'll be left wud thah wan racin round like a March
hare in her nightdress and Ded atin hees dinner like a
dog at the duur and Daddy blusterin and butcherin all
the small helpless creatures a the fields. Even work
horses nades a day off every wance in a moon.

Shalome (*getting up, fixes her hat, gathers suitcase*) I'll
call to see you once I'm settled in Kinnegar.

Dinah Ah would ya geh up to bed.

Sorrel Leh her off, she never gets further than the end a
the lane.

Dinah Daddy'll go mad. Come on you till I settle ya
again. You're tired now, aren't ya?

Shalome But I wrote Daddy I'd be arriving this evening.

Dinah Just lie down for five minutes and then ya can
commence your travels.

Shalome (*allowing Dinah to lead her up the stairs*) All my life I've waited for my life to start, somehow it never has.

Dinah I know, I know, Granny.

Shalome Did I ever tell you that once a German officer asked for my hand in marriage? In the Gresham Hotel. I was only fourteen, was in my school uniform.

Dinah Imagine thah, now hould the banister.

Shalome I could be in Bavaria right now. I could've met Dracula. Instead here I am. This is the thanks I get for being a good girl, these old stairs, this old hill.

> *And they're gone by now.*
> *Enter Red Raftery with two shot hares around his neck. Gun. An imposing man in his sixties. He is followed by Isaac Dunn, sly, quirky, also in his sixties, also carrying a gun.*

Red I smell cowdung . . . Ded was here, wasn't he?

Isaac That's noh a cowdung smell, that's the stink a' all a' them dead sheep and cattle ya just lave maggotin the fields.

Red He was here wasn't he now?

Sorrel Aye, for hees dinner, we had to coax him in.

Red Knew I was righ. Sih in there Isaac and rest them bones. Sorrel, whiskey. (*Flings the hares at her.*) And ya may gut them, young wan.

Sorrel I will noh. No wan ever tell ya ud's bad luck to shooh a hare, not to mind two?

Red Auld wives' tales. Skin them now young wan and gut them. I want hare's soup for me breakfast.

Isaac And he went into the lair after them and strangled the leverets. Seven little babbys all huddled in a ball. Ya don't hunt fair, Red.

Red They've the land ruined.

Isaac Ud's not the hares has the land ruined and you wud a stinkin carcass in every field. You'll turn this beauhiful farm into an abattoir.

Red (*pours two large whiskies, slams one beside Isaac*) Would ya drink thah and stop bendin me ear. Dinah? Where's Dinah?

Sorrel Settlin Granny.

Red Serve up the dinner, Sorrel, there's a girl.

Sorrel goes to the pantry to get the dinner.

Isaac (*after her*) Aren't ya all grown up, Sorrel, and I member I used thrun ya over me back.

Red None bar Dara Mood may lay a hand on her now.

Sorrel (*coming on with one plate*) There's only wan plahe in the cooker, may divide ud ouh between yees.

Red I tould Dinah Isaac'd be atin here tonigh. (*Shouts up.*) Dinah!

Dinah (*coming down*) Would ya kape ud down, Daddy. I've just goh her to slape.

Red Where's Isaac's dinner, you?

Dinah Ud's there in front a' him.

Red Whah? . . . Then where's mine?

Dinah I fed ud to the pigs. I forgoh Isaac was comin, alrigh, went clane ouh a me mind.

Red (*knocks on her head*) What's in there? Wool? Friggin moths.

Dinah I forgoh, okay!

Red What's wrong a' yees, women?

Isaac Lave ud, Red, sure I'm noh even hungry.

Red You want to disgrace me! Thah's what you want! Ya want word goin round thah Raftery kapes a sparse house, ya want me to have no company bar you.

Dinah Ah, would ya shuh up you're givin me a migraine.

Red Donten you talk to me like thah, ya lazy rip ya, wud your skinny arms and your lunatic drames a somewan takin ya off a this Hill. I wouldn't use ya for silage.

Dinah I'm noh listenin to your pisined pulp. (*And exit Dinah up the stairs.*)

Red Come back here, you!

Isaac Christ almighy can't ya lave the girl alone?

Red Girl! She's nearly forty. (*Pushes plate to Isaac.*) You ate thah, I've no stomach after thah wan. (*To Sorrel.*) Whah're you lookin ah, young wan?

Sorrel Nothin.

Red Ya want a whiskey?

Sorrel Alrigh.

Red Then get yourself a glass and stop gawkin ah me.

Sorrel goes to get a glass, sound of Ded's fiddle.

Isaac And there's Ded on hees fiddle. The lad can play, Red.

Red (*listens a minute*) So could hees mother . . . Me only son Isaac, me only son is a halfwih who lives in a cowshed.

Isaac Ud's noh righ spakin abouh your own like thah.

Red Any other father'd have him in an asylum. Not me though, whah am I to do wud the farm, Isaac? Three hundred acre a the finest land this side a the Shannon and west a the Pale. And me only son and heir can't tell nigh from day, oak from ash, he'd milk a bull and drink ud in his tay and never know the differ. And I swear I seen him talkin to the corn, kissin ud and carressin ud as if ud were a golden wench swayin in the sun.

A knock on the door.

Come in.

Enter Dara Mood, a young man in his twenties.

Well if ud isn't the young fancier come to plunder the heart a me daugher.

Dara Boss. Isaac. Sorrel. (*Nods at each of them.*) Be a dirty winter for the trees is stripped already and October still in nappies.

Red (*to Sorrel*) Geh him a whiskey.

Dara Ya should clear them fields, boss, the wind takes the stink all over the Valley.

Red You look after your little farm and I'll look after mine.

Dara Ud's shockin that's whah ud is. I hear Rosie's noh well, Isaac.

Isaac I'll tell ya now Dara, women is a breeze compared to cats.

Dara Thah so?

Isaac I can do nothin righ for Rosie. She's like a prima donna ouha the operehha, wailin and flailin on the bed. Nothin would do her last nigh only hop me ouh on the fluur and her wud the whole bed to herself. And would thah sahisfy her? Noh a bih of her. There's me freezin on the fluur so I puh on me cap to trap the bih a hate goin at the top a me head and next thing Rosie's glarin ah me from under the sheets wud her paw rachin for me cap. So I says, 'Rosie ya cranky yoke ya, you're noh getting me cap as well,' and she goes into a tantrum, tears rollin off a her whiskers and poundin the pilla. In the end I found an auld scarf used belong to the missus and tied ud round her head and thah contented her for she went off to slape after a while.

Sorrel Whah age is Rosie now?

Isaac Sixteen and a half. Her kidneys is gone.

Red Too auld for a cah. I'll puh her down if ya want.

Isaac Ya'll do no such thing. Me and Rosie is goin to the grave together like the Egyptians, have ud in me will, Philomena knows what to do, wrohe her a lehher wud burial instructions.

Red Ah would ya shuh up abouh thah stupid auld cah.

Isaac She's Padgkins Disase, same as the Elephant Man had, her bones just kapes growin, eventually all her bones'll be on the outside, kinda like a birdcage.

Red Any news from the Valley, young Mood?

Dara Only bad news.

Red The Brophy young wan?

Dara Yees heard abouh her trouble?

Red We heard alrigh.

Dara And yees heard she had the stillborn son there last wake?

Isaac The poor misfortunahe girl.

Dara Well she goes down to Clonloon cemetery last nigh and digs up the child.

Isaac Ah no. Ah no.

Sorrel I was in school wud Sarah.

Dara So the word goes ouh she's missin. Found be her father in the small hours, sittin on the coffin tryin to fade the child, couldn't say which a them bluer. Brophy throws hees coah over her and tries to take her home buh she refuses to go wudouh the child. Eventually they geh her into bed wud the corpse a the infant and she goes into some sourt a fih and dies this afternoon.

Isaac Whoever goh her into difficulty and just left her like thah should be . . .

Dara Well, here's the worst part, Brophy goes round the neighbourhood howlin for a priest. Meself and Gerrity had to hould him down, and he's whisperin thah ud was all a mistake, thah he only ever went near her the wance, thah he wanted to die as well. He's beyond in Ballinasloe now in a straihjackeh and they may watch him or he'll do away wud heeself.

Isaac You're noh sayin the child was Brophy's a' ya?

Dara I am and may God forgive him for none in the Valley will.

Red Don't belave ud. Don't believe wan word of ud. Sarah Brophy goh whah was comin to her. Now I'm sorry the child had to die, wouldn't wish thah on anywan.

Buh blamin Brophy's all wrong. Ya don't know whah you're talkin abouh, young Mood. Ud's gossips like you destriys a man's good name and reputation.

Dara I heard the admission from hees own lips, wouldn't call thah gossip.

Red Ud's only your word again our beliefs, thah righ, Sorrel?

Isaac Find ud hard to believe Dara and thah's noh callin ya a liar, sure Brophy has allas been the kindest a men.

Dara Ud all adds up in my mind anyway.

Sorrel Allas thought the child was Gerrity's.

Dara So did lots and called him a spineless weasel for lavin Sarah the way she was. But Gerrity tould me early on thah Sarah broke ud off wud him up on a year ago.

Red Trouble in the Valley anyway. There was allas skullduggery in the Valley. Yees should take a draught a the air up here on the Hill.

Dara Aye and keel over wud the stink a rotten sheep and cows.

Red Ah g'wan cuurtin would yees, can't kape yeer eyes off a wan another. Jay, Isaac, if eyes was hands the pair a' them be stripped and pantin on the table.

Sorrel Would ya give over, Daddy.

Red Sorrel's getting embarrassed now. G'wan will yees or are ya a man ah all? Is he, Isaac?

Isaac Lave the chap alone.

Red Well, what's kapin him then?

Dara I take exception to other men's talk and presumptions on a subject is none a their concern.

Isaac There's your answer, Red, was never a Mood as couldn't express heeself.

Red Sorrel is my daugher first and everythin concernin her, concerns me, includin marriage proposals. Thah said I was only jossin ya. You're too quick to hotten, and if I do laugh ah the fumblins a young lovers ud's only because I member me own. D'ya know whah ud manes to be young, Dara Mood? Do ya? Manes your slate is clane, manes the muck on your boots stays on your boots and don't sape up to your unploughed soul. Manes ya know fuck all abouh the dirty world, how and why men and women fall. G'wan, young Mood, and enjiy yourself while your guardian angel's still around, for wan a these mornins ya'll wake and she'll be gone.

    And exit Dara and Sorrel.

Isaac (*getting up*) I'll be away too.

Red Ya'll stay. Thah's whah Dinah'd like, to banish everywan and have us all gloatin round her.

Isaac You're too rough on her, way too rough altogether.

Red I have to be, otherwise she'd puh an apron on me. I'm tellin ya, Isaac, give em an inch next thing you're wearin a bra.

Isaac There's worse things than wearin bras. (*Finishes drink.*) Nigh.

Red Have wan for the road?

Isaac Have to geh back to Rosie.

Red Ya prefer animals to humans.

Isaac Whah's wrong a' ya? Donten ya like your own company?

Red G'wan home to your cah, call up for ya tomorra.

Isaac Why? Ya don't even like me.

Red Whah's like got to do wud anythin?

Isaac Nigh.

And exit Isaac. Red sits there a minute, drinks, goes to stairs, calls up.

Red Dinah.

Silence.

Dinah.

Dinah Shuh up will ya, ya'll wake herself.

Red (*sings up to her*)
Come down the mountain Kahie Daly,
Come down the mountain Kahie do,
Oh can't ya hare me callin Kahie Daly,
I want to drink your Irish mountain deweeweew.

Dinah I'm radin.

Red I'm thinkin a signin the farm over to ya.

Dinah I'll geh ud in the end anyway.

Red Will I bring ya up a whiskey?

Dinah No.

Red (*mutters to himself*) Cranky cunt.

Ded's fiddle starts up, Red listens a minute, goes to the door.

Ded.

Fiddle stops.

Geh in here, you.

Ded I'm aslape.

Red Then slapewalk yourself in here or do I have to go ouh and drag ya in?

Ded appears at the door with a blanket around him, blinking, shaking, looking down.

Hould up your head, you.

Ded (*does*) Is ud me fiddle playin thah's anniyin ya? I'll stop. Here, cuh off me hand.

Red Whah do I want wud your girly fiddler's hands. Stop blinkin will ya. You're noh a hare a' ya.

Ded No.

Red No. You're mad as Alfie Horgan, thah's what ya are. And whah happened to him?

Ded Can I go back to the shed now?

Red I says whah happened to him?

Ded To who?

Red To Alfie Horgan, whah happened to him?

Ded He choked on hees tongue in the lunatic asylum.

Red Thah's righ, he choked on hees tongue from tellin too many lies. Would you like to end up like thah, would ya?

Ded Dunno.

Red What ya mane, ya dunno?

Ded Whah's the righ answer?

Red Ya'd drive anywan mad!

Ded I should be puh away.

Red Would ya shuh up would ya.

Ded jumps terrified.

And listen here you, I know ya come in the house when I'm noh here.

Ded I do noh. I do noh.

Red Don't lie to me, I smell cowdung everywhere.

Ded I don't come in, ud's the girls makes me ate me dinner in here, otherwise I'd starve.

Red You come in here in the middle a the nigh and ya drink my whiskey and ya smoke in the cowshed.

Ded I don't. I swear I don't.

Red Would ya listen would ya, I'm glad ya come in the house even if ud's only the middle a the nigh, I'm glad ya drink me whiskey, I'm glad ya smoke in the cowshed.

Ded Then I'm glad too.

Red Christ, you're noh listenin! I'm glad! Ya know why I'm glad? Because ud manes you're noh a total animal yeh.

Ded (*confused, getting very upset*) So am I to smoke or noh to smoke? Whah? Am I to come in the house or noh? Whah? Am I to drink your whiskey or noh? Whah're ya sayin, Daddy? Just lay down the rules, don't kape changin them. Don't. I don't know whah to do to make ya happy. And I want me mother, I miss her fierce so I do. She'd kape ya away from me, she promised me she would. I'd liefer she'd pulled me into Heaven after her. (*Begins to wail.*)

Red (*through Ded's wails*) Did you take your tablets today? Would ya whist would ya? I says whist! Whist up now, ya big babby ya!

Claps a hand on Ded's mouth. Ded freezes.

Thah's behher. Take her handy now. Handy handy. D'ya want a whiskey?

Ded Can I go back to the shed?

Red Ya want an auld record player in the shed?

Ded I just want to go.

Red Ya want a new fiddle? The farm? Ud's yours if ya want? Jaysus, whah do ya want!

Ded Just to go back to the shed.

Red (*hits him a slap on the head*) Go then, go to be dammed!

Ded runs out. Red kicks the door shut after him. Enter Shalome across the landing, just out of bed, nightdress, bed socks, cardigan, suitcase, down the stairs and heading for the door.

Off to Kinnegar.

Shalome (*surprise*) How did you know?

Red A wild guess.

Shalome You were always so clever, Redmond. Always. I wanted you educated, I wanted to send you away to the Jesuits, away from this terrible Hill. But no, Old Raftery wanted you rough and ignorant like himself. (*Looks at him.*) You haven't turned out the way I planned, Redmond Raftery. Why you're older than Daddy.

Red Shut the duur, Mother, have a drink before your travels.

He closes the door, leads her to table, pours her a drink.

Shalome You could've amounted to something, Redmond, if old Raftery had let me have my way. Please don't think I'm a snob, I've nothing against the people around here, they're just not our sort, Redmond, never were. Old Raftery with his dirty hurler's hands and the stink of cowdung off him. Well he never laid a hand on me. Thirty years of marriage and not once did I touch him. How many wives can boast of that? Hah?

Red I'll wager thousands.

Shalome No Redmond, your father, your real father was an English captain.

Red Ah would ya give over them lies abouh your fancy German officers and English captains!

Shalome German, English, what does it matter, my dear, as long as it wasn't old Raftery?

Red Who was me father? I want to hear ya say ud.

Shalome Your father, Redmond, was a beautiful-looking man with soft brown eyes and the gentlest of ways.

Red No, really, who was he?

Shalome I told you he was an English officer.

Red He wasn't.

Shalome He was! He was! Don't you dare contradict me, young man! He was from Yorkshire. He was lovely. I would've married him except for mean old Daddy.

Red You're a lyin witch!

Shalome Don't you raise your voice to me! I hate it, young man, I hate it. I hate this world. People are just awful! They're so ridiculous with their noses and their necks and their hands and their stupid, stupid legs! I mean, what are legs actually for?

Red G'wan back to bed will ya, ya've me scutcheoned wud your lies and tales a' woe.

Shalome I'm never sleeping in this house again. I'm going back to Kinnegar and from there I shall return to India.

Red Then g'wan back to India, ya mad wide heifer ya!

Shalome You're not the son I wanted, not by a long shot, and don't ever presume you are!

And exit Shalome dragging suitcase out the door, as Dinah comes down the stairs in her nightdress.

Dinah Geh back here, you! I'm noh goin after her again! (*Drinks from Red's glass.*) Christ, does anywan slape in this house any more.

Red (*takes his drink back*) Get your own glass.

Dinah You geh ud for me.

Red Alrigh, only kape your lips off a mine.

Goes to get glass. Dinah looks after him.

Dinah (*half to herself*) Skanky auld goat.

Red Ya talkin to me?

Dinah Just nohicin how auld ya've gotten. Ya've a stoop in your shoulders and a hop in your carriage.

Red You're no Easter bunny aither.

Dinah Damn righ I'm noh. No spring for me nor summer aither. I had no summer in me life, Daddy. Just auhum, allas auhum. Christ, I'm goin to die on this Hill.

Red Have to die somewhere.

Dinah The philosopher.

Red Were you drinkin upstairs?

Dinah No, I was sayin me rosary. A cuurse I was drinkin upstairs, how else could I face the lug a you. Whah were ya torturin Ded abouh?

Red He starts ballin for your mother.

Dinah Thah wan.

Red Ya remember much abouh her, do ya?

Dinah Mostly silences and headaches. May she roast like a boar on a spih in the courtyards a Hell.

Red I'll drink to thah.

Dinah And people round here still talks like she was an angel. Some angel. To everywan else maybe. Everywan bar me.

Red And me.

Dinah Ya know whah we are, Daddy?

Red Whah?

Dinah Granny was talkin abouh gorillas earlier. Thah's whah we are, gorillas in clothes pretendin to be human, goin back to bed. (*Gets up.*)

Red Ya want to go into town someday this week?

Dinah For whah?

Red I d'n know, buy a dress, get your hair done, whahever ud is yees women likes spendin money on.

Dinah Whah do I want wud a hair do or a new dress except you to ogle ud off a' me.

Red Buuks. Ya like radin. Ya want buuks?

Dinah Can get them from the mobile library. Nigh.

Red Stay a while.

Dinah Look, I'm in no mood for ya tonigh.

Red G'wan then, ya contrary rip ya.

Dinah (*pauses on the stairs*) Don't touch Sorrel.

Red I won't ever . . . I swear.

Dinah Nigh so.

> *Enter Shalome with her suitcase, muck all over her.*
> *She sits on her suitcase facing the door. Red watches*
> *this a while.*

Red To Kinnegar and back already?

Shalome (*still facing the door, defeated*) I'm waiting until it's light, dear. These Midland nights. You'd see better in the coffin. I fell into the pigsty.

Red (*cleaning her face and hands with a dishcloth*) Ya must have the constitution of an ox. Any other auld wan'd be dead be now.

Shalome Far be it for me to say anything good about Old Raftery, but I will say this much. He kept this farm clean, you could eat your dinner off the yard if you were that way inclined. Now it's just a river of slurry and rotten animals. The smell from these fields. Poor Old Raftery, I'd watch him from here, scouring the yard and all I could think was how much I hated the shape of his back. I was cruel to him, Red, crueller than necessary to keep him at bay. And the crueller I was, the bigger and sadder his eyes. In the end he just stood in ditches and stared, died that way, standing in a ditch, staring at God knows what.

Red He was no Padre Pio himself.

Shalome You married a good woman too, and the way you butchered her.

Red I married a lunatic wud an antique violin and an eternal case a' migraine. If Christ heeself slid onto the pilla she'd plead the migraine. (*Leading Shalome to the stairs.*)

Shalome No, I can't go up these stairs.

Red If you were a cow or a sick dog ud'd be perfectly lagle to put ya ouh a' your misery, but you're an auld woman and ya can do nothin to women these days. Now geh up them stairs.

Shalome Just let me stay down here, I'll be gone at first light.

Red Just lie down, Mother, and ya can commence your travels in the mornin.

Shalome You and I, Red, what we've done to this beautiful Hill, it was beautiful and yet we're entirely blameless. What sort of monsters must we have been in a past life to suffer like this?

Red We were big loose monsters, Mother, hurlin through the air, wud carnage in our hearts and blood under our nails, and no stupid laws houldin us down or back or in.

Shalome Speak for yourself.

Red Exactly whah I'm doin.

And they're gone. Hold a minute, enter Sorrel and Dara Mood.

Sorrel He's gone to bed, come on in.

Dara Just for wan more hould a you.

Comes in, pulls her to him, kisses her, long and sweet.

In a couple more months ya'll be all mine, won't have to be lavin ya to anywan else's duur, no more jouncin haystacks or milkin parlours or tombstones.

Red has entered on the landing, stands there watching and listening.

Sorrel I may miss thah.

Dara I'll build a haystack in the bedroom for ya, and a milkin parlour. I'll plant roses on your pilla. I'll have a cherry blossom lanin over the bed tryin to kiss ya and I'll ate ya for me breakfast, me dinner and me tay. And sometimes I'll go away from ya for an hour or two, just to savour ya privahely and let ya echo through the four chambers a me heart. (*Sniffs.*) God, the smell a these fields.

Sorrel Hardly nohice ud anymore.

Dara Your auld fella seems to have lost ud altogether. I don't know how he gets away wud ud.

Sorrel He's pushin on, he's no interest in the farm any more.

Dara Such beauhiful land. Why doesn't he sell ud? I've enough saved to buy half ud as ud is and the banks'd give me the rest. Wan day I'll own all this, Sorrel, you'll see.

Sorrel Daddy won't part wud ud aisy.

Dara He can't g'wan like this forever, y'ax me he looks like a man thah's finished, the way the flesh rides down hees face.

Sorrel Ya don't like him, do ya?

Dara D'ya like him yourself?

Sorrel He's me father, isn't he?

31

Dara Buh if he wasn't?

Sorrel I never think abouh him, really. D'you like your father?

Dara My father's wan sad picnic in the rain. He never speaks to me mother, just kind a grunts and pints and sits in the corner drinkin cans a condensed milk and sighin to heeself. Me mother now is a different kittle a fish.

Sorrel Men and their auld mammies.

Dara Aye, I'm me mother's molly cuddle and glad to be. Only for her I'd be full a stingy silences like my auld fella or perverse rages like yours.

Sorrel Daddy doesn't have perverse rages, does he?

Dara I seen him cut the udders off a cow noh two wakes ago. Down in the River Field. And then he shoh ud, and then he dragged ud to the river wud a rope, a job should take three men to do. And then he pushed ud over the bank into the river. Cows is the most beauhiful creatures, gentle and trustin and curious, and they've these greah long eyelashes. This wan walked up to him and starts nuzzlin him and he goes ah her wud a knife.

Sorrel He did noh!

Dara I seen him, Sorrel, and all the time he's cursin and scramin abouh auld Raftery and the Fairyfort, couldn't make head nor tail of ud.

Sorrel Whah're ya tellin me all this for? I don't want to hear this kind a gore.

Dara There's times I fear for ya in this house. I can't wait to geh ya under me own roof, in wan piece, perfect, the way God made ya. Don't trust him, Sorrel, and don't believe him when he gives ouh abouh me, he does, doesn't he?

Sorrel Sometimes.

Dara Look, in a couple a months ya'll be safe wud me.

Sorrel I'm safe here, Daddy's allas been good to me. Ya shouldn't be sayin things like thah. Ud's noh righ.

Dara You're way too innocent.

Sorrel Look, I'm just fed up a you and Daddy givin ouh abouh wan another. I'm the wan stuck in the middle tryin to smooth everythin over. Just don't talk abouh him any more. He's auld, he'll be dead soon and you can buy hees farm and we can live and brathe and enjiy ourselves.

Dara I won't mention him again. (*Kisses her.*) I'll be away, I've a mart in the mornin.

Sorrel See ya tomorra?

Dara Ya will aye.

Kisses her again and he's gone. Red comes down the stairs.

Sorrel Oh Daddy, ya puh the heart crossways in me . . . Were you listenin to us?

Red (*paring his nails with a pocket knife*) A man can stand on hees own stairs, in hees own house, surrounded be hees own fields thah Dara Mood'll never geh hees scrubber hands on . . . And I never went after e'er a cow wud e'er a knife.

Sorrel Well, Dara's noh a liar.

Red And I am?

Sorrel Ud's so horrible ud has to be true.

Red Dara Mood has lots a rasons to lie.

Sorrel I think I'll g'wan to bed.

He is blocking her on the stairs.

Can I geh by . . . please?

Red Please. (*Laughs.*) Ya'll stay where ya are, young wan, till I give ya lave to go.

Sorrel You're drunk, Daddy.

Red I'm sober and I'm watchin you and I heard ya wishin me dead.

Sorrel I did noh.

Red I heard you and Dara Mood schemin again me, tryin to stale me farm, next thing yees'll pisin me.

Sorrel This is crazy talk, Daddy.

Red Did you gut them hares, did ya?

Sorrel I don't know how to gut a hare.

Red Donten ya? Alrigh, I'll show ya how to gut a hare.

Grabs her suddenly and holds her in a vice grip.
Sorrel struggles pointlessly against the strength of him.

Sorrel Ow! You're hurtin me, Daddy.

Red (*cutting the clothes off her with the knife*) First ya skin the hare . . .

Sorrel Daddy! Stop!

Red Ya do thah slow and aisy . . .

Sorrel Whah're ya doin! Whah're ya doin!

Red (*holding her in the vice grip, all the time cutting the clothes off her*) Ya do thah slow and aisy so ya don't nick the flesh . . .

Sorrel Would ya stop! Daddy!

Red I've allas been too soft on you and look where ud's goh me.

Sorrel (*yells*) Dinah! Dinah! Come quick! Dinah! Ded! Daddy, stop! Stop will ya! Dinah! Granny!

Red (*still cutting the clothes off her*) Dinah won't come and ya think Ded's comin? (*A mad laugh.*) And Granny's noh comin. And your precious Dara Mood can't help ya now.

> *Red continues cutting the clothes off her. Sorrel gesticulates and struggles pathetically. Her voice has betrayed her. We hear the odd animal moan or shriek. Now Red has her down to her slip. He pauses, looks in satisfaction at his work.*

And you all the time prancin round like the Virgin Mary. (*He pushes her across the table, cuts the straps of her slip.*) Now, this is how ya gut a hare. (*Stabs knife in table.*)

> *Blackout.*

Act Two

Night. Three weeks later.
  Sorrel sits at kitchen table. Ded puts his head around the door.

Ded Ne'er a sign a Daddy?

  Sorrel looks at him, looks away.

Give us a buh, g'wan give us a buh.

  Sorrel opens drawer, throws a packet of cigarettes at him.

And a flame?

  Sorrel passes him matches. He lights his cigarette, smokes nervously, jauntily, quickly.

Whah're ya thinkin abouh, Sorrel?

Sorrel Noh thinkin ah all.

Ded Y'are so, can hear your brain whisperin.

Sorrel Can ya?

Ded Dara Mood comin to see ya tonigh?

Sorrel Aye.

Ded He bringin chocolahe for me?

Sorrel Doesn't he allas.

Ded That's alrigh so.

Sorrel Dinah won't talk to me any more . . . I tried to tell her, Ded.

Ded I think I may go back to the cowshed, thanks for the buh.

Sorrel Ya heard me callin, Ded . . . why didn't ya come?

Ded Ya see now, Daddy, I'm just a little bih wary a him, but same as you were to remove him, ya wouldn't know me.

Sorrel Then why don't ya remove him?

Ded I've a crowbar filed if he comes near me. I'm no girl to be played wud.

Sorrel I don't think Daddy's choosy. He just wants to bate us all inta the dirt.

Ded Ud's Dinah decides everythin round here anyway. Dinah's Daddy's cattle daler. You and me is only the cattle, Sorrel.

Dinah (*coming down the stairs with a wedding dress*) Am I now?

Ded First thing I'll do when I get this farm is peg you off of ud.

Dinah Why'd'n you just fuck back to the cowshed where ya belong?

Ded I'll go when I'm good and ready.

Dinah Ya'll go now or I'll tell Daddy ya were in here guzzlin hees whiskey and causin trouble.

Ded You tell him anythin' about me and I'll puh a mate hook through the turkey neck a ya.

Dinah And I'll ring the lunatic asylum and they'll take ya away and squaze ya like a bull calf and cut bits ouha your head.

37

Ded I'm getting the guards, tell them all abouh you and Daddy.

Dinah G'wan get the guards! G'wan get them! And tell them what ya done to me while you're ah ud.

Ded I done nothin to you only clane up the mess after Daddy!

Dinah Geh ouh! Geh ouh! Lave me alone!

Ded Thunderin trollop, that's what ya are!

Dinah Geh ouh! Geh ouh!

Runs for him. He runs out.

(*To Sorrel after a minute.*) Ya goin to try this yoke on? (*Wedding dress.*)

Sorrel Ud'll be grand.

Dinah Just let me check the hem's righ. (*Holds it up against Sorrel.*) Knew ud was too long. Why'd'n ya just try the bleddy thing on!

Sorrel throws it off.

(*Going up the stairs with the dress.*) Well don't blame me if you're a holy show.

Sorrel You're me mother aren't ya?

Dinah Whah?

Sorrel Ya heard me.

Dinah You'd want to stop all this nonsense and moonin abouh or your groom'll flee the altar.

Sorrel Suppose I allas knew ud . . . buried in me though.

Dinah Our mother died givin birth to you . . . now stop all a this for your own sake.

Sorrel You and Daddy.

Dinah Whah're ya on abouh?

Sorrel (*a suppressed sob*) Nothin I suppose . . .

Dinah You're nervous about the weddin, aren't ya now?

Sorrel Aye.

Dinah Don't you worry, ud'll all be fine. I'll make sure your dress is beauhiful and I've all the flowers planned. Cornflowers for your hair, them is your favourihe, aren't they now?

Sorrel Aye.

Dinah And a big bunch a lilies on the altar, and Daddy says we're to spare no expense, he wants ya to have a astoundin day . . . he can be very good, Daddy, can't he now?

Sorrel Yeah.

Dinah And we're to go into Brown's Hotel wan a these days to decide on the menu for the weddin breakfast and even Ded says he'll come to your big day. Isn't thah somethin, Sorrel?

Sorrel I won't be comin back to this Hill ever again, ya may come and visih me in the Valley.

Dinah Sure I will, sure I will Sorrel . . . anythin . . . anythin to gladden ya up.

Sorrel Why'd'n you ever get married?

Dinah No wan ever axed me, besides who'd look after yees all?

Sorrel Can look after meself.

Dinah Now ya can, buh when ya were a babby, no wan to mind ya except me. Granny was allas useless.

Sorrel Whah was me mother like?

Dinah Whah was she like? Good lookin, like you. I take after Daddy.

Sorrel Whah else abouh her?

Dinah She was allas sick, long as I can remember anyway . . . lyin in the back parlour wud a dish cloth on her head . . . never liked the woman, may God forgive me.

Sorrel Did ya noh?

Dinah Fierce selfish, and Ded was her favourihe. Any attention I goh was from Daddy. He used take me up the fields wud him, up on hees shoulders, thought I was a giant. I went everywhere wud him, he'd be mendin fences and I'd be playin wud me dolls beside him, or savin the hay, he'd throw me up on the haycocks and I'd roll down them and he'd ketch me, taught me to fish . . .

Sorrel Taught me to fish too.

Dinah Taught me all the names a the trees, ash behind the house, sycamore in the Church Field, yew and oak in the Calla, sycamore, elder, blackthorn, the River Field, beech the Lower Field, beech the Haggard, beech the Fairyfort . . . I remember the names a trees like no wan. . . . And I'd make him tay before I was the size a the range, he'd have to lift me up and hould the kettle so I wouldn't scald meself, and then he'd drink it, swill it round his mouth and say, well I declare that's the best cup a tay this side a the Shannon and west a the Pale. And I'd stand there watchin him, as proud a meself . . . He knew how to build up a child's heart . . . Daddy, never forgeh him for thah.

And exit Dinah up the stairs with wedding dress.
Enter Red and Isaac, guns, hunting bags and flasks.

Red Ah Sorrel, you're up and abouh, ya over thah flu?

Sorrel And whah flu is thah now?

Isaac Musta been a fierce dose ya goh.

Sorrel Oh fierce, Isaac, fierce.

Red Pour us whiskeys, there's a girl.

Sorrel goes to pantry, comes back with two glasses.

Seems to me be the longest winter of all the winters I have lived.

Isaac I remember worser winters than this wan.

Red This wan fluurs them all. (*To Sorrel.*) Jine us, why don't ya.

Sorrel looks at him, goes up the stairs.

Isaac Eighy-wan, now thah was a winter put manners on lovers, the whole mountain and valley courtin with gloves on. Eighy-wan, the missus dead and snow to the rafters, couldn't geh up the road to bury her. Slept beside her three nights tryin to warm her up. Be asier hotten the wastes of Antarctica or melt the pakes of Everest.

Red I'd say thah.

Isaac Anyway, if'n ya ax me, winters has nothin to do wud weather. I seen men freeze on Midsummer's Day. Jack Frost nor the Ice Quane does be sittin on the front duur a their heart.

Red There's gravel in thah . . . me father, now come the winter'd sih out there in hees Morris Minor, member ud?

Isaac I do.

Red Called ud hees smokin saloon, he'd sit there for hours, lookin at nothin . . . d'ya know I can't ever remember talkin to him.

41

Isaac I often spoke to him and I passin.

Red And whah used he talk abouh?

Isaac The weather, the football, the hurlin, who's dead, who's dyin, normal conversation.

Red Hmmh.

Isaac Sure wasn't he the greahest hurler ever to come ouha this county, and then wan Sunday he doesn't show up. Shockin bad blood over thah and the tame creahed around him.

Red Over somethin thah was said at the time, that's what thah was abouh.

Isaac Forgeh now, it's a long time ago.

Red Like hell ya forgeh and you wud the biggest lugs in the parish. Ud was all over somethin thah was said abouh me mother and abouh me.

Isaac Only auld gossip . . . ya heard Brophy drank a mug a weedkiller.

Red I heard thah.

Isaac Still find ud hard to believe.

Red Sure, even if he done to Sarah what they're all sayin he done, what did he have to go and down a mug a weedkiller for?

Isaac Mebbe the lavins of Christian dacency made him do ud.

Red Wouldn't your auld Christ forgive him?

Isaac They say he forgives everywan exceptin devils. Dependin on whether ya'd class Brophy as a devil or noh . . . still it's a loh to ax forgiveness for.

Red Aye, if you're wan a them as hankers after forgiveness.

Isaac Me own daugher now . . .

Red Philomena.

Isaac Don't see much of her any more, buh I can't imagine how any father could do thah to hees daugher.

Red Well, I can't imagine anywan wantin to do anythin to Philomena.

Isaac The bleddy nerve a ya talkin abouh Philomena like thah!

Red Ah I'm only jokin ya! Buh admih ud, the girl's a wagon, noh her fault, but she is. Where's your sense a humour, the cah taken thah too?

Isaac Talk about your own how ya like, but noh about mine.

Red Can't a man make a joke any more?

Isaac Brophy disgusts me! Monster, that's whah he is! And them's my unchristian thoughts on the mahher.

Red And doesn't your God make monsters too, for all the righteous to look down on? Didn't he create Lucifer for the sole pleasure of flingin him ouha Heaven?

Isaac Monsters makes themselves. They were hopped into the world clane as the next. The Grakes however has a different opinion of the mahher. Zeus and the missus . . . whah was her name? . . . Hera, Zeus and Hera, sure they were brother and sister and they goh married and had chaps and young wans and the chaps and young wans done the job wud the mother and father and one another, and sure the whole loh a them were ah ud mornin, noon and nigh, I suppose they had

43

to populahe the world someway. Is ud any wonder the stahe a the country and them for ancestry. (*Finishes his drink.*) I'll be away.

Dinah (*coming down the stairs*) Home to Rosie, Isaac?

Isaac Rosie died last nigh, five past three, peacefully. I'm thinkin of havin a waistcoah made ouha her.

Dinah So ya can stroke her from time to time?

Isaac Mebbe . . . nigh.

Dinah Nigh, Isaac.

And exit Isaac.

Red Well the young wan's up . . .

Dinah just glares at him.

She alrigh, is she?

Dinah She's noh wan bih alrigh . . . just cries and cries, won't ate anythin, just keeps takin a bah.

Red She's only sulkin.

Dinah Wan thing I axed you to do me whole life! Lave Sorrel alone. Whah we need here is the guards, the social workers, the whole shootin loh a them. I'm thinkin a tellin Dara Mood the class of an animal he'll have for a father-in-law.

Red You start peggin muck, I've plenty to peg back.

Dinah Noh again me ya haven't. I'll get Sorrel to back me.

Red Lave the young wan ouh of ud.

Dinah Was you brung her in! Where are ya goin to stop Daddy? Where?

Red At the end a cuurse, where else.

Dinah And where the hell's thah?

Red Would ya stop grousin over nothin. I barely went near her.

Dinah Barely did ya! There's marks on her as hasn't haled in three weeks!

Red You didn't hear the things she said abouh me.

Dinah For eigheen year I watched thah wan like a hawk, protected her from you, and what does the stupid little bitch go and do? Gives ouh abouh you under your own roof. Christ, doesn't she nohice anythin? Doesn't she know you be paddin round the duurs and landins, wud your cloven toes, spyin on everywan, waitin to pounce? I seen pictures a your toes in books, books abouh devils wud their toes all stuck together.

Red You're involved here too, missus, layin ud all on me, I barely touched her.

Dinah (*dives for his neck, throttles him, he laughs*) Don't small talk me, you! Save ud for them as doesn't know ya! Whah are ya! Whah are ya!

Red You're jealous is all.

Dinah Jealous a you is ud, wud the big stumpy jaw a black molars on ya!

Red You're no Marilyn Monroe aither, missus.

Dinah I'm noh even forty till next year and look ah the stahe a you, sure you're eligible for the auld age pension and ya need a hearin aid.

Red I hear fine so I do.

Dinah Why couldn't ya a just lave her alone? The wan perfect thing in this house.

Red I was only puttin manners on her, somewan had to, you've leh her run wild . . . here. (*Gives her a big wad of money.*) G'way and spend thah for yourself.

Dinah (*takes the money, puts it in her pocket*) Ya think a big fist a dirty tenners solves everythin.

Red Ya want more? How much do ya bleddy want?

Sorrel crosses the landing.

Dinah Ah Sorrel, ya comin down?

Sorrel Goin for a bah.

Dinah Ya'd wan already today and two last nigh.

Sorrel Well, I'm goin for another wan.

Red Ya may lave me some hot waher for my bah.

Dinah What do you want a bah for?

Red Never you mind now, nosey parker.

Dinah To smell nice for me is ud?

Red Can't a man dunk heeself in his own bah withouh a runnin commentary?

Dinah All the Shannon wouldn't wash you clane, Daddy.

Red (*shouts up to Sorrel*) Young wan!

Sorrel Whah?

Red High time you goh dressed and joined the land a the livin.

Sorrel I'm noh well.

Red We'll let bygones be bygones young, wan. Just apologise to me now and we'll say no more abouh ud.

Sorrel Apologise to you!

Dinah Ud's high time yees were greah agin, come down and make ud up wud him, I'm the wan stuck atwane yees tryin to keep the pace.

Red Mother Teresa's only trottin after ya. Get down here, young wan, I've had enough a your ghost act and your double dalin and your vicious attack on me.

Sorrel Just lave me alone. (*And exit Sorrel to bathroom.*)

Red Is she goin to start spreadin lies?

Dinah Doubh ud . . . she's a Raftery, a double Raftery, well versed in subterfuge.

Red Look, Dinah, we'll turn things round here, clane them fields, get the ground ready for spring.

Dinah We should be allas workin the farm and there'd be none a this, everythin goes bockety when we don't be ouh workin the fields and the cattle and the pigs.

Door opens. Enter Shalome, bedraggled, lugging her suitcase after her.

Shalome (*sticking her head around the door*) Oh sorry, wrong house. (*Goes back out.*)

Dinah Geh in here, you. (*Goes after her, pulls her in.*)

Shalome No, let me go, I thought I was on the road to Kinnegar.

Red Come in before ya ketch ammonia.

Shalome (*allowing herself to be brought in*) Kinnegar, will I ever get back there?

Dinah It's only twenty mile down the road. If ya really wanted to go there ya'd go, it's all a figary just to geh at me.

Shalome You're not as nice to me as Sorrel, poor little Sorrel, I wanted to stop it. Is she alive still?

Dinah Sih down will ya till I get ya a bun.

Shalome When I tell Daddy all I've had to put up with. Did you know Daddy used to take me boating on Lilliput Lake? Every summer, boating on the lake, we don't have summers like those any more, dragonflies on the water, the sun bursting the sky, and Daddy would row and say, 'Are you tired, darling?' And I'd lie there looking at him through my fingers, and once he said, 'Shalome, look at the heron feeding in the rushes.' Shalome. No one has ever pronounced my name nicer than Daddy.

Ded (*off, shouts outside the door*) You and your fuckin Daddy! D'ya ever talk abouh anythin else do ya!

Red (*goes to door, opens it*) Geh in here, you. Ded! I said geh in. And where's your shirt gone to? (*Pulls him in.*) Dinah, geh him wan a my shirts.

Ded What do I want wan a your stinky shirts for?

Red Ya been skippin your tablets again.

Ded What's tablets got to do wud anythin, there's nothin wrong a me.

Red Come on sih in, have a whiskey till we warm ya up.

Ded (*to Shalome*) And you, missus, where the fuck were you when ya were naded!

Shalome Such filthy language in my presence. You apologise this minute, young man.

Ded I'll tell ya where ya were, up in your bed, dramin a your Daddy. Perverts the loh a' yees.

Red That's enough poetry ouha you now.

Ded I was the wan had to do ih all. I was the wan had to take Dinah to the cowshed, member thah, do ya, Daddy?

Dinah (*on the stairs*) Aye he remembers alrigh, Ded.

Ded And you – (*To Shalome.*) – suckin your Fox's Glacier Mints and playin patience and the roars a Dinah and blood and every bleddy thing comin ouha her.

Red I says thah's enough, Ded, you're ravin is all, thah's whah happens when ya don't take them tablets, drink up your whiskey there, good lad, ya want a buh do ya? (*Offers him a cigarette.*)

Ded And do yees know the worst, the worst of ih all? Mother never spoke to me again, I never seen her again. Yees wouldn't even leh me go to her funeral.

Dinah Here puh this on (*shirt*) before ya freeze.

Ded Are you still cross wud me, Dinah?

Dinah And whah would I be cross wud ya abouh?

Ded I d'know . . . everythin . . . I was only doin whah Daddy tould me, buh I never done nothin to you, sure I didn't.

Dinah No ya didn't, Ded, ya never done nothin to me.

Ded Thah's alrigh so, I geh inta a swill sometimes, geh all mixed up abouh thah time buh I'm noh an animal sure I'm noh?

Dinah No, it's not you is the animal, Ded.

Ded As long as I never harmed ya.

Red Would ya shuh up would ya! No wan harmed anywan. No wan!

Ded I'm next, amn't I? It's my turn next.

Red And whah would I want wud you, wud your sissy fiddle, ya can't even look after a shed a cattle.

Ded I've axes and billhooks and a plastic yoke a strychnine I'll peg in your eye if ya come near me. I'm never comin inta this house again. Dinah, ya may lave me dinners at the shed duur. (*To Red.*) And you, you're barred from the cowshed. (*And exit Ded.*)

Red Jaysus, whah a threat. (*To Dinah.*) Go after him, you, and see he's alrigh.

Dinah goes out after Ded.

Shalome He's an absolute disgrace, that fellow, you didn't give him a proper rearing, Red.

Red He was reared as well as the next. Ded's me thorn. Every man has wan, every woman too. I'm yours. G'wan to bed will ya, ouha me sigh.

Shalome I'm hungry.

Red A' ya, Dinah'll fade ya when she comes in.

A knock on the door.

Ud's on the latch.

Enter Dara Mood. Fiddle music starts up from the cowshed.

Dara Boss. (*Nods.*) Mrs Raftery. (*Nods.*)

Shalome Shalome, call me Shalome, that's my name.

Red (*shouts up*) Sorrel, himself is here.

Shalome You'll make someone very happy, Dara Mood, but it won't be Sorrel because you see we're strange creatures up here on the Hill. And strange creatures, aberrations like us, don't make for lifetime companions.

Sorrel That's enough ouha you, Granny.

Red I suppose you're wonderin what's goin wud her?

Dara What do ya mane?

Red Don't play innocent wud me, Mood. Ya know righ well I'm not goin to peg her into the world like a broken cup. (*Produces papers and envelope from his pocket.*) There's the deeds a Fifty Acre there and a cheque for twenty grand. (*Throws them on the table.*)

Dinah (*entering*) Me or Ded never goh any fifty acre or twenty grand.

Red (*to Sorrel*) That's all you're getting so don't come lookin for more when they put me bones down.

Dinah Come on, Granny, and lave them to their bribery and blackmail.

Shalome Could I have some toast and jam first?

Dinah When you're settled ya can.

As they exit up the stairs:

Red And I'm tellin ya now, Mood, ya may keep your trap shuh as to how I run me farm, see how well you'll manage now you've a hundred acre to work.

Dara I'm not sure I want your fifty.

Red Sure ya do.

Dara As a mahher a fact I don't.

Sorrel Dara!

Red You're a bigger fool than Ded.

Sorrel Take the Fifty Acre, Dara, and the cheque. Look, you're allas sayin if ya'd more land what ya'd do wud ud. now's your chance.

Dara I'll buy me own land, Sorrel, don't like handouts, especially them that's given in such an ungracious way.

Red Oh the pride a the Scrubber Moods.

Sorrel Well ud's mine. I'm owed ud. I'll take ud.

Red Owed ud are ya! And whah have you ever done to deserve me two best fields?

Sorrel Done plenty so I have.

Red Aye, ya have, ya little upstart ya.

Dara If you want them, Sorrel, take them, they're yours to take buh I won't touch them.

Sorrel I don't need you to tell me whah I can do. They're mine and dearly paid for. (*Takes the papers and cheque, runs upstairs with them.*)

Red That's righ, take the money and run, ya kite ya. Be careful, young Mood, for I've rared up an avaricious little thing wud pound signs lewin in her eyes.

Dara You've the knack a reducin everywan to dirt.

Red No, lad, you've ud all wrong, ya see women, ya may watch them, watch your back, lad, for fear they stick a knife in ud.

Dara You're nothin, only a bull on crutches.

Red (*drinks a large whiskey*) G'wan and cuurt your greedy bride and grow rich on the fah a my fields. There was a time I'd shooh a man who'd dare to walk across me River Field withouh permission. Noh any more. Ud's yours now and ya may breed rats on ud for all I care. (*Puts on his coat, gets his gun, hunting flask.*)

Dara I'll noh touch your River Field, Red Raftery, noh if ud was harvestin nightingales and gold.

Red Big words from the small farmer. Raftery's Hill fed yees all through the Greah Hunger, sould yees yeer fifty acre a scrub and marsh, 1923. You'll take me River Field, young Mood, and me churchyard field, and me daugher, for the Moods was ever opportune and you're wan a' them.

Dara You'll never see my plough on your cursed land.

Red (*as he exits*) You may see mine on yours.

Dara Whah?

Red is gone.

(*Goes to stairs, calls up.*) Sorrel?

Sorrel comes onto the landing.

Dara What's goin on here?

Sorrel There's natin goin on here except you decidin things in swell a pride thah concerns me.

Dara Your father, Sorrel, I have to say ud. I can't abide the man.

Sorrel Well, hees blood runs through me so what you're really sayin is ya can't abide me.

Dara Ya know righ well that's noh whah I'm sayin. (*Goes up the stairs to her.*)

Sorrel Go way from me, you, now.

Dara Sorrel!

Sorrel No! Go way from me! There's natin wrong a Daddy. Ud's you! Think ya know everythin abouh everywan! Well, ya know natin, Dara Mood.

Dara Then tell me.

Sorrel Why couldn't ya a just taken the land and the money? Why couldn't ya a? Ya gone and ruined

53

everythin so ya have. Anyway I don't want to be a small farmer's wife. With this fifty acre we'll have somethin. (*Shakes papers at him.*) And wud this (*cheque*) we'll be rich and have standin in the communihy instead a been scrubbers from the Valley.

Dara So that's whah I am, a scrubber from the Valley.

Sorrel Ud came ouh wrong.

Dara Buh ud came, strange that's the exact phrase your father used noh ten minutes ago. I allas thought I came to ya as an equal, Sorrel.

Sorrel There ya go again wud your stupid pride! Only for you ud'd all a gone smooth, allas givin ouh abouh Daddy and under hees very roof and all. Ya know of old hees manner is gruff, buh he manes natin by ud. He's good at the back of ud all, leastways hees instincts are, and for you to be puttin him down to hees daugher is wrong! Same as I was to start in on your family, how'd ya like thah?

Dara Well, if your Daddy's as good as ya say he is mebbe ud's him ya should be marryin.

Sorrel Well, I know wan thing, I won't be marryin you.

Dara That's a bih extreme isn't ud?

Sorrel Ya've ruined everythin, Dara Mood, ya gone and ruined everythin.

Dara Ruined whah?

Sorrel I don't know. I don't know anythin any more . . . The world's gone ouh like a ligh and I can't see righ abouh anythin any more.

Dara Let's not figh.

Sorrel Ud's over, Dara. Don't come here again. (*And exit Sorrel from the landing.*)

Dara Whah? . . . What do ya mane? . . . Sorrel?

Dinah crosses the landing and down the stairs.

What's goin on in this house?

Dinah We're just tryin to live like everywan else, don't ya know how hard thah is sometimes, Dara Mood, just to live. What's wrong a ya? A tiff wud Sorrel?

Dara Sorrel's not righ in herself this last few weeks, she's gone schaways altogether. Did somethin happen her?

Dinah (*pouring whiskey*) Ya want wan?

Dara Naw.

Dinah Sorrel'll be fine. She's young, her whole life ahead a her wud a beauhiful young husband like you by her side. Me now, what do I have to look forward to? (*Drinks.*)

Dara Sure, hadn't you the pick a all the lads wan time? Didn't ya dangle me own brother on a string for the longest while. . . . he still axes after ya.

Dinah How is he?

Dara The finest. Another babby comin in June.

Dinah That'll be three he'll have.

Dara Aye ud will.

Dinah In another life they'd have been mine . . . I broke ud off wud Jimmy fierce sudden and fierce hard . . . things was rickety for me thah time. Ud's allas the wans you're fondest of ya drop the axe on . . . Sorrel'll be fine, I'll knock sense into her, g'wan home and come back in a few weeks.

Dara Alrigh, if ya think I should stay away for a while.

Dinah I do.

Dara Nigh so.

Dinah Nigh, Dara. (*Looks up the stairs and exits.*)

Dinah sits at table, Shalome comes onto landing and down the stairs in Sorrel's wedding dress.

Shalome (*to herself*) You left Kinnegar in your wedding dress so it's only right you should return in it.

Dinah Christsake, Granny! That's Sorrel's! You've ud ruined.

Shalome I'm going back to Daddy in Kinnegar.

Dinah Ya'd put years on Father Time heeself.

Sorrel comes down the stairs.

Sorrel Lave her, Dinah.

Dinah And leh her ruin your dress in the yard and the lanes?

Sorrel I won't be needin ud.

Dinah What do ya mane, ya won't be needin ud?

Shalome escapes out the door.

Shalome Bye Raftery's House, bye Raftery's Hill . . .

Dinah Don't come back here tonigh you! I'm not puttin ya down again. (*Slams door on her.*) Whah were ya fightin wud Dara Mood abouh?

Sorrel Just tould him I won't be marryin him is all.

Dinah And why noh?

Sorrel Why do ya think?

Dinah Ud's not the end a the world just because hands was laid on ya thah shouldn't a. Why couldn't ya a just been more careful?

Sorrel So ud's all my fault!

Dinah I'm noh sayin ud is, only I never had anywan lookin ouh for me the way I looked ouh for you.

Sorrel Some lookouh you are and ya listenin behind the duur to the whole thing.

Dinah For eigheen years I watched you and minded you and kept ya safe! Ya know how many wishes and drames thah is brushed aside. Eigheen years, the best part a me life and noh wan bih a grahitude from you! No, ya go and fling ud in me face. I had a whole life before you came along, missus, no wan ever stood up for me. Ya know whah my mother done? She sent me into the bed aside him. I was lanin on the fridge in the pantry and she comes in behind me and says ouh a nowhere, you're to sleep in wud your father tonigh. She didn't want him so she sends me in. I was twelve.

Sorrel And since?

Dinah What do ya mane, 'and since'?

Sorrel Innocent as a lamb aren't ya? Don't think I don't know your and Daddy's nocturnal carryin ons. Whah is ud? Wance a month? Wance every two months? A period a guilt and atonement for yeer sins and then yees are back ah ud again.

Dinah So we do ud from time to time, allas in the pitch dark, never a word, ud's no wan's bleddy business. Who's ud hurtin? And we want ud to stop. You don't believe thah. You don't believe anythin good abouh me and Daddy, we don't aither buh we want ud to stop. Ud's just like children playin in a field ah some awful

57

game before laws was made, buh you're noh goin to end up like me, you're goin to marry Dara Mood and geh off a' this hill if I have to run ya off.

Sorrel Ya'd have me in a poh a lies wud Dara Mood.

Dinah Ud's not lyin, ud's just noh tellin him things. Ud's just sayin the opposite of whah you're thinkin. Most goes through their whole life sayin the opposite a whah they think. What's so different about you?

Sorrel I won't do ud.

Dinah Then what'll ya do? Rot up here? Go tearin round in your nightdress like Granny?

Sorrel I won't pretend wud Dara.

Dinah Well, ya behher noh start tellin him lies abouh us. We're a respectable family, we love wan another and whahever happened ya happened ya be accident. D'ya honestly think we'd harm wan another?

Sorrel Spare me your Legion a' Mary canter. We're a band a gorillas swingin from the trees.

Enter Red with Shalome in muddied wedding dress.

Red Would yees look ah the stahe a' Sorrel's dress.

Shalome (*to Red*) Do you think will Daddy recognise me after all these years?

Red I tould ya a hundred times he's dead. Dead, Mother! Dead.

Shalome No . . . you must be thinking of someone else.

Red Don't ya remember hees funeral? Ya took me, I must a been whah? Twelve, thirteen, the army out blowin their bugles, a woman came up to me and said, God, but you're the spih of him. (*Laughs.*)

Shalome Daddy dead? What a lark. Daddies never die, they just fake rigor mortis and all the time they're throwing tantrums in the coffin, claw marks on the lid.

Dinah Did ya ketch anythin?

Red Only this auld bird. I nearly shoh her.

Dinah Why didn't ya?

Red (*to Sorrel*) I hope you knocked some sense inta young Mood.

Sorrel Oh I sourted him ouh, Daddy, don't you worry, I sourted him ouh for ever more.⌐

Music from Ded's fiddle, and fade.

End.

ARIEL

Ariel was first performed at the Abbey Theatre, Dublin, in association with Fiach MacConghail, on 2 October 2002, with the following cast:

Fermoy Mark Lambert
Elaine Eileen Walsh
Sarah Joan O'Hara
Hannafin Des Cave
Boniface Barry McGovern
Frances Ingrid Craigie
Ariel Elske Rahill
Stephen Dylan Tighe
Verona Caitríona Ní Mhurchú
Young Stephen Paul McGovern, Shane Murray Corcoran
Young Elaine Siobhán Cullen, Lydia Rahill

Director Conall Morrison
Designer Frank Conway
Costume Designer Joan O'Clery
Lighting Designer Rupert Murray
Fight Director Renny Krupinski

Characters

Fermoy Fitzgerald

Frances Fitzgerald
his wife

Ariel Fitzgerald
their daughter

Elaine Fitzgerald
child of twelve and young woman

Boniface
monk, Fermoy's older brother

Stephen Fitzgerald
child of ten and young man

Sarah
aunt of Fermoy

Hannafin

Verona
interviewer

Cameraman / Woman

Soundman / Woman

Time and Place

ACT ONE: the present
ACT TWO: ten years later
ACT THREE: two months later

Dining room of the Fitzgerald home:
table, drinks cabinet, CD player,
chairs, two entrances

Theme Music

'Mors et Vita' from Gounod's *Judex*

Act One

Curtain up. Lights up as Fermoy, Frances, Ariel, Elaine, Boniface, Stephen and Sarah stand around a birthday cake on the table. The cake is lit with sixteen candles. All are singing:

All
    'And so say all of us,
    And so say all of us,
    For she's a jolly good fella,
    For she's a jolly good fella,
    For she's a jolly good fella,
    And so say all of us.'

Ariel blows out the candles, claps and cheers.

Frances Happy birthday, sweetheart. (*Kisses her.*)

Boniface Sweet sixteen and never been kissed. (*Kisses her.*)

Fermoy We hope, we have our doubts.

Ariel What ya don't know won't bother ya. Does this mane I get the keys a the car, Daddy?

Fermoy Mebbe ud manes ya get your own little banger.

Ariel Whah?

Fermoy Look ouh the winda.

Ariel runs to window followed by Elaine.

Ariel Ah, Daddy, you're mad, you're mad.

Fermoy gives her the keys, lifts her up, sings to her, dancing around the room.

Fermoy
'Whin first I seen the love ligh in your eye
I thought the world held nough buh jiy for me
And aven though we drifted far apart
I love ya as I loved ya,
Whin ya were sweet, whin ya were sweet sixteen.'

(*Puts her down.*) You're noh a child any more buh we'll hould onta ya long as we can, won't we, Frances?

Frances Leh go, Stephen, leh go a me dress. (*To Fermoy.*) Yeah, a cuurse we will.

Ariel Can I go drivin now?

Fermoy Were ya drinkin wine?

Ariel Just a glass.

Frances Yeah, come an, I'll go for a spin wud ya.

Exit Ariel, Frances, Stephen.

Sarah Anywan for cake?

Frances When we come back.

Sarah (*exiting, muttering to herself*) Was up half the nigh makin thah. Whin I was a girl we had wan cake ah Christmas, now ud's cake all the time, cake and more cake, swear ud was Versailles yees were brough up in.

Fermoy Elaine, g'wan wud your mother, good girl.

Elaine Sing a song to me, Daddy, sing sweet sixteen to me.

Fermoy Whin you're sweet sixteen, darlin, then I'll sing sweet sixteen to you.

Elaine Sure thah's years away.

Fermoy Ah g'wan for a drive in Ariel's new car, good girl.

Elaine Will ya gimme a puff a your cigar if I go?

Fermoy Whin ya come back I'll give ya a puff.

Elaine And a swig a brandy?

Fermoy Two puffs and two swigs if ya lave me in peace for five minutes.

Elaine Alrigh so. I'll be back shortly to hould ya to your word.

Exit Elaine.

Fermoy I've no doubt ya will. God, they'd drive ya mad, kids. I spind the whole day duckin them.

Boniface And me thinkin ya were an adorin father.

Fermoy And I am, an adorin father who doesn't know what to do wud em. I can't waih for Mondays. Wakinds should be banned. More paple gets murdered on Sundays than any other day a the wake. Whah does thah mane?

Boniface I suppose ud's wan way a passin the time after the roast beef and the trifle.

Fermoy (*pouring brandy for himself*) Ya still on the wagon?

Boniface Liver like a newborn. For whah, I ask meself.

Fermoy (*pouring a Coke for Boniface*) And how's things up ah the monastery?

Boniface The last a the Mohicans. I'm the only wan under sixty. Spind me days changin nappies, ferryin thim to hospitals, funeral parlours, checkin they take their medication, givin em glasses a whiskey to shuh em up, breakin up fights over armchairs and toffees. They go ah wan another like three-year-aulds. Caugh Celestius goin for the back of Aquinas' head wud a hommer last wake. I swiped ud ouh a hees hand just in the nick a time. Noh today, I says to Celestius, noh today, and he gives me this avil grin and slinks off. And Aquinas manewhile is oblivious to the whole thing, he's dribblin and droolin away to hees horse. He has this horse goes everywhere wud him.

Fermoy Noh a rale horse?

Boniface No, no, ud's all in hees addled little head. Him and the horse does everthin together, makes room in the bed for him and all. There's a place seh for him ah the table, betwane me and Aquinas. No wan else'll sih beside the horse. Ya'd want to see Aquinas fadin him rashers. I don't enquire whah goes on in bed betwane em. I'm afraid he'd tell me. And Bonaventura is in intensive care, thanks be to the Lord God.

Fermoy He's the wan calls ya Mammy?

Boniface Thah's him. And whin he's lucid he's worse. Wint inta see him yesterda, gev him a Padre Pio relic and he flings ud back ah me. Whah do I want wud Padre Pio's britches, says he. Well, is there anhin I can get ya, says I. There is, he says, me youh and Billie Holida. And then he goes into a swirl abouh bein cremahed, thah he's noh a Catholic any more, thah he never belaved in the first place, and him takin chunks ouha the chalice hees whole life. And despihe all the lunacy they cry like babbies at nigh, hare em whingin in their cells. Some part of em knows ud's over and they goh ud all wrong and still they hang on.

Fermoy Well, wouldn't you?

Boniface Apparently I am. Are ya goin to swing ud this time?

Fermoy Ud'll be a dogfigh.

Boniface Aye, Hannafin's mug is everywhere, he's some cowbiy, had the nerve to come canvassin me ah the monastery.

Fermoy Whah had he to say for heeself?

Boniface Asked me to talk sinse to you. Tould me to tell ya ya don't stand a chance, that you're ony makin a fool a yourself.

Fermoy Four votes. Four. That's all was in ud last time.

Boniface He still has the whole machine behind him. You're on your own.

Fermoy I've God behind me and what's a little civil war coven compared to God backin ya. I'll geh in this time alrigh. Been havin powerful drames lately. Drames of a conqueror.

Boniface Have ya now?

Fermoy Oh, aye. Dreamt last nigh I was dinin wud Alexander the Greah, Napoleon and Caesar, and we all had tigers' feeh under the whihe linen tablecloth. Ud was brilliant. And ya know thah famous portrait a Napoleon, up on hees whihe horse, the fah legs of him diggin inta the flanks, off to destriy the world? Well, I can't stop dramin abouh thah picture, ony I'm the wan on the whihe horse instead a Napoleon.

Boniface Noh another wan wud a horse. You should take up wud Aquinas.

Fermoy Laugh away. Me and God's on a wan to wan.

Boniface Oh, excuse me. And whin did this greah event occur? Ud wasn't in the papers.

Fermoy Ya think I'm jokin. I'm tellin ya I've direct access to him.

Boniface Well, you're the first I meh thah has. Tell him to scahher a few bars a gold in my pah next time yees are houldin hands.

Fermoy The last person ya should ever talk to abouh God is wan a the religious. Yees are the most cynical, rational, mathemahical shower I ever cem across whin ud comes to God.

Boniface Ya have to be mathemahical when you're dalin wud mystery.

Fermoy Well, yees have him ruined for all true belavers.

Boniface What do ya expect? Facts are he hasn't been seen for over two thousand year, for all we know he's left the solar system. We're goin on hearsay, gossip, the buuk. Times I wonder was he ever here.

Fermoy Well, if he wasn't none of ud makes sinse.

Boniface There's many belaves wasn't him med the earth ah all, thah ud was Satan and hees fallen armies, thah we were masterminded in hell, only Lucifer's pawns to geh ah God. Now I wouldn't go thah far meself, ih'd be too frightenin if thah was the case, buh for you to claim the privilege a God's ear is ouhrageous. Ud's blasphemy. Does paple belave in blasphemy any more?

Fermoy I do.

Boniface Well, if ya do why're ya claimin God's talkin to ya?

Fermoy I'm claimin natin, forget the whole thing.

Boniface No, ya've me curious now. And whah does he say to ya?

Fermoy I'm noh tellin ya, forgeh ud, cheers. (*Raises his glass, drinks.*)

Boniface I've offindid ya.

Fermoy I'm sick a ya talkin down to me from the heights a your canon law and the foosterins a the Pope a Rome and your cosy mehaphysics and your charihy. For all your religion ya know natin abouh the nature a God.

Boniface And you do?

Fermoy I know a couple a things.

Boniface And tell me, what's he like, this God a yours?

Fermoy Oh, he's beauhiful. When he throws hees head back hees hair gets tangled in the stars, and in hees hands are seven moons thah he juggles like worry beads. Hees eyes is shards of obsidian, hees skin is turquoise, and hees mouth is a staggerin red, whah the first red musta been before ud all started fadin. I'm noh capturin him righ, for how can ya parse whah is perfect.

Boniface My God is an auld fella in a tent, addicted to broccoli.

Fermoy No, God is young. He's so young. He's on fire for us, heaven reelin wud hees rage at not bein among us, the eternihy of eternihy hauntin him. Time manes natin to him. He rises from an afternoon nap and twinty centuries has passed.

Boniface No, no, no, he never slapes. Christianihy is based on God never slapin. You're wrong there, God does noh slape.

Fermoy My God slapes.

Boniface How d'ya know, did ya tuck him in? Rade him a bedtime story?

Fermoy Didn't I see him, a mountain slapin on a mountain.

Boniface Ah, you've had too much brandy.

Fermoy Don't you try pullin rank wud me, wud your cross and your robes and your broccoli God. I entered the landscape a God before you, long before. You can't tell me anhin abouh God.

Boniface Ya talkin abouh Ma, a'ya?

Fermoy No, I'm noh talkin abouh Ma. Why d'ya have to brin her up every time?

Boniface Do I brin her up every time?

Fermoy Wudouh fail.

Boniface And is thah a crime?

Fermoy Was thirty-five year ago, Boniface. She's gone, she's gone.

Boniface And whah an exih.

Fermoy She was never the suurt was goin to die in her bed.

Boniface She'd a died in her bed if she'd been leh . . . I remember goin home to see you wan time, soon after, and Auntie Sarah was sittin ah the table wearin Ma's clothes, the hair up in wan of her slides, prancin round the kitchen like ud was hers.

Fermoy Someone had to wash the dishes.

Boniface Now ud's comin ouh.

Fermoy Whah?

Boniface Thah I didn't lave the novitiate to look after ya.

Fermoy Auntie Sarah looked after me fine, fierce good to me, a packet a biscuits and a bottle a red lemonade every nigh before I wint to bed, whah more could ya ask for?

Boniface A wonder ya've a tooth in your head. No, shoulda been me looked after ya, ony I was a maniac for religion ah the time. I goh the full benefih a Ma's Christianihy, no douh abouh thah, a novice ah seventeen. Ya know ud never occurred to me to go agin her. At last ya were spared thah, buh I shoulda looked after ya.

Fermoy I grew up, didn't I? Furthest thing from me mind righ now. I've an election to win. D'you think I stand a chance?

Boniface Hannafin has the core vohe. He's held thah seat for twenty year. Be hard budge him.

Fermoy Nearly done ud last time. This time I will.

Boniface Whah makes ya so sure?

Fermoy Horse sinse and God. That's all ya nade to get by in this world, horse sinse and God. That's whah goh me this far and thah's what'll take me to the moon.

Boniface Ya may geh past Hannafin first.

Fermoy Ah, ud's noh Hannafin's the crux ah all, ud's meself, allas meself. Hannafin's a gombeen, like the rest of em. Why do they all want to be nice? What's so greah abouh bein liked? Am I missin somethin here? Swear ud was beahification they were after and em all cut-throats in their own kitchens. All chirpin the wan tune like there's no other – aqual wages, crèches in the workplace, no ceilin on the women, the pace process, a leg up for

75

the poor, the handicapped, the refugees, the tinkers, the tachers, the candlestick makers. In Sparta they were left on the side a the hill and that's where I'll lave em when I've the reins. I swear to God I'm goin to brin in a new religion, no more guilt, no more sorrow, no more good girls and good biys, just the unstoppable blood path a the soul.

Boniface Ya wont win an election on thah speech.

Fermoy Migh surprise ya to know how many agrays wud me. The earth's over, paple knows thah in their bones, ozone layer in tahhers, oceans gone to sewer, whole world wan big landfill a dirty nappies. We're goin to lave this place in ashes like the shower on Mars.

Boniface I don't belave in much any more. Gardenin, if ud was puh to me and me back to the wall I'd say I belave in cornflowers. I'd like to think whahever happens us thah this ground will survive us.

Fermoy The age a cornflowers is dead and gone. Last two thousand year a complahe farce. Well, ud's nearly over. We'll pick up where we left off.

Boniface And where's thah?

Fermoy The mortal sins is back in fashion. Welcome back, we missed yees. Age a compassion had uds turn, never took rooh. Well, way past time to banish the dregs to heaven's dungeon. The earth is ours wance more and noh before time.

Boniface If thah's your manifesto I may start prayin ya don't geh in.

Fermoy Ud's mine for the takin, I know ud is, all ud nades on my part is a sacrifice.

Boniface Whah suurt of a sacrifice?

76

Fermoy A sacrifice to God.

Boniface Buh whah suurt?

Fermoy The only suurt he acknowledges. Blood.

Boniface Blood?

Fermoy This thing's been edgin me to the cliff all year. And there's more. If I don't offer up this sacrifice he demands, he's goin to take ud anyway. And me for good measure. Whichever road I take is crooked. Thah's the price a God. If I make the sacrifice, then ud's all mine. Buh the cost, the cost. Impossible. Buh if I refuse this sacrifice, I'm facin the grave meself and, worse, facin him after refusin me destiny and, worse agin, after refusin him the wan thing he asks as payment for this enchanted life.

Boniface Spakin a blood, ours is streaked, Fermoy. You know thah well as me. The auld fella.

Fermoy This is different. We're talkin a different league here. We're talkin whah I was puh on this earth for.

Boniface No wan knows whah they're on the earth for.

Fermoy I do. I'm on this earth to rule. Was born knowin ud. Timidihy has held me back till now. Ud'll hould me back no longer. I refuse to spind any more a me life on the margins. I refuse to succumb to an early exih. I'll give him whah he wants for ud's hees in the first place anyway.

Boniface And whah is ud he wants?

Fermoy I tould ya, blood and more blood, blood till we're dry as husks, then pound us down, spread us like salt on the land, begin the experiment over, on different terms next time.

77

Boniface We've moved beyond the God a Job, Fermoy. Two thousand year a civilisation has taken us to a different place. Now I'm noh sayin this is Utopia or anywhere near ud, buh we have advanced a few small steps along the way. And for you to call up the auld God is terrifyin. I don't care how beauhiful he appears. He's a wolf and ud's a wolf you'll be growlin wud if ya dredge him up. You're playin dangerous games here. God does noh do dales, ah laste the God I know doesn't. I mane whah exactly is this blood sacrifice? Is ud some suurt a pagan calf ritual or are we talkin somethin far older and more sinister here?

Fermoy Can't a man air the festerins of hees soul withouh bein convicted?

Boniface No, I don't think he can. Thah's why there's such a thing as custody a the tongue. Thah's why our thoughts is silent, so we can do away wud em before they're spoken. And ud's a mighy short journey from sayin a thing to doin ud.

Fermoy Ah, forget the whole bleddy business.

Boniface Ih'd fit yourself behher to forgeh ud.

Fermoy Alrigh. Alrigh. Ud's forgotten. Gone. I'll lave ud wud the nigh where ud belongs and hope ud'll lave me. In the manetime I've an election comin and I've a problem wud the hospitals, wonderin could ya help me.

Boniface If I can.

Fermoy Ud's all the wans dyin in their beds wud their faces to the wall, nade their votes.

Boniface Ah, would ya lave em alone.

Fermoy Ya think I want to be botherin thim? There's only a spider's leg between me and Hannafin. Whah would ya say to a dyin person thah'd make em vote for ya?

Boniface Say natin ony sih and talk to em.

Fermoy I'm noh the Sisters a Mercy, talk to em abouh whah?

Boniface I'd'n know . . . heaven, mebbe?

Fermoy Whah? Say natin abouh votin ony soother em wud eternihy? Alrigh, I've a good workin knowledge of eternihy. I'll melt em wud pictures of uds silver avenues and uds houses a tarnished gold and the blue waher lappin offa the whihe marble pier as the brass-bodied angels grates em wud mugs a tay. If they don't serve tay in heaven there won't be an Irish person in the place.

Boniface And ya call yourself religious.

Fermoy Yes, I do, buh my eternihy is noh for the herd.

Boniface The herd's eternihy will do fine for me.

Fermoy No douh ud will, a swate little postcard heaven. Have you any idea of the vastness of heaven? Your heaven would fih on a stamp. Mine cannoh be measured.

Boniface Then I think ud's a dangerous thing noh to have the square rooh a heaven in your mind.

Fermoy Look, I nade to wrihe a lehher to thah eegih thah runs the health buurd. Whah's this hees name is agin? The wan wud the coconuh hair?

Boniface Alloni.

Fermoy Thah's him, noh returnin me calls. I nade the run a the hospitals, auld folks homes, day cintres, thah suurt a thing. You should know the kind a lehher thah'll

geh him. He's givin Hannafin free rein and he won't leh
me in. What's hees pisin anyway?

Boniface Bates the wife. Mebbe he's stopped. See her
goin round wudouh her sunglasses, perfect face on her.

Fermoy Anhin else?

Boniface He puh wan a hees kids in hospital a while
back. Med em take ouh her appendix, noh a thing
wrong a the girl.

Fermoy I suppose if ya run the health buurd ya can have
the whole family operahed on for free.

Boniface Mebbe ud was a sign of affection.

Fermoy Or a birthday present. Come an down to the
den and we shape this lehher. (*Upwards.*) I'll geh in yet,
sir, wud or wudout ya. (*Exiting by the cake.*) Ya want a
slice a cake?

Boniface Naw.

Fermoy Me aither. Hate cake, so does the kids.

He smashes the cake.

Allas wanted to do thah to a cake. Ah, Auntie Sarah,
spyin agin.

Sarah Wanta be fierce bored to be perchin on your
conversation. I hear Hannafin's goin to win.

Fermoy Ya won't rise me, missus.

Sarah Only tellin ya the word abroad.

Fermoy I won't be countin on your vohe so.

Sarah And the missus is votin Green, heard her on the
phone.

Fermoy Ah, the little protest vohe. The Granes'll come back to me ivintually. She'll vohe for me in spihe of herself. Why does all the women in this house want to kill me?

Sarah Law a the world, don't take ud personally.

Exit Boniface and Fermoy as Ariel enters, talking on her mobile. Sarah tries to fix the cake.

Ariel (*on her mobile*) Yeah, a suurt of a buhherfly yella . . . brand new, I swear . . . Yeah . . . Whah're y'up to? . . . Yeah, I seen ud, fierce, isn't ud? . . . Ya love ud? Ah, ud's wocious, ya still belave in Noddyland, ah, Stephanie . . . Yeah, yeah, whah time yees matin ah? . . . No, they'll never leh me, never leh me anywhere, afraid somewan'd run off wud me. I wish . . . Did he say he'd be there? . . . Damn ud . . . Sunda nigh they'll never leh me . . .

Frances (*entering*) You're goin nowhere in the dark, Ariel, so don't bother askin.

Ariel (*exiting*) Ah, Ma . . . (*To Stephanie on the mobile.*) Ya heard thah, did ya? Look, tell him I'll see him in school tomorra . . . Yeah, yeah. (*She's well offstage by now.*)

Frances Whah happened the cake?

Sarah Didn't heeself puh hees fist through ud.

Frances (*to Stephen who stands beside her, looking at her*) I said no, Stephen, you're noh getting ud.

Stephen Just a sup.

Frances I'm noh a lollypop.

Stephen (*climbing on her knee*) Come an and don't be so manchey wud em. (*Going for her breast.*)

Frances I said, no. (*Stops him.*) No, Stephen, no. (*A struggle.*)

Sarah Ah, leh him suck away. If there was wan goin I'd be suckin on ud too.

Frances (*struggling with him*) No way, Stephen. Whah would your Daddy say?

Stephen Don't you dare tell him!

Frances I'll tell him righ now if ya don't stop.

Stephen Alrigh, alrigh, just leh me lie up agin ya. (*Lies up against her.*)

Frances Don't fall aslape on me now, I'm warnin ya. (*To Sarah.*) Here, give us a bih a cake, love cake, I'd ahe ud all down to the plahe.

Sarah gives her a lump of cake. Enter Elaine.

Ya want a bih a cake, Elaine?

Elaine No. (*Stands there watching Frances.*)

Frances Damn ud, he's aslape.

Elaine He's ony pretendin.

Frances Wake up, Stephen, come an, wake up, love. (*To Elaine.*) What do ya want, peh?

Elaine Natin, just lookin at ya.

Frances Did ya like Ariel's birthday?

Elaine No.

Frances And why, migh I ask?

Elaine Birthdays is ony interestin when they're your own.

Frances A'ya lookin for a scrap, are ya?

Elaine Yeah, I am.

Frances Ya'd too much Coke, that's what's wrong a ya.

Elaine Daddy tould ya noh to be doin thah thing wud Stephen.

Frances Whah thing? I'm noh doin anhin wud him.

Elaine You're a liar. A big liar.

Frances Don't you call me a liar, and stop givin me the avil eye. I'm tired, Elaine, I'm tired.

Elaine stands there looking at Frances.

Sarah She's like her grandmother, thah wan, she'd stare the world down, biggest eyes y'ever seen. I goh the hands, she goh the eyes.

Elaine And where is me grandmother?

Sarah Never you mind where she is.

Elaine She's ah the bohhom a Cuura Lake where me grandaddy puh her, in a bag wud a boulder, nowan ever found her.

Frances If ya know why're ya askin?

Elaine Want to hear her say ud. She's ah the bohhom a Cuura Lake where me grandaddy puh her. Love the sound a thah.

Sarah Ya do, don't ya, ya babby witch in the cauldron. Thah child knows too much.

Elaine And where were you when ud was happenin, Auntie Sarah?

Sarah Never you mind where I was.

Elaine Ya were warmin me grandaddy's bed, that's where ya were.

Sarah And what's ud to you if I was?

Elaine Ud's information and information is useful.

Frances Thah's enough, Elaine. G'wan ouhside the duur and don't come back in till ya say sorry to Auntie Sarah.

Elaine Well, ud's true, isn't ud, what's to be sorry for when ud's true? (*Squeezes Frances.*)

Frances Ow, ya rip, ya!

Elaine Thah's for the last twelve years.

Frances Geh ouh!

Elaine (*sauntering out*) Ya think ud bothers me goin ouhside the duur? Love ud ouh there. Can't waih to be ouhside your duur forever.

Sarah There's a madam. I'd like to see her whin she's twinty-wan.

Frances Thah child hates me, I don't know why ud is, buh thah child hates me.

Sarah Mebbe she'll grow ouh of ud.

Frances Ud's noh natural. From the very beginnin she wanted rid a me. Times I think she's me penance for James. Isn't thah an awful thing to think?

Sarah High time you stopped torturin yourself over James.

Frances Why will no wan in this house leh me talk abouh James? Fermoy goes mad if I mention him, he thinks I'm blamin him. If I wanted to I could, for James' death was as much hees fault as mine. I wanted to brin him on the honeymoon. Fermoy says no, lave him wud your aunts. And oh . . . when they rang and tould me . . . three thousand miles away and James dead from the belt

of a hurl . . . still can't belave ud. (*Produces locket.*)
Look ah him. And hees father. I wasn't good to thah
man. Two calves they were. Look at them.

Sarah Seen ud before, Frances, seen ud before, many,
many times.

Frances Aye . . . and these tears is natin to the wans I'll
shed in the future. I still have to pay for James. Every
mornin I ask meself is this the day the roof's goin to fall
in for whah I done to James. And if I as much as look
ouh the winda a second too long or pause in the hall of
an avenin, Fermoy goes inta a reel of how I loved James
and the first husband more than him. Well mebbe I did.
Fermoy threw the dust in me eyes. These two I loved.

Sarah (*exiting with dishes*) The beauhiful dead, the
beauhiful dead, everywan loves em.

Elaine (*head around the door*) I've a fierce destiny, Ma,
and you're in ud.

Sarah (*shoos her out*) Away wud ya and lave your
mother alone.

*Frances sits there with Stephen asleep on her knee,
looking at locket. She looks from locket to Stephen to
locket. She strokes his head.*

Frances You've a look of him alrigh. The eyes, yees boh
have my eyes. Buh ya don't have hees black curls, you've
Fermoy's hair. James had the most beauhiful, beauhiful
head a blue black curls. Paple'd stop us in the street to
touch hees curls. I had to puh a clip in your hair to kape
the curls ouha your eyes and still I wouldn't cuh em.
Whin a' ya goin to cuh thah child's hair, they'd ask.
Never, I'd say, never, and I never did. Five years a black
curls wint inta thah grave and me wud em.

Enter Boniface.

Boniface I'm away, Frances. Ah, the child, the child, is there anhin lovelier than a slapin child?

Frances There is, aye. A dead wan. (*Closes locket.*)

Boniface Is thah so?

Frances If he doesn't geh in this time there'll be war.

Boniface He's overdue a dressin down.

Frances Help him, will ya, Boniface? He's us all driven mad here, you know everywan, geh em to vohe for him. He's noh a bad man, just all wrong, behher than Hannafin.

Boniface Ah, Hannafin's harmless, he's the auld school, sell the whole country down the Swanee for an extension to hees bungalow and a new jape.

Frances Well, I'm the wan'll suffer if he doesn't geh in. I'm the wan'll be blemt.

Boniface I've an awful falin he's goin to swing ud. He's down there in the den rattlin on abouh blood sacrifice and destiny and vision. God help us all if he gets in, thah's whah I say. The auld fella was a tyrant too.

Frances I only meh him the wance, thought he was a fine auld gintleman.

Boniface He'd the charm a forty divils alrigh. They allas do, buh back a the charm was the stuck-up rebellis heart of all a Lucifer's crew. Does he ever talk to ya abouh the auld lad?

Frances Me and thah man doesn't talk ah all. Wance ya go past hello wud Fermoy he wants to kill ya. Asier say natin.

Boniface Ask him abouh the auld lad and Ma sometime.

Frances God, no, don't want to open thah buuk a butchery. Sooner leh an ud never happened.

Boniface Oh, ud happened, and me man in there in the middle of ud all. Auld fella med him hould Ma down.

Frances He was ony a child, wasn't he, wasn't hees fault.

Boniface I'm noh sayin ud was. All I'm sayin is somethin like thah is bound to take uds toll on a person's view a the world. I don't like the way he's goin an.

Frances And why did your father do ud?

Boniface In cuurt he said ud was to save her the trouble a dyin laher an. Figure thah wan ouh at your leisure.

Frances And whah had she done? I don't mane she deserved to be puh in a bag and pegged to the bohhom of a lake, buh whah was goin an?

Boniface He tried to make ouh she was havin an affair. She wasn't. Thah woman was in love wud wan man and wan man only. Padre Pio of San Giovanni.

Frances Hard compate wud Padre Pio.

Boniface Her party piece was Padre Pio hearin her confession. And ah the end of ud he puh hees hand through the curtain and the stigmaha bled onta her blouse. She had the blouse folded in tissue paper wud lavender sprigs all over ud. And if ya were really good she'd take down the blouse and leh us trace our fingers over the blood. That's eternihy you're touchin, she'd say. That's eternihy, be careful wud ud. Christ, I could tell ya stories abouh thah woman, never a dull moment, and the eyelashes on her and the big dark mane of her, like a horse, like a beauhiful Egyptian horse. And the auld lad doesn't know whah to do wud her so he does away wud her.

Frances And Fermoy there in the middle of ud all. The size a the nigh in thah man is past measurin.

Fermoy has entered.

Fermoy Is ud now? . . . Was he on ya agin?

Frances He's ony sittin on me knee.

Fermoy Know you're lyin. Can smell the milk.

Frances You slape better ah nigh thinkin I'm a liar.

Fermoy I certainly do. (*Takes Stephen.*) C'mere, me little man, till we snake some gristle inta your drames.

Frances Whah'd ya go and mash the cake for? Ya know I love cake.

Fermoy And ya love withholdin ud. I'm married to a nun, Boniface, a born agin virgin. Ud's noh every man can say he's hitched hees cart to the reverend mother.

Boniface Ya may lave me ouha the sheets.

Frances I'll take off me wimple when you learn how to trahe a woman righ and noh before.

Fermoy And where am I supposed to learn? On a rockin horse?

Frances Ya know natin, Fermoy Fitzgerald.

Fermoy Then tell me, missus! G'wan, tell me! Listen to this now, Boniface, listen to wan of her dirges on love.

Frances Waste a breah dirgin you.

Fermoy Sure, the only rason I married ya was so I could have ud on demand. And all she does is talk abouh ud, talk abouh ud wud this lad here latched onto her. Look ah hees teeth, he's whah? Ten, and he still has hees milk teeth. They won't fall ouh till she weans him. Buh she won't wean him. Ya know why? Because then she'd have to dale wud me. I've the length a you, missus. I know whah's goin on in thah little bantam head a yours. You should be tratin me like a king steada grindin me down to bone male.

Frances You and your auld election. Ya never have a nice word. Ya never have a word. (*Exiting.*) In and ouh like a fox. Sooner be palin a bag a spuds.

Fermoy (*goes after her, yanks locket from her neck*) Knew ud! Just knew ud. Sure there's no talkin to ya when ya've thah yoke round your neck.

Frances Gimme thah back if ya value your life.

Fermoy (*fending her off*) Look whah she wears round her neck.

Frances Give us ud.

Boniface Ah, would ya give the woman her locket.

Fermoy Look ah him! Look whah I have to puh up wud. The first husband. Pugnacious puss of him.

Frances Gimme thah back now, ya gone too far.

Fermoy High time ya forgoh abouh them. They're dead. Dead as stones. I'm your husband. There's your son. (*Stephen.*)

Frances (*pointing at locket*) And there's me other son. Look ah him if ya dare. The wan ya killed.

Fermoy Oh, here we go.

Frances You killed him or as good as.

Fermoy How, tell me how did I kill him and I on another continent?

Frances Wud black thinkin and wishin him away.

Fermoy Brin him wud us, I told ya. Brin him on the bleddy honeymoon for all I care.

Frances Like hell ya said brin him wud us. You're greah ah re-jiggin the past, allas wud yourself as the haroh. Give him to me, ud's me favourihe picture, give him to me.

Fermoy Well now, missus, you shoulda taken the edge off of me this morning.

Exit Fermoy.

Boniface Y'alrigh?

Frances This is ony the warm-up. This is natin.

Boniface Ya want me to get your locket back?

Frances No, thah's whah he'd like. Leh him cool hees jets. He'll be back for another round.

Boniface Righ, I'm away durin the calm.

Frances Nigh, Boniface.

Frances wakes Stephen.

C'mon, peh, up to bed.

Stephen Whah am I doin noh on your knee?

Frances Your Daddy was nursin ya.

Stephen Ya didn't tell him, did ya? Make a holy show a me.

Frances No, I didn't tell him.

Stephen I'm givin y'up for Lint, ya may puh up wud me till then.

Frances Alrigh, ya mane thah now, do ya?

Stephen I do. Will ya come up and say goodnigh to me, I'll be fierce fast.

Frances Alrigh, me little man.

She kisses him. He walks sleepily from the room as Ariel stands in the doorway.

Ariel Ah, Ma, leh us ouh for five minutes, will ya, want to show Stephanie the car.

Frances Buh ud's dark, love.

Ariel I'll be wary. Ah, Ma, ud's me birthday, I'll be righ back.

Frances Ya enjiy your birthday?

Ariel Aye, never thought I'd see sixteen.

Frances Swear ya were ninety.

Ariel I know ud's mad, buh I never thought I'd make me sixteenth birthday. I've this thing abouh a girl in a graveyard, don't know where ud cem from, buh just before I go to slape and me mind's blanked ouh, this sintince kapes comin. Girl in a graveyard, girl in a graveyard, I tap ud ouh on the pilla, puts me to slape like a lullaby. Mad, isn't ud?

Frances Ud's somethin. G'wan then to Stephanie. I'm timin ya.

Ariel You're a great little ma.

She blows her a kiss and she's gone. Frances sits there eating the cake. Hold a minute. Then enter Fermoy with a CD. He puts it on. Stands there listening to it, looking at her. Dancing.

Fermoy Ya wanted some romance, missus.

Frances Take more than Spanish eyes to romance me.

Fermoy (*dances towards her, for her*) You're the wan, you're the wan. I'm just busy, busy, you're lookin ah the next Taoiseach. Go aisy on me a while, will ya, and then I'm yours agin.

Frances Where's me locket?

Fermoy takes locket from his pocket, gives it to her, dancing all the time. She examines it.

What's your phoho doin here?

Fermoy I left in the child's phoho. Don't be getting thick over natin agin. I don't mind ya wearin a phoho of the child but noh heeself. I'm the wan should be straddlin your heart.

Frances And what ya do wud Charlie's phoho?

Fermoy On me desk.

Frances Ud's important to remember whah has been lost.

Fermoy (*pulling her to him*) I know. I know.

Frances Like hell, ya know. Ya don't remember yesterda, you're thah suurt of a man.

Fermoy (*dancing with her*) Oh, I remember everythin, don't you ever fear, buh ud's important to forget too.

Kisses her, a long lovely kiss. Enter Hannafin, stands there watching and listening.

Frances We started on the wrong fooh, Fermoy, no way to puh ud righ.

Fermoy Ud was meant to be.

Frances I wish I could be as certain as you. Facts are me goin wud you cost me me husband's life, me son's life and forever more me peace a mind.

Fermoy Whah happened James and Charlie was strokes a destiny.

Frances Strokes a destiny?

Fermoy Aye, natin to do wud you or me. The man above cleared the way, is all. Ony for destiny you'd a ran back and forth between me and Charlie. Ya'd be runnin still. Ya should be grateful the chice was med for ya.

Frances And James?

Fermoy James was left field, I'll admih thah. James' death shook me to the core. And then I began to understand the God we're dalin wud. He was boulsterin us for things to come.

Frances Whah things to come?

Fermoy We mustn't be afraid, we mustn't baulk, ony dance to the music till the music's done. And when I'm Taoiseach you'll be there wud me, where ya belong. That's whah's wrong a the country, noh enough sex. I'm goin to creahe a new ministry, the ministry a sex. You'll be the minister and I'll be your assistant. We'll give em demonstrations on the national airwaves, we'll be the new Angelus.

Hannafin And put the whole nation off their tay.

Fermoy Hannafin . . . Whah do we owe this pleasure to?

Hannafin Look, Fitzgerald, ya won't geh me seah offa me. I've the core vohe wrapped up, whole county in me fist.

Fermoy Four votes, Hannafin. All I naded last time, four votes. Thah's never happenin agin.

Hannafin Ya want to play dirty. Alrigh. I'm the Baron a Dirt when ud's called for.

Fermoy I'm squaky clane, and ya know ud. Thah's why you're here whimperin like a girl.

Hannafin Squaky clane. Whah abouh your father and mother?

Fermoy Whah's thah got to do wud me?

Hannafin Everywan knows you were there.

Fermoy I was there alrigh. But you're noh criminally responsible ah seven. Ya don't know your law.

Hannafin I know me law and I know the pulse a the paple. The apple doesn't fall far from the tree. And here, I've the figures a the new poll. (*Produces fax.*)

Fermoy That's noh ouh till the mornin.

Hannafin For the likes a you, mebbe. For us in the know any information can be goh. I'm miles ahead a ya. Here, look ah ud yourself.

Fermoy (*hits it away*) Them polls, allas wrong.

Hannafin smiles, lets poll sheet fall to the floor.

Hannafin And how is the lady a the house?

Frances Very well, thank you.

Hannafin Was visihin the mother's grave today, do thah every Sunda, brin the auld daffodils to lay on her bones, and I passed be your son's grave, tiny little yoke of a yoke, fierce neglected lookin, reminded me a you. Just who do yees think yees are? Yees think the wind is in yeer favour just because yees built the big house wud the Grake columns and the fountains goin full blast and the lions roarin on the gates and the money pourin in from the cement and gravel. Ud's my wind yees goh a whiff of and be careful ud doesn't blow yees away. You're messin wud my votes, Fitzgerald, the hurlers on the ditch who'd go wud me if you weren't banjaxin everythin. Back down now before ya make a hames of ud all. Sure they're ony laughin at ya. The murderer's' son for this county. That'll never happen. Back down now and I'll owe ya wan.

Fermoy The county's sick a ya, Hannafin, and ya know ud. Ya do natin ony drink whiskey and lap-dance. Whin's the last time you spoke in the Dáil apart from tellin them to close the winda?

Hannafin Alrigh, I asked ya nicely. Now we'll do ud the hard way. If you don't back down I've an interview done that'll put ya in your place. All I have to do is make a call and ud'll be all over the mornin papers.

Fermoy I know what's in ud. You're noh the ony wan can geh information. Natin, ony hoh air abouh me laineage. Me mother and father, Frances' son and first husband, me brother Boniface and hees addictions, long cured, ya didn't put thah in. Thah's all ya have, thah's all there is. Pathehic. Oh, aye, there's me greah grandfather, they say he ate a child durin the famine. So did everywan's durin the famine. So did yours.

Hannafin Well, if he did, he didn't ate wan of hees own.

Fermoy Hunger is hunger. Laineage manes natin any more. You're the auld generation thah'd like to kape us in our place forever. We new wans comin up judge a man for whah he is in heeself, noh where he cem from. We judge a man these days be hees own merit, as if he'd ne'er a smithy bar God heeself.

Hannafin The pipe drames of the self-med. You were forged in a bloodbah, Fitzgerald, and the son allas carries the father somewhere inside of him. I know thah much, he carries the Da inside of him sure as he carries hees kidneys, the family jewels, the heart. And ud's time

the paple beyond this parish knew the gruesome
blacksmith hommered you to earth and the symmetry
can be predicted from there.

Fermoy And whah abouh your own symmetry,
Hannafin, and your father dancin up the field the last
three year of hees life, waltzin wud the sheep, or your
mother stealin jars a coffee from every shop for miles
around? Whah was ud abouh coffee thah everthin
collided in her over jars a coffee? Or your grandmother
walkin inta the silver river ah eighy-seven? Christ, if ya
could puh up wud ud all till you're eighy-seven and thah
new asbestos plant, there's noh a lake or river we can
swim in any more, thanks to you. And thah piggery,
who's been fundin thah all these years? There's lots a
questions to be asked concernin you if ya want to play
ud thah way.

Hannafin And there's a few inquiries to be med as to
how the cement and gravel empire goh off of the ground.

Fermoy The cement and gravel was grown from the air
be me and Frances and ya know ud. I heard ya been
snoopin round our accounts, whadlin the tax biys, and
ya found natin because there's natin to find. I'm warnin
you, Hannafin, you open your gob abouh my personal
life and I'll take ya to the claners.

Hannafin There's somethin rotten in you, Fitzgerald. I
know ud, know ud like me own hand. I just can't puh a
finger on ud yeh. Buh I will before long. In the manetime
thah interview goes ouh in the mornin. That'll get the
ball rollin. If ya've any thoughts to the contrary ya know
me number. I'll give ya an hour, no more.

Exit Hannafin.

Frances (*poll sheet*) Is these polls accurahe?

Fermoy Accurahe enough.

Frances Well, I'm noh looking forward to radin abouh meself in the papers. Me aunts'll go through the roof. Peg in the towel, Fermoy, ud's obvious he's goin to win. Ring him, geh him to cancel thah interview.

Fermoy A'you goin to start layin inta me as well?

Frances Everywan says he's goin to hould hees seah. Look, we been through this before wud Hannafin.

Fermoy Ya don't same to know how important this is, missus.

Frances I know whah ud's like livin wud you after a defeat.

Fermoy I'm noh losing this time. Geh thah inta your head.

Frances You're the ony wan thinks thah.

Fermoy I suppose ya'd like me to lose agin.

Frances I'd like a bih a peace round here. I'd like a bih a help wud the cement. Ya know, mebbe too many bad things has happened, Fermoy, for you to win. Mebbe you losin agin is God tellin us our golden reprieve is over.

Fermoy Kape your auld guilt trip to yourself. Charlie and James have natin to do wud this and they've natin to do wud me.

Frances You tould Charlie abouh us. You tould Charlie abouh us though I begged ya not to.

Fermoy Somewan had to tell him. You weren't goin to.

Frances I would have. In me own time.

Fermoy Like hell ya would. Ya'd still be stringin the both of us along.

97

Frances You just couldn't waih to hurt somewan. You knew thah man loved me.

Fermoy And I don't?

Frances He was my husband. You were just a fling, a fling thah wint wrong.

Fermoy Then whah're ya doin wud me this seventeen year?

Frances You're the father a me children. That's whah I'm doin wud ya.

Exit Frances. Fermoy sits there brooding. Hold a minute. Enter Ariel.

Ariel Meh Hannafin in the lane.

Fermoy Aye, he was here.

Ariel The car's mad.

Fermoy Is ud?

Ariel Yeah. Thanks. (*Kisses the top of his head.*)

Fermoy Whah'd Hannafin to say for heeself?

Ariel He puts wan a hees cowbiy boots up on the bonneh, lanes in the winda, pats me on the head, 'Aren't you the fine girl, Ariel Fitzgerald, considerin who spawned ya?' Tould me to give ya this.

Fermoy examines it.

Whah is ud?

Fermoy Ah, ud's an auld newspaper cuttin abouh me father's trial.

Ariel Whah was he really like?

98

Fermoy Whah was he really like? He was really like whah he really was, a man in a navy raincoah thah butchered me mother . . . Ya know whah he done after?

Ariel Whah?

Fermoy Lih a cigarette, puh me up on hees shoulders, all the way up from the lake, across the fields to the Sea Dew Inn. We sah at the counter, him drinkin four Jemmies, the eyes glihherin, glancin from me to the glass to the fluur, then lanin over and whisperin 'Time to be turnin ourselves in.'

Ariel And what did you say?

Fermoy Don't remember if I said anhin . . . All I remember is lookin ah him, the low sounds of Sunda evenin drinkin, the barmaid puttin an lipstick and him smilin, yeah, smilin. How can ya describe thah to anywan?

Ariel He shouldn't a said 'we'.

Fermoy Ya think noh?

Ariel A cuurse noh.

Fermoy No, 'we' was righ. I was there too. And though I was only seven, an excuse on this earth, I was also seven thousand and seven millin, for the soul is wan age and mine just stood and watched. I'd seen him drown a bag a kittens, blind, tiny pink tongues and fairy teeth. Really this was no different.

A pause. Fermoy studies Ariel.

Ariel Whah? Whah is ud, Daddy?

Fermoy Ya want to take me for a spin in your new chariot?

Ariel Alrigh. Where do ya want to go?

Fermoy Anywhere.

Ariel Then anywhere ud is. Will we brin Ma?

Fermoy Gone to bed.

Ariel I'll puh ouh the ligh so.

She looks out. Puts out the light. 'Mors et Vita' music. Blackout.

Act Two

'Mors et Vita' music as curtain comes up. Ten years later.
Fermoy sits centre stage. Beautifully groomed. An
interview is in progress. Verona, the interviewer, sits to
the side. Cameraman, Soundman, to the other side.
Elaine stands watching, in a suit, taking notes.

Fermoy Yes, I've held three ministries over the past ten
years.

Verona And of the three, Minister, do you have a
favourite?

Fermoy They're all very different. I enjiyed tremendously
Arts and Culture though I was only there for a year. Ih
was an area I knew very little abouh when I took over
the brief. I used look up to artists and poets before I got
to know em. Ih was a greah education to realise they're
as fickle and wrongheaded as the rest of us. Thah said,
ih was a huge learnin curve for me and, I'll tell ya, it's
hard to beah a pride a poets and a tank a wine for good
conversation.

Verona And what is it, Minister, that's just so great
about their conversation?

Fermoy It's noh aisy puh a finger on ud, buh I think ud's
their attempts, mostly banjaxed mind you, buh an
attempt anyway to throw eternihy on the table.

Verona You're a great believer in eternity, aren't you,
Minister?

Fermoy Yes, I am.

Verona You said it was divine providence that won you your seat ten years ago.

Fermoy I said ih was divine grace.

Verona With all due respects to divine grace, Minister, didn't you rise in proportion to Hannafin's fall?

Fermoy A cuurse I did, but thah doesn't diminish divine grace. If that scandal had broken a week laher, Hannafin would've kept hees seat.

Verona There were suggestions at the time, Minister, that you were instrumental in the breaking of that scandal.

Fermoy Malicious gossip.

Verona And still the rumours persist, Minister.

Fermoy Yeah, by them thah'd like to take me down. Facts are I was elected fair and square by the people. Why make a mountain ouh of a molehill?

Verona I wouldn't call the suicide of a highly respected politician a 'molehill', Minister.

Fermoy I wasn't referrin to Hannafin's suicide as a 'molehill'. I was referrin to how I was elected. Hannafin's suicide was tragic. We weren't exactly bosom buddies but ud wint hard wud me thah he thought ud necessary to take hees own life. And ud has been devastatin for hees wife and children.

Verona No doubt it has. However, you went on to become Minister of Finance after Arts and Culture. How did you find that transition?

Fermoy Well, there's more fiction written in Finance than in Arts and Culture, so the transition wasn't that difficult.

Verona I remember, Minister, the outrage at the time, both within your own Party and from the Opposition, when you were appointed. They said you were untried, untested, too green.

Fermoy They said a loh of other things too, not fit for public consumption.

Verona The former Taoiseach took a big risk on you.

Fermoy Ih turned ouh to be no risk. My term in Finance was wan of the most successful in the history of the State.

Verona And it begs the question why you haven't remained in Finance.

Fermoy I'd learned all I had to learn there.

Verona It's on the record, Minister, that you said of Finance, and I quote, 'I'm fed up being the nation's handbag.'

Fermoy Thah was said in a private conversation, on Christmas Eve, after seven brandies. Are ya goin to crucify me for thah now?

Verona You're also on the record as saying that your term in Finance left you feeling like Granny on pension day with the bag of gobstoppers.

Fermoy Look, I spent five and a half year in Finance. I brough ud kickin and screamin inta the twenty-first century. I brough money inta the country from places yees didn't know existed and in ways ye'd never dreamt of. I done me service in Finance. Ih was time to move on.

Verona But your refusal to remain in Finance caused a huge rift between you and the former Taoiseach.

Fermoy Yes, ud did, but don't forgeh I served him faithfully for the best part of eight year. He taught me everythin I know.

Verona Was it a question, Minister, of the pupil outstripping the master?

Fermoy Ih was more complicahed than thah.

Verona Whatever it was, it led to the no-confidence motion in his leadership last year.

Fermoy Mebbe ud did.

Verona Come on, Minister, the whole country knows you were behind that no-confidence motion. The word abroad is that the present Taoiseach, Mr Dudley, is your puppet and that very shortly he'll get the axe too.

Fermoy Well, the word is wrong. As usual. I wish I knew as much abouh me self as yees reporters know. The facts are very different.

Verona And what are the facts, Minister?

Fermoy There's an optimum moment for everywan, few recognise ud when ud comes and fewer still recognise when the moment is gone. Never to return. The Taoiseach was jaded. The party had lost direction and the party cannoh be sacrificed to wan individual, whahever our privahe estimations of thah individual may be. And belave me when I say I held him in the highest esteem and will always. Hard decisions cost us all and I know more than most the price a those decisions. You think I enjiyed the public humiliation of a close friend. You're wrong. You're very wrong.

Verona It's not over yet, is it, Minister?

Fermoy What d'ya mean?

Verona Dudley's leadership has been disastrous.

Fermoy That's a mahher of opinion.

Verona The electorate is losing patience, Minister.
They'd rather you came clean.

Fermoy I've no idea what you're talkin abouh.

Verona That you have your eye on the leadership. That
it's only a matter of time before Dudley goes. The Party's
in such a state right now they'll give you the reins. That
you've the whole place in uproar. You control the
Cabinet as it is. You are Taoiseach in everything but
name.

Fermoy You overestimahe my power. I'm Minister for
Education. That's my job.

Verona Can you categorically state you will not be
orchestrating a no-confidence motion in Mr Dudley's
leadership in the next week or two?

Fermoy That's somethin for the Party to decide.

Verona Could you answer the question, please,
Minister? Are you or are you not interested in
Leadership?

Fermoy Well, a cuurse I'm interested. I wouldn't be
where I am if I wasn't. But I'm noh interested in power
ah any price. I love power, yes, I love ud, buh I love ud
as an artist loves ud.

Verona You love power as an artist loves it. You're
quoting Napoleon, Minister.

Fermoy I'm paraphrasin him.

Verona Are you comparing yourself with Napoleon,
Minister?

Fermoy Who can compare wud Napoleon? I can't, aven if I wanted to, because I'm born inta the wrong century, surrounded be the wrong people. If you're a Napoleon lover you'll know whah he said as he was dyin on St Helena, 'If I had sailed for Ireland instead of Egypt, where would England be now, and the world?' This country has missed ouh on everythin, overlooked be Alexander the Greah, overlooked be Caesar, overlooked be the Moors. Overlooked, overlooked, overlooked. The rest a the world gets Napoleon, we get a boatload a Vikings, a handful a Normans and the English. We get the nation a shopkeepers.

Verona Napoleon's verdict on the British. Are you anti-British, Minister?

Fermoy No, a cuurse I'm noh. I'm talkin abouh imagination. If ya have to be colonised ya migh as well be colonised by somewan wud a bih a vision. I'm talkin abouh a way of lookin at the world. D'ya look ah ud from behind a till or d'ya look ah ud from the saddle of a horse on a battlefield? And, like ud or noh, the legacy the Brihish have left us is the till, whereas for Napoleon the world was wan big battlefield. He talked abouh hees battlefields like they were women. Which a the battlefields was more beauhiful than the other. That's the stuff we nade to learn, or rather re-learn, we knew ud wance. Aven Caesar while butcherin the Celts had to acknowledge whah a strange tribe he was dalin wud. 'They measure periods a time be nights, noh be days.' That's whah he said abouh us. Wance we had a calendar, markin out time be the nigh. Them were the biys had the perspective. Look, the outsize ego a this nation is built on sand and wind, a few dramers, natin else. We nade to go back to first principles. We nade to re-imagine ourselves from scratch.

Verona You've been much criticised by the Opposition for precisely this going back to first principles, Minister, which you've outlined in your Education Papers.

Fermoy It's the Oppositions's job to oppose so I don't take them too seriously.

Verona They're not the only ones unhappy over some of the contents of these Papers.

Fermoy I'm noh interested in cosmehics. If you're goin to do somethin, do ud righ or don't do ud ah all. Learned thah on me mother's knee. Look, I chose to go inta Education. Lots has seen thah as a step down. Well, ud's noh. I chose Education because ud all begins and ends wud education. And my business righ now is to re-educahe a nation. Thah won't be done in a day.

Verona Some of us think we don't need to be re-educated, Minister, not to mind your refusal to consult with the experts. A sizeable portion of the public is alarmed by the last three Papers your party has pushed through.

Fermoy There's natin to be alarmed abouh. I think we've proved over and over we have this country's interests at heart.

Verona But your Theology Paper, Minister, has caused uproar.

Fermoy I belave in God well as the next.

Verona Come on, Minister, your God is as far from the traditional notion of God as it is possible to be.

Fermoy Yes, he is, and I make no apology for thah.

Verona The Church has spoken out against you on several occasions, and I quote a recent statement from the Archbishop's office. 'What the Minister proposes is the antithesis of the nature of God. What he proposes is ancient, barbaric, and will take us back to the caves.'

Fermoy What does he mane, 'take us back to the caves'? Does he think we've left em?

Frances enters, coat, briefcase, stands listening.

Verona The statement refers to your Paper on the nature of Christ. Could you clarify what you meant by that Paper, Minister?

Fermoy I though ih was clear enough ah the time. I was talkin abouh the sullen nature a Christ, somethin thah has been hushed up for centuries. Somethin I'd long suspected and was brough home to me by a particular paintin by Piero della Francesca. His *Resurrection*. Puts manners on them thah tries to tell us that the deah a Christ was for us. That the resurrection a Christ was for us. Let's noh mix words here. The deah a Christ was by us, noh for us, and the resurrection a Christ was for heeself. Look ah this paintin and you'll see whah I mane. It's magnificent. A big, cranky, vengeful son a God plants a leg like a tree on hees new opened tomb. He looks ouh inta the middle distance and hees eyes say wan thing and wan thing only. Ye'll pay for this. Ye'll pay for this. No forgiveness in them eyes. The opposihe. Rage, and a staggerin sense a betrayal, as if he's sayin, I've wasted Eternihy on ye band a troglodytes thah calls yeerselves the human race. Children should be taught this along wud Barney. So I get shot down for tryin to introduce a little balance inta the education system. Well, I'm used to bein crihicised and thankfully I don't suffer from the national disase.

Verona And what's that, Minister?

Fermoy Wantin to be liked. Ya'd swear thah was the politician's job these days. To be liked. Well, ud's noh.

The politician's job is to have a vision and to push thah vision through, for wudouh a vision the people perish.

Verona I suppose, Minister, whatever else they say about you, you're not afraid to speak your mind.

Fermoy Ud's ony slaves thah fear to speak their mind.

Verona Perhaps. Ten years ago, Minister, you were running a cement factory and now you're tipped as the next Taoiseach. Do you ever stop for a minute and say to yourself, this is a dream?

Fermoy Well, ud's all a drame, isn't ud? Wan beauhiful heart-breakin drame, but, no, I don't ever stop, and I'll tell ya why. Fate gev me the hand, I hardly have to play ud.

Verona And the hand fate dealt you hasn't always been so good, has it, Minister?

Fermoy No, ud hasn't.

Verona Alongside what can only be described as your meteoric rise is a huge personal tragedy.

Fermoy Yes . . . Ariel.

Verona Your daughter. I know this is difficult, but could you tell us what happened to Ariel?

Fermoy Ariel walked ouha this house on her sixteenth birthday to show a friend her new car that we'd goh her as a present. She never cem home.

Verona They never found her?

Fermoy They never found her, no.

Verona Have you given up hope, Minister?

Fermoy Yes, I have.

Verona You believe she's dead.

Fermoy I know she is.

Verona How do you know, Minister?

Fermoy In me bones. Don't ask me how I know, buh I know and wish I didn't and wish ud was otherwise. I would give me life for her to walk through thah duur agin. Buh that's noh goin to happen.

Verona It's an appalling thing at the centre of your lives.

Fermoy You have no idea.

Verona Thank you, Minister.

Fermoy Thank you.

Verona (*stretches; to Cameraman*) You got all that?

Cameraman nods.

Fermoy Elaine, what do ya think?

Elaine Three things. Ya can't admih ya love power. Thah has to go. God. Paple's fierce touchy abouh God. We may pare thah back. And three, Ariel. Ariel's your trump card. Play ud. Ya nade to go wud the emotion of ud more. Thah's whah paple wants, details of your personal life. Don't be afraid to give ud to em. Don't be afraid to give em Ariel.

Verona No, no, the Ariel section was fine. If you want people to feel for you, you hold back a bit yourself. Your instincts are spot-on there, Minister.

Elaine I'm noh so sure, buh I'm prepared to lave Ariel the way ud is if ya edit the lovin power bih and the God speech.

Verona All right. I'll pull back a bit on God without losing the whole thing, but the loving power stays. I think it's refreshing to hear a politician admit they love power. Everyone knows you do. What's the big deal?

Elaine Dudley'll be gone by Friday. We have to geh this wan righ. Daddy?

Fermoy Lave ud. Migh as well be hung for a sheep as a lamb.

Verona Great.

Elaine There's a bite to ate in the conservatory. (*Hands papers to Fermoy.*) Sign these.

Fermoy Whah have we here?

Elaine Ya can just sign. I've been over em.

Fermoy I'll jine ya in a minuhe, Verona.

Exit Verona and Elaine. Fermoy gets up, throws the papers aside, stretches, turns, sees Frances.

Ah, Frances.

Frances How do you know she's dead?

Fermoy Ten years, Frances, ten years.

Frances Buh ud was the way ya said ud. Ya sounded so certain.

Fermoy No wan shows up after ten years.

Frances And now she's your trump card. I thought her memory would be more . . . sacred to ya. Today is her tenth anniversary. Have you no respect?

Fermoy I know today is her tenth anniversary. Why d'ya think I'm here?

Frances You're here because the press has descended like crows on the church to phohograph the big bronze lug a ya glowerin inta your daugher's empty grave. Ariel's a good phoho opportunihy. The gravin father wud hees arms tightly around the gravin mother. Don't you touch me ah her Mass this avenin. I'm goin up to geh changed. Ud's ah six.

Fermoy I know ud's ah six.

Frances Ya'd never think ud.

Exit Frances. Fermoy looks after her, begins signing papers, lights a cigar, puts on a CD, dances around, smoking, drinking, signing papers. Stephen appears in the doorway, dressed in black.

Fermoy Stephen, ya look like an undertaker.

Stephen Ud's the way Ma wants ud.

Fermoy Anhin strange?

Stephen Naw . . . Yourself?

Fermoy I'd love to walk down Grafton Streeh and just drink coffee. Sick a watchin other people live. I'd love to walk inta a shop and buy me own newspaper and then noh read ud, forgeh ud somewhere. Were ya at the match on Sunda?

Stephen Ya know I've no interest in Ga.

Fermoy Well, you're the first Fitzgerald thah hasn't. How's college?

Stephen shrugs.

You're graduatin this year, aren't ya?

Stephen Yeah.

Fermoy Ya studyin?

Stephen Yeah.

Fermoy Ya never call inta see me any more.

Stephen You're busy.

Fermoy Not thah busy. Drop inta me next week, we'll go for lunch.

Stephen There's no pint.

Fermoy Why noh?

Stephen Because ya'll cancel ud.

Fermoy Ah, Stephen, Stephen, Stephen, you're all grown, when did thah happen?

Boniface (*we hear him before we see him*) Lilies for the dead. Lilies. Lilies for sale. Lilies for the dead. Whihe lilies for all the whihe dead.

Enter Boniface.

Stephen How is Boniface?

Boniface Don't ever geh auld, Stephen, promise me thah.

Stephen Thah's a promise.

And exit Stephen.

Fermoy I thought you were above in Pat's dryin ouh.

Boniface And I could die up there before you'd come visih me. Pour us wan a your fortified, rectified, sanctified thousand-year-auld brandies there like a good lad.

Fermoy I haven't been called a good lad since the last time I seen you.

Boniface Well, mebbe ya should see me more. If natin else I'd remind ya of where ya cem ouh of.

Enter Frances, dressed in black, coat, handbag.

Frances Boniface. Was wonderin would ya show.

Boniface Haven't missed Ariel's anniversary yeh. Used to be the birth a Christ was the big wan. Gets whittled down, ud all gets whittled down. Now ud's the death a me niece is the feast a feasts.

Fermoy Ring a taxi and have him driven back to Pat's.

Frances Ring wan yourself.

Boniface has moved to drinks cabinet, about to pour.

Fermoy (*stays his hand*) You've had enough, sir.

Frances Give him a drink. Give him a drink. Let somewan be intoxicahed round here. (*Pours for Boniface.*) I drink to forgeh buh wud each glass ud all comes clearer.

Boniface Does ud?

Frances Too clear, too clear to bear.

Boniface For Ariel. (*Lilies.*) Grew em meself. Stripped the hoh house this mornin. I know her grave is empty. We do these things for ourselves.

Frances They're lovely, Boniface, thanks. (*Lays them on the table, straightens them.*)

Boniface May God have mercy on your carcass, and may he have mercy on mine. Up Offaly. (*Drinks. Pours another, stands at drinks cabinet, drinking and pouring, pouring and drinking.*)

Fermoy (*watching Frances fixing the flowers*) Ya miss me ah all?

Frances Miss ya?

Fermoy Tell the truth for wance in your life.

Frances Alrigh. Yeah, I miss ya, noh you in yourself, noh you now and the riddled pelt a ya, buh the spangled idea I had a ya which is the best part a love.

Fermoy I miss you too.

Frances Aye, wud your cartload a virgins spread across five continents.

Fermoy You're noh exactly livin like a nun yourself.

Frances I bed the min whin the fancy takes me which isn't often.

Fermoy Ya tryin to make me jealous?

Frances I'm past your jealousy. Way past.

Fermoy They're welcome to ya, snow quane that y'are, turn any man to ice. You're noh the ony wan is beddin them down. I've more women than votes linin up for me. Beauhiful young women, bodies a bronze, minds a gold, sophisticahed, beauhiful women, teeth like delph, high-bellied, tauh as fish on a line. And ya know somethin? They like me. Ud's ony here I'm treahed like a dog. I step out this duur and I'm a king.

Frances (*pushes him violently*) Then go to your high-bellied hoors. You're safer wud them and whah they don't know about ya.

> *Exit Frances. Fermoy stands there looking after her. Boniface watches him from the drinks cabinet.*

Boniface Tell me this and tell me no more, was ud worth ud?

Fermoy Was whah worth ud?

Boniface And whah about me?

Fermoy Whah about ya?

Boniface You tould me, ony I didn't understand what ya were sayin, ya tould me, Fermoy, thah nigh ya were goin an abouh blood sacrifice, in this very room.

Fermoy I've no idea what you're talkin abouh.

Boniface No. No. Listen. Listen. Listen. I can't stop drinkin. Can't slape, can't ate, garden be moonligh, go to bed in the mornin. I'm afraid I'll tell me psychiatrist, thah it'll just spill ouha me. They don't know what's wrong a me. Me soul, I tell em, me soul, ud's hurtin me fierce, like bein flayed from the inside. They think I'm some suurt a religious nuh. Burst a blood vessel in me eye, bled blood down me face for two days, they couldn't stop ud. You're the wan should be in Pat's. You're the wan should be bleedin from the eyes.

Fermoy Take ud aisy, take ud aisy, you're ouh a your mind wud drink and tranquillisers. Take ud aisy.

Boniface Take ud aisy! I'm facin me maker wud this on me immortal soul. Do you aven realise whah ya've done! Why didn't ya listen to me when I tried to stop ya, though I didn't know whah I was tryin to stop. Why didn't ya listen? All we have in this world is the small mercies we can extend to wan another. The rest is madness and oblivion. Haven't ya learnt thah much? Haven't ya learnt thah much on your travels?

Fermoy Oh, aye, I learnt thah much alrigh, but like everythin worth learnin, ud's learnt too lahe. Everythin comes when you've no more use for ud, must be a law.

Frances at the door in her coat.

Frances We're goin to be lahe, geh an your mournin, will ya.

Fermoy Don't you talk to me abouh mournin. (*Takes out electric shaver, mirror, shaves himself.*) Most gets up offa the ground sooner or laher, dusts themselves down, rejines the land a the livin. Not you though. Everythin thah happens to Frances Fitzgerald has to be momentous, spectacular. Her jiys could never be the same as anywan else's and her grafes must be inconsolable. Live! Live! Live! That's whah we're here for. Do somethin! Anhin! Ya'll have all of eternihy for pussin in the dark.

Frances You're noh browbatin the Opposition now.

Fermoy Amn't I? . . . This funeral parlour I come home to every time.

Frances Ya were home wance this year. Two hours for your Christmas dinner.

Enter Elaine, dressed in black, holds out mobile.

Elaine Himself wants a quick word.

Fermoy (*takes phone*) Will ya organise thah fella back to where he cem from. (*On the phone.*) Boss . . . No harm done . . . Whah is ud?

And exit Fermoy.

Elaine What ya want to do, Boniface?

Boniface I'll go back to Pat's after Mass.

Elaine Alrigh, I'll drive ya, goin back tonigh meself.

Frances (*sitting, muttering, drink, coat on, handbag*) Twenty-six . . . twenty-six years of age . . . (*Shakes her head.*)

Boniface Whah?

Frances Ariel . . . She'd be twenty-six if she was here today . . . I don't think I slept a nigh straight when I was carryin her. Had meself convinced I didn't deserve her on account a James. Kept thinkin this child's goin to come ouh wrong, this child's goin to come ouh wrong. Nighmare ridin nighmare she be deformed, no face on

her or wan a thim frog babbies or birdy-headed little
creatures ya see phohos of, or she was goin to have no
arms or die ah the last minuhe as happens oftener than
paple knows. Buh ouh she cem wud everythin ya nade to
look human. And for ages after I'd look ah her and
whisper, thank you, God, thank you, God. For along
wud the night sweats I still dared to hope I be given
another chance. And for a while I thought I had. Buh the
man above was ony playin wud me . . . ony playin wud
me, is all.

Elaine And did ya have nighmares when ya carried me?

Frances No, belave ud or noh, you were aisy. The
trouble wud you started after ya were born. Though I
had to have a jar a beetroot every nigh when I was
carryin you. I'd wake up in the middle a the nigh dyin
for beetroot . . . Kept a jar beside the bed. 'Another
beetroot party, missus?' Fermoy'd guffaw from under the
quilt. Buh I didn't care, I'd sih there in the dark atin
beetroot and then I'd drink the vinegar. Mebbe that's
why you're so bihher.

Elaine Am I bihher, Ma?

Frances As a field a lemons.

Elaine Sure ud's noh yourself you're talkin abouh and ya
shrunk to a pip over your two dead children.

Frances You'd have me forgeh em like your father.

Elaine I'd have ya cut your grafe accord in to your cloth.

Frances You'd have me grave to a timetable, throw Ariel
and James aside like a pair of auld gloves or an umbrella
left after the rain.

Elaine Your empire a sorrow doesn't convince me and
ya cuttin dales like a shark down ah the cement every

day a the wake. Ya switch ud on, Ma, ya switch ud on when ud suits.

Frances And whah would you know abouh sorrow and ya dry-eyed at your sister's funeral?

Elaine I know wan thing abouh sorrow. I learned ud watchin you. Sorrow's an addiction like no other. You won't be full till you've buried us all. Well, ya won't bury me, Ma. I'm here, thrivin, your unlovely daugher is thrivin, your unlovely daugher that ya'd swap like thah for Ariel to return. She's noh comin home, Ma. She's noh comin home. Ud's just me now, me and Stephen.

Frances How do you know she's noh comin home?

Elaine Thah's none a your business.

Frances Do you have information you're kapin from me?

Elaine And if I had?

Frances You and your father, swear ya were married to him. You tell me now what you know!

Elaine I know natin, Ma, natin ya don't know yourself.

Enter Sarah.

Sarah Ah, Boniface, ya do a runner agin?

Boniface The savage loves hees nahive shore.

Sarah And what d'ya think a the antics a your little brother? They're goin to puh him on the throne. I used change that fella's nappy. Seen ud all now. (*Watches as Boniface pours another drink for himself.*) Ya were thirsty as a child too, a bottle in each fist as ya snoozed in the coh. Your Ma used love watchin ya guzzlin. The little sounds of him, she used say, isn't he like a little bonamh?

Boniface You'd reminisce the future, missus, if ya though ya'd geh away wud ud.

Sarah Aye, I would and noh wan a yees would belave me.

Stephen has entered.

Stephen It's ten to six.

Elaine Give him a minuhe. We'll make ud, they'll wait for us.

Boniface Stephen, I hear you're the new John Ford.

Stephen I wish.

Elaine He won a prize and all.

Boniface Didn't I rade abouh ud in the paper.

Stephen That's only because a Daddy.

Boniface A prize is a prize. These things is important. Never won as much as a turkey meself. Whah was the film abouh anyway?

Stephen Ma'll tell ya, she's fierce proud of ud.

Frances Ah, ud was disgustin, Stephen, no two ways abouh ud. Near fainted when I seen ud. Ya've this mother and her son and ud's the son's weddin day and then the son goes missin, and the bride is lookin all over the hotel for her new husband. And where does she find her new husband? In the bridal suihe, on the bridal bed, bein breast-fed be the mother. Now what's thah abouh, I ask ya? What's the pint in makin a film about thah?

Stephen Does there allas have to be a pint, Ma?

Frances I'll tell ya what the pint was. The pint was to geh at me.

Stephen You think everthin comes back to you. Ud doesn't.

Frances Then why did ya call the mother Frances in your film? Why was she dressed like me? Why was she drivin an auld Merc? That's whah I drive. I don't nade this, Stephen. Pack a lies, the whole thing.

Stephen Ud's noh a pack a lies. Ud happened.

Frances Didn't happen here, me bucko.

Stephen Buh ud happened. Read abouh ud in an Italian newspaper. Ya don't have to make anhin up.

Boniface Thah's for sure. Everythin ya can possibly imagine has happened already or, if ud hasn't, will shortly.

Frances And manetime the cement is waitin on ya.

Stephen I'll puh a bullet through me head first.

Fermoy stands in the doorway. He has changed into his mourning clothes.

Fermoy Righ, are we off?

Frances You come back here after Mass. Don't go scurryin away, ya hear?

Fermoy I've a seven o'clock meetin in the mornin.

Frances You come back here or I'll folly ya to Dublin. (*To the others, exiting.*) Come an, we're lahe, we're lahe.

Exit Frances followed by Boniface and Stephen.

Elaine A'ya alrigh, Daddy?

Fermoy Your mother.

Elaine Don't mind her, brazen ud ouh, we'll be gone straih after Mass, won't have to see her for another year.

Fermoy Have Bernard drive yees down. I'll walk.

Elaine We should all arrive together.

Fermoy I nade two minutes to meself, Elaine.

Elaine Alrigh, alrigh, I'll send Bernard back for ya.

Exit Elaine. Sarah pours a whiskey for herself.

Fermoy Ya noh goin down to dunk your soul?

Sarah A millin Masses wouldn't bleach ud.

Fermoy Nor mine.

Sarah Nor yours. (*Raises Fermoy's chin with her hand.*) That's ih. Never leh em see ya wud the harness off.

Exit Sarah. Fermoy stands there a moment, gets out pocket mirror, checks himself in it, teeth, hair, eyes, a long look.

Fermoy Who are ya, sir? Who are ya and from where do ya come? Geh a hould, stranger, geh a hould. (*Clicks mirror shut. Takes a deep breath.*) Righ, let's rock and roll.

The phone rings. Note on Ariel's voice: once convention of the phone has been established, let Ariel's voice come from everywhere. Fermoy does not talk into the phone after the first couple of exchanges.

Yes?

Ariel Hello.

Fermoy Elaine, I'm on the way, tell her I'm on the way.

Ariel Ud's me.

Fermoy Who's me?

Ariel Me, Ariel.

Fermoy Ariel . . . Who is this? I'm in no mood for . . .

Ariel No, ud's me, Ariel.

Fermoy Buh ud can't be . . . ud can't.

Ariel Buh ud is.

Fermoy Oh, Ariel . . . you're alive . . . you're alive.

Ariel Come and get me, will ya? Ud's awful here, ud's awful. There's a huge pike after me, he lives in the belfry, two rows a teeth on him and teeth on hees tongue, bendin back to hees throah. He won't rest till he has me. Come and get me, will ya?

Fermoy How? Tell me how can I come and get ya?

Ariel (*sounds of terrible weeping*) I don't know . . . I want to go home . . . I just want to go home. Please, just brin me home.

Fermoy Ariel . . . Ariel . . . don't . . . don't.

He listens as the sound of Ariel's weeping fades and fades to silence. Fermoy stands there. Let him stand there, utterly still, looking out. Then enter Frances. She stands in the doorway, in her coat, out of breath. Fermoy registers her after a while. They look at one another for an age.

Ya cem back for me. I'm comin, I'm comin.

Frances No more Masses.

Fermoy Well, I'm goin. Where's Bernard? Come an and we get this over wud.

Frances You're goin nowhere. Ud was you, wasn't ud? Ud was you.

Fermoy Y'ony realisin thah now? I thought ya knew for years.

Frances Knew whah for years?

Fermoy Frances . . . ya didn't . . . Look, this is noh the time for this conversation.

Frances You. Allas you and me scourin the world for her. You. And me gone to ground wud grafe. You. And ony last nigh I dreamt she walked in the duur and ten year a madness just fell away. She had wan life. Wan. Are you tellin me you took ud?

Fermoy Ariel was a drame hopped among us from start to end. We had the privilege of her company a while buh she was never really ours. We brough somethin inta the world thah didn't belong here and so we gev her back.

Frances Gev her back? We gev her back? Gev her back where?

Fermoy Remember them wings she was born wud?

Frances Wings? Whah wings?

Fermoy Them wings on her shoulder blades.

Frances Whah are ya talkin abouh? Whah wings? On her shoulder blades? Them growths on her shoulders, is thah what you're talkin abouh?

Fermoy They were the start a wings.

Frances They were balls a hardened bone and gristle, thah's all, benign, tiny, we had em removed.

Fermoy You're callin them everthin except what they were. Leh me tell you somethin, Frances. Before I ever laid eyes on you, long before thah, I had a drame, a drame so beauhiful I wanted to stay in ud till the end a time. I'm in a yella cuurtyard wud God and we're chewin the fah and then this girl wud wings appears by hees side. And I say, who owns her? And God says she's his. And I say, give us the loan of her, will ya? No, he says, she's noh earth flavour, like he's talkin abouh ice-crame. And stupidly I say, I'll take her anyway. Alrigh, he says, smilin ah me rale sly, alrigh, buh remember this is a loan. I know, I know, I says, knowin natin. And the time'll come when I'll want her returned, he says. Yeah, yeah, I say, fleein the cuurtyard wud her before he changes hees mind. Ariel. Thah was Ariel.

Frances Just tell me where she is.

Fermoy I'm tellin ya, thah was Ariel I fled the cuurtyard wud. And then I wake and the enchantment begins. You, Ariel, Elaine, Stephen. All the trinkets of this world showered on us. We had ten good years, hadn't we? Them were the years and we didn't know ud. He gev, he gev, he gev, and then like the tide he turned and took ud all away.

Frances (*a heartbroken wail, weeping like we've never seen, stands there heaving and choking and wailing*) Ariel . . . Ariel . . . Ariel . . . How could ya? . . . You loved thah child . . . How could ya? (*Shakes him.*)

Fermoy I had to! I had to!

Frances You had to!

Fermoy Yeah, I had to. Ya think I wanted to sacrifice Ariel? I had to.

Frances Sacrifice? Ya sacrificed her? What did you do to her?

Fermoy I tould ya, I returned her to where she cem from.

Frances She cem from here, from you, from me.

Fermoy She rode ouha God from nowhere and to God she returned.

Frances You sacrificed her! Aaaagh. Why didn't ya
sacrifice yourself if he wanted a sacrifice? Why didn't ya
refuse?

Fermoy A cuurse I refused. I fough him till I couldn't
figh him any more.

Frances Thah was no God ya med your pact wud. No
God demands such things.

Fermoy My God did.

Frances Blem God, blem the world, anywan bar
yourself. Ud's all comin clear now, clear as a bell. Ya
done ud for power, didn't ya, some voodoo swap in the
dark for power. You laid my daughter on an altar for
power. You've flourished these ten years since Ariel.
You've flourished on her white throat. You swapped her
to advance.

Fermoy Yes, I did. Yes, I did. I had to. Ud was the price
demanded.

Frances And you dare to stand here tellin me fairy
stories abouh her.

Fermoy Frances, I know whah I have done. I know my
portion a blame, buh when I'm hauled before him I'll
fling hees portion ah him, where ud belongs. I have lived
my life by hees instructions. He asked the unaskable and
I obeyed, and then he departs, lavin me here in ashes.
And my greahest fear is he won't be there whin I go. No,
I've wan greaher, thah he will.

Frances (*softly*) Buh Ariel . . . Fermoy . . . This is Ariel
you're talkin abouh.

Fermoy Don't make ud more difficult for me than ud is.

Frances Ya med ud difficult yourself. This was your
playground well as anywan's.

Fermoy This is no playground and never was. This is where he hunts us down like deer and flays us alive for sport.

Frances Whah was ud I seen the day I first wint wud you?

Fermoy I'll tell ya what ya seen. Ya seen a man capable of anhin. And thah seh fire to your little bungalow life. Ya seen a man that could do away wud your children and ya ran towards him, noh away from him. That's whah drew ya the first time and that's what kapes ya swirlin round me. Tombstones, headstones, graveyard excitement and the promise of funerals to come.

Frances You'll say anhin for company in your carnage.

Fermoy You wanted me, missus, and ya still want me. Ud's any your pride is stoppin ya.

Frances I wanted me first husband. Was through wud you before the honeymoon started. You stole me life from me, me children from me, everythin I though I was from me and I a glazed fool flung open the duurs for the plunder. Never agin.

Fermoy You want a divorce? Yours for the askin.

Frances Ya think ya'll geh off thah aisy? Where is she?

Fermoy Thah you'll never know.

Frances I cem from gintle people, me father used rescue spiders from the bah, mice he'd carry ouh in hees hand and leh go in the field, gintle people, Charlie, James, Ariel, gintle, gintle, gintle, no place for em in this nest a hooves. Where is she? (*Stabs him.*)

Fermoy (*reels*) Frances.

Frances (*another stab*) Where is she?

Fermoy You think you can do away wud me . . . Gimme thah.

A struggle. Frances stabs him again.

Frances And you thought I was afraid a the knife. (*Another stab.*) Where is she?

Fermoy (*falls to the ground. She gets on top of him*) No . . . Frances . . . no . . . Stop . . . stop . . .

Frances And did you stop when Ariel cried ouh for mercy? Did ya? Tell me where she is.

Fermoy This wasn't . . . this . . . Sweet God in your . . .

Frances Tell me. Where is she?

Fermoy (*whispers as he dies*) Cuura Lake.

Frances Cuura Lake.

She throws down the knife. 'Mors et Vita' music, and blackout.

Act Three

*'Mors et Vita' music continues from end of Act Two.
Two months later. A coffin lies centre stage. Elaine lies
on the floor in T-shirt and tracksuit bottoms. She's
asleep. A drink beside her. Enter Stephen, suit, folders,
takes in the coffin, goes to it, has a long look.*

Stephen Elaine . . . Elaine . . . (*Shakes her gently.*) Ya
should go up to bed.

Elaine Ah, Stephen. (*Yawns.*)

Stephen When did ud arrive?

Elaine This mornin . . . (*Stretching.*) What time is ud?

Stephen After five.

Elaine Oh, God. (*Lies down again.*)

Stephen (*goes back to coffin*) Thought she'd be behher
preserved, Cuura Lake bein a bog lake and all.

Elaine She looked behher when they took her up first.
Forensics scraped her down.

Stephen Hard to square this wud Daddy.

Elaine Ya think?

Stephen Don't you?

Elaine I knew for a while ud was him.

Stephen Did ya?

Elaine Didn't you?

Stephen No, a few stray thoughts. Never wahered them. How did ya know?

Elaine He tould me . . . Well, I asked him abouh her wan time. Venice. Some conference. Drink on the table in a little restaurant lookin on to the Rialto. And he tould me the whole thing. Very emotional he was too. Ariel was the stroke a destiny, he said, woven into him from the beginnin. Ariel was Necessity udself, the thing thah's decided ouhside a time. And he tould me all abouh Necessity. How before ya come to this world, Necessity and her sisters weaves a carpet for ya. And ya watch as they weave so ya know how things will fare ouh below. And then ya turn your back and Necessity puts a twist in the weave. Thah's the wan thing ya can't foresee and thah's the wan thing will define your stay here. And then you're flung to earth wud this weave and this twist in the weave thah some calls fate.

Stephen Ya belave thah?

Elaine Belaved ud thah nigh. The lights on the waher, ud's hard to be rational in Venice.

Stephen Ma wants to puh her in beside Daddy.

Elaine If thah wan as much as touches a pebble of my father's grave.

Stephen Well, you shouldn't a puh up thah headstone, her name noh even on ud. Ma wanted to puh up hees headstone. You're like an Alsatian the way ya guard hees grave.

Elaine And you're still slurpin ah her altar after all she's done.

Stephen There was a pair a them in ud. She keeps askin for ya, Elaine, to go visih her. Ya wouldn't know her. She's still our mother.

Elaine Ariel's the ony wan she cares abouh. Ariel and James, her dead children, while she bates her livin inta the dirt.

Stephen Thah's noh true, sick a ya givin ouh abouh her.

Elaine And I'm sick a you makin your weekly pilgrimages to her, bringin information abouh me. I warned ya noh to tell her anhin abouh me. I'll live like a tinker in me own house if I want, me father's house. She's natin to me any more. Natin.

Stephen Well, ya certainly proved thah, ravin agin her in cuurt.

Elaine Ya know I wish I'd said more agin her.

Stephen A spew a lies.

Elaine I tould ud as ud happened.

Stephen Like hell ya did. Anyway ud's been struck.

Elaine I knew ud would, buh ud was still heard. You don't seem to understand whah's goin on here, Stephen. She killed our father, slashed him till blood ran down the walls. I had to bury him in pieces. I was the only mourner ah hees funeral. Me, Boniface, Auntie Sarah. You were too busy swaddlin Ma to go to your own father's funeral. Such as ud was. She wouldn't aven allow him a public funeral. Paple loved Daddy. You saw the size a the removal. She aven tried to stop thah. But she couldn't. They just kept comin.

Stephen They kept comin to have a gawk.

Elaine They cem because they loved him. You never seen Daddy in hees element. You never seen him the way he seen himself, the way he was born to be seen, the way he could work a room, the way he held himself when he spoke, the big mellifluous vice, ya'd hear a pin drop. He was goin to run this country. He was goin to cahapult the whole nation ouha sleaze and sentimentalihy and gombeenism. I'm goin to take this country to the moon, he used say to me, and he would've, only for her. And she's still noh happy havin done away wud him. No, now she had ud in her head to take away hees name and mine wud ud and yours, though ya don't seem to care. Draggin this yoke up ouha Cuura Lake. All to destriy what's left of hees reputation. All to make her look like a martyr.

Enter Frances and Boniface.

Stephen Ma, we weren't expectin ya till tonigh.

Frances They let me ouh early to avide the press. Hello, Elaine.

Elaine looks at her.

I was hopin we could be civil for Ariel's funeral.

Elaine Were ya?

Frances goes to coffin. Looks. Leans in. Kisses Ariel. Leans in for ages.

Frances (*whispers*) Ya'll soon be the girl in the graveyard ya tould me abouh wance. Ya'll soon rest aisy. Who picked ouh her dress?

Stephen Elaine did.

Frances Thank you.

Elaine Was in her wardrobe. They had to staple ud on to her. I didn't do ud for you.

Boniface Elaine. Elaine. Elaine.

Elaine You're goin to geh off on insanihy, a cuurse y'are, ya can shooh a baby in the face these days and geh off on insanihy.

132

Frances Well, if I do ud'll be no thanks to you.

Elaine Ud was murder. Cold-blooded murder, and if you geh off on insanihy I'll open me own cuurtroom here.

Frances You weren't aven here and ya med out ya were.

Elaine I was here. He died in my arms. You were standin in the hall lookin at the radiahor.

Frances And would you have done different if he done to wan a yours whah he done to Ariel?

Elaine Yes, I would.

Frances Oh, ya would, would ya?

Elaine Yes, I would. I can tell the difference between a crime of eternihy and a low, blood-spahhered, knife-frenzied revenge. And then your coward's insanihy plea on top of ud. Whah my father done to Ariel had the grandeur a God in ud. Pure sacrifice. Ferocious, aye. Buh pure. Whah you done to him was a puckered, vengeful, self-servin thing wud noh a whiff of the immortal in ud.

Frances So your father spills blood and he's a haroh. I spill ud and I'm a coward. You've spint too long around the min, me girl, too long cavortin the corriduurs a power to understand the first thing abouh justice. Ya know, there's ony wan thing I regreh. Thah I didn't do ud sooner. And I won't apologise to you for thah or for pleadin insanihy. I'll plead whahever ud takes to geh my freedom back. And don't tell me you'd do different if you were in my shoes.

Elaine I'm as different to you as the auld world is from the new, sem as my father was. Oh, to be Joan of Arc goin up in a blaze to me maker.

Frances Then go up in a blaze to your maker, ony lave me alone. I've wan nigh here, wan night's freedom to

mourn my daugher, to puh her in the clay tomorra
beside her father.

Elaine She's noh goin in wud him. My father's grave
stays the way ud is. Can't ya just lave him alone?

Frances She's goin in beside him and thah's the end of
ud, Elaine. Ud's whah he'd have wanted.

Elaine Whah he'd have wanted?

Boniface Ud is, Elaine, ud's whah your father would've
wanted.

Elaine Whah my father wanted was to be above the
ground, noh under ud. Above ud! You're noh shovellin
her in on top of him. You stand here givin orders abouh
hees grave. I organised hees burial. I picked the ploh,
under the elms, near the path so he won't be too lonely. I
paid for hees headstone. You weren't aven ah hees
funeral.

Frances I wasn't fit to go, Elaine.

Elaine But you're fit for Ariel's. You're ony here to
swing the jury. Don't touch hees grave. Ud's mine. Ud's
all ya've left me wud. I'm warnin ya now.

Frances Keep your grave. I've a new ploh arranged.
Your father's moving, lock, stock and barrel as we spake.
Ariel's goin in wud him. And I'll arrange the headstone
this time. You think you can kick me when I'm down.
I'm down, aye, righ now I'm lower than the lowest low.
Buh I'll rise agin in spihe a your efforts to wipe the
ground wud me. Why don't ya go and stay in the hotel
tonigh, be asier for all of us. I'll be gone tomorra.

Elaine I'm stayin here, to haunt ya.

Frances You? Haunt me? Oh, Elaine, you're ony the
fallouh. We never goh on, I don't know why I want us to

134

now. This skirmish betwane us is ancient. Y'ever feel thah? Seems to me we been battlin a thousand year.

Elaine I'm goin down to hees grave and I hope for your sake there's natin disturbed.

Exit Elaine.

Frances Where did I geh her from?

She pours a drink.

Boniface (*looking at Ariel in coffin*) The divers found the remains a seven people and they draggin the lake. Wan wud a boulder tied round the skelehon of a wrist. Most a them just an assortment a bones. Found the skelehon of a pike too, massive, musta been over two hundred pound, all the teeth intact.

Frances Did they find your mother?

Boniface We don't know yeh. They're tryin to date em all. I tould em, she's the wan wud the boulder, but they want to do their tests. (*To Ariel.*) I liked you, little girl.

Frances (*to Stephen*) Shouldn't you be down ah the cement?

Stephen I was, cem home early because a the day is in ud.

Frances I been goin through the figures. Big losses these last two months.

Stephen They don't listen to me.

Frances Make em listen. Tell em ud's comin down from me. Ud's your inheritance.

Stephen I'll sell ud soon as ya sign ud over.

Frances Ya too much of a swank wud your film degree to lower yourself to the cement and gravel.

Stephen I don't have me film degree yeh, thanks to certain events round here.

Frances Well, mebbe ya should think abouh jackin in the films and start turnin your mind to cement.

Stephen Thah's noh goin to happen, Ma.

Frances Me and your father built thah cement up from wan lorry smuggled in from England, an auld shed and the lase of a quarry. Cement built this house, cement gev ya your education, your fast car, your designer clothes, your foreign holidas. Cement finances your arty films. You think you're above the cement and gravel? Well, you're noh. You're med of ud like the rest of us. Sure ya were nearly born in wan a the lorries. Me and your father drivin through the nigh, big delivery, me follyin him along the weh roads. Elaine aslape beside me, Ariel in front wud Fermoy. Me bapin like a madwoman for Fermoy to pull over, him bapin back thinkin I'm messin, and you surgin to be born. I fling open the winda, wavin and yellin. He sees me in the mirror and pulls over. Me in a panic, geh me to the hospital, geh me to the midwives. Him laughin ah me, I'll be your midwife, missus, and the rain as balmy on him and the head of him thrown back, laughin, just laughin . . . Was fierce sorry after I didn't leh him be me midwife. He'd a done ud too. Thah man was afraid a natin.

Stephen Ya boltin the stable now and your horse is gone.

Frances Doesn't everywan?

Stephen No, they don't, some knows when they're happy ah the time. You had your chance, Ma, now ud's mine, and I won't be buried under a ton a cement on your whim. I tould ya I'd help ouh till the trial's over. And I will. Buh then I'm gone.

Frances Is thah a threah?

Stephen Ud's a fact.

Frances Ya been listenin to Elaine. She's turnin ya against me.

Stephen Can make up me own mind, Ma. Count yourself lucky I can stand in the same room as ya.

Frances So that's the way ud is. I thought ya were on my side.

Stephen Ya though wrong. Ud's time ya stopped pullin ouh a me, livin through me.

Frances I don't live through ya! How dare you! I've never lived through anywan, to me own greah cost. Allas I've resisted. Allas! When ud'd be asier bow down. Whah are you sayin to me?

Stephen I'm sayin . . .

Frances All month long I been dramin I'm breastfeedin a snake. I thought ud was Elaine, buh ud's you. And insteada milk comin ouh ud's blood. And ya kape suckin though I'm roarin wud the pain. Ud took me ten year to wean you. Ten year I didn't have. And now you tell me thah doesn't count.

Stephen Ten year pretendin I was James. Ten year I went along wud ud. I used pray to die so you'd be given back James, I loved ya thah much. When strangers'd ask me me name, I'd say, James, me name is James, I'm James of the blue black curls.

Frances Whah are you talkin abouh, Stephen?

Stephen Don't pretend ya don't remember.

Frances I know I'd never win Mother a the Year, buh, Christ, Stephen, I wanted you as I wanted all me children. I swear, in me heart, what's left of ud, there's a tahhered chamber for each wan a ya. And them chambers is of equal measure.

Stephen And if they are, then why did ya kill my father?

Frances You know why.

Stephen Tell me.

Frances You know why, you know, because of her. (*Coffin.*)

Stephen Wudouh a thought for Elaine or me. Wudouh a care of how thah rippin away has shahhered us. Ya did ud for Ariel. For James. There was ony ever two chambers in your heart, Ma, two dusty chambers, me and Elaine tryin to force our way in. Our playground was a graveyard, Ma, we ran among your tombstones like they were swings, we played hop, skip and jump on the bones a your children, your real children, while we whined for ya like ghosts. Isn't thah the way ud was? (*Gestures to coffin.*) Isn't ud the way of ud still?

Frances Stephen . . . where a'ya goin?

Stephen (*exiting*) The thing is, I'm goin.

She runs after him, tries to hold him back.

Frances Ariel's funeral, me trial . . . Stephen! Don't, sweetheart, don't. Don't do this to me now. Please. Noh now. Noh now.

Stephen stands there, immovable. Frances withdraws eventually. Exit Stephen. Frances stands there distraught, disbelief.

(*Whispers.*) He's gone . . . he's gone . . . my baby is gone.

Boniface And leh him. Whah I shoulda done forty year ago. Good man, Stephen. How did ya do thah? Mammy's off the menu for ever more. Thah's how ud's done. Like thah big fah cluckin Mammy owl I seen on National Geographic the other nigh. And this Mammy Owl is huntin like billy-o to fade Owl Junior. And she comes back to the nest this nigh, big rah in her mouh, all important like, I'm fadin the young lad, aren't I a model Ma. And Junior's gone, fled when her back was turned, no goodbyes, thah's the way to do ud. Or salmon, sure salmon has ne'er a Ma ah all, and y'ever watch them, lords a the waher, sun shinin for em. Or trees, don't get me started on trees. Seems to me everythin worth lookin ah in this world has ne'er a Ma ah all, ud's just there be udself in a flowerin gorgeousness, orphaned and free.

Frances Geh ouha my house, you.

Boniface Whah?

Frances You call yourself a man a God. Fermoy wud all hees divilry had more religion. Prancin around in your robes, watchin me like a hawk, cheerin on me ony son's departure.

Boniface Frances, I was talkin abouh meself.

Frances You knew all along and ya never said a word.

Boniface Whah could I have done? I'm payin for this too.

Frances Spare me your remorse. I rue the day I ever seh eyes on the Fitzgeralds.

Boniface I think we can return the compliment.

Frances Just go.

Boniface I'm charged wud your care.

Frances The place is crawlin wud cops. I'm goin nowhere. Just go. I want five minutes on me own wud Ariel.

Boniface I'll sih in the car. If ya nade anhin, I'll be in the car.

And exit Boniface. Frances goes to coffin, looks in.

Frances (*whispers*) Mother a God, ya could be anywan.

Enter Elaine, stands there watching Frances.

Elaine So ya dug him up.

Frances Elaine, please, no more, no more, our love affair wud the knife is over.

And exit Frances.

Elaine (*to herself*) Alrigh. Lave her alone. Lave her alone. Say natin. Do natin. She'll be gone tomorra and ya can just dig him up agin. (*Wanders to coffin, looks in.*) Mebbe I'm unnatural buh I never fell under your spell. Then the wrong things has allas moved me . . . and if there's such a place as paradise, leh ud be empty, oh leh ud be empty.

Sarah has entered, listens.

Sarah I've an inklin of whah you're plannin.

Elaine I never plan anhin, Auntie Sarah.

Sarah Don't ya? (*Looks into coffin.*) God, she's wizened to a nuh. Wud a squaze ya'd fih her in a fishbowl.

Elaine She's after diggin him up.

Sarah So? He was her husband, noh yours, and this is her house, noh yours, and a body can do whah they like behind their own front duur.

Elaine Whah planet were you brough up on? Behind your own front duur's the wan place ya can do natin ya like. Behind your own front duur's where ya face em all down wud your tail to the wall. And by God I'm goin to face thah wan down before long.

Sarah There's a divil the size of a whale inside you. Where in God's name is this hatred a your mother comin from?

Elaine If I knew thah . . . I can't look ah her for too long or me head swims. She appals me, allas has. (*Shudders.*) Her eyes, her shoulders, everythin abouh her. I look ah her and I think there's somethin missin. I don't know is ud in me or in her.

Sarah And whah is ud ya think is missin?

Elaine I think she has no soul.

Sarah And since when have you become the decider a souls? A cuurse she has a soul, if she hadn't a soul she wouldn't be alive.

Elaine They say there's some born wudouh em and I think she's wan a them. She tells me we been slashin wan another since time began. Well, if we have, this here is my turn, this is my opportunihy to geh a good go ah her and silence her till Judgement Day.

Sarah And on Judgement Day what'll ya tell the man above wud hees seven eyes level on ya? Ya won't face him down so aisy.

Elaine You dare to talk to me abouh God and you the first thah coaxed the darkness in. I know you of an auld dahe. Addicted to nigh is what y'are, slobberin over ud like the cah wud the crame. But ya won't grab your own piece a nigh, no, ya covet mine from the corner. You ud was watched the first murder in this house. You watched your sister die, ya watched me grandfather tie her wud stones and ya said natin and ya done natin, ony watched in a swoon, black flowers sproutin ouha your chest. Yes, ya whispered, yes, I'll watch anhin, I'm the woman who'll watch anhin.

Sarah You don't know the first thing abouh me and me sister and your grandfather.

Elaine I know ya married him.

Sarah Thah was the ind! Thah was the ind! I'm sick a bein judged on the ind. Whah abouh the start? Ya think I was never young? Ya think I like these auld hands, wud the veins risin on em like rivers in flood? Ya think I never burned? Ya think the world started wud you? I loved my sister. I adored thah woman.

Elaine Aye, and ya adored her man wud your grady plain Jane heart. Oh aye, ya loved her alrigh, loved her so much ya wanted her life, her eyelashes, her children, her husband. And some goblin in me grandfather heard your prayers and answered em.

Sarah Ud was me he wint wud first. Me! Ya didn't know thah, did ya! And she took him from me wudouh a by your leave, wudouh an apology. And I took him back. Fair is fair.

Elaine And you try to bate me over the head wud God, like you're hees favourihe, like you'll be sittin on hees knee on Judgement Day, wud me prostrahe before yees. God won't like me. I know thah. Buh he'll have more time for me than he will for you. You married your sister's husband as she turned to bog oak in Cuura Lake. Ya watched Ariel die, ya watched me father die. Is there anhin ya wouldn't watch?

Sarah To watch a thing is only to half wish ud. And to half wish a thing is a long way off from doin ud. Buh I'll watch no longer. I'm bowin ouh here. I'm no match for ya any more.

Exit Sarah.

Elaine (*after her*) Good. Good. Good.

Elaine goes to coffin. Takes out skull of Ariel, with a few strands of hair attached to it. She holds it up.

(*To skull.*) I drame abouh you all the time. Strange, wakin there's no animosity, we're friends, friendly as sisters can be, buh aslape we're enemies, enemies till the end a time. Whah does thah mane? Remember them black dolls we had when we were scuts and how we used torture em on Sahurday mornins, line them up on the bed and tear em limb from limb? That's what ya remind me a now, them black dolls. Did ya go aisy, Ariel? Or did ya figh him ah the end? Or did ya think ud was all a game, smokin hees cigar and swillin hees brandy as the stars leant down to watch?

Fermoy stands in doorway, dressed as he was at end of Act Two. Covered in blood. He watches Elaine dancing. She finally registers him, backs off.

(*A whisper.*) Daddy.

Fermoy (*advancing*) Whah?

Elaine Go way, keep away.

Fermoy Who are you?

Elaine Ya don't know me?

Fermoy Don't I? I thought ya were familiar, walkin up the drive, the lawn, the fountain, thought I recognised this place from somewhere. Who are ya?

Elaine Ya never give the dead your name.

Fermoy Am I dead?

Elaine Oh, you're dead alrigh.

Fermoy Dead as thah? (*Points to skull.*)

Elaine Yeah.

Fermoy Who's thah?

Elaine Me sister . . . Ariel . . . Ya remember her?

Fermoy Who?

Elaine Ariel.

Fermoy No, should I?

Elaine No.

Fermoy Then why did ya ask me?

Elaine Never mind.

Fermoy Look, I'm tryin to find this place, ya may be able to help me.

Elaine And whah place is ud you're tryin to find?

Fermoy I don't know the name of ud. (*Thinks.*) Ud's a cuurtyard, yella, or the ligh in ud is yella. There's some girl there I have to meeh. D'you know the place I'm talkin abouh? Is ud anywhere 'round here?

Elaine I never heard if ud is.

Fermoy Ya sure?

Elaine Yeah.

Fermoy I have to get there . . . I have to meet this girl. No wan seems to know where ud is. I may kape goin.

And exit Fermoy as Frances enters.

Frances Elaine.

Takes skull off Elaine, who looks after Fermoy.

Just whah d'ya think you're doin . . . maulin her like thah?

Puts skull back in coffin.

Elaine I tould ya not to touch me father's grave. Tould ya ih'd disturb everythin. But ya wouldn't listen, would ya?

Frances Just geh ouh! Geh ouh a this house and don't come back. You're so full a your own hate ya don't nohice the hate of others. Some zebra stallion grafted you onta me. I wanted a son to make up for James. And I goh you. Now g'wan wud thah piece of information and leh ud sustain ya on your travels. G'wan, geh ouha me sigh.

Elaine Aye, some zebra stallion grafted me onta ya alrigh, and I festered there, bidin me time. Ya say ya prayed for a son to make up for James. Well, I am James. I'm James returned. And I'm me father that ya butchered to hees eyeballs. And I'm Ariel. And I'm Elaine wud your deah on me palm, carved inta my plain a Mars like stone. Whah a relafe to be finally livin ud.

Stabs Frances in the throat.

Frances (*reels, falls*) Elaine . . . no . . . no . . . no more . . .

Elaine (*watching her reel, die, flounder*) After this, no more.

Frances No . . . (*Tries to get up, holds her throat, blood spilling from her mouth.*) Had to . . . had to . . . puh ud off . . .

A massive effort to get up, gets up, holds on to coffin, looks into it, a blood-curdling wail.

No . . . no . . . Don't . . . don't leh me . . . don't leh me . . . don't leh me . . . don't leh me go . . .

Falls against Elaine, who lets her slide to the floor. Elaine stands there. Throws down the knife. Looks out.

'Mors et Vita' music, and blackout.

145

WOMAN AND SCARECROW

Woman and Scarecrow was first performed at the Royal Court Jerwood Theatre Upstairs, London, on 16 June 2006. The cast was as follows:

Woman Fiona Shaw
Scarecrow Bríd Brennan
Him Peter Gowen
Auntie Ah Stella McCusker

Director Ramin Gray
Designer Lizzie Clachan
Lighting Designer Mischa Twitchin

Characters

Woman

Scarecrow

Him

Auntie Ah

The Thing in the Wardrobe

Set

A bed. A chair. A wardrobe. A CD player

Time

Now

Act One

Woman lies in bed gaunt and ill. Scarecrow watches her.

Woman I ran west to die.

Scarecrow You ran south and you didn't run, you crawled.

Woman I ran west. West. Why would I go south?

Scarecrow You got lost.

Woman I thought you were the navigator.

Scarecrow He found you under a bronze statue of a man with his arm pointing out to sea.

Woman Did he? . . . Oh yes, and his eyes fixed beyond the horizon and I remember thinking before I passed out, if I can't see the horizon myself at least I'm near something that can. Why didn't you help me get back west?

Scarecrow We're not cowboys.

Woman I started out west. I'd like to finish there.

Scarecrow When you could've gone west you refused.

Woman No, listen to me. If I could get across the Shannon once more maybe the air would perform some kind of miracle . . . I might live.

Scarecrow You think crossing the Shannon is all it takes? Once perhaps, long ago, that would have been the thing to do.

Woman What you asked was impossible at the time.

Scarecrow I would've looked after you. The world would have looked after you. I was getting used to it here. I'm only settling in and now you're going to cart me off with you.

Woman Suppose we headed west, for good this time. Let's get up and walk. One foot in front of the other till we reach the river.

Scarecrow Walking is no longer an option. He's waiting in the wardrobe. Can't you hear him sucking his oily black wings?

Woman In the wardrobe? In my wardrobe?

Scarecrow He moved in while you were away. Do you want to meet him?

Woman No. Good God no. He's not really here? Tell him to go away.

Scarecrow goes to wardrobe. Opens door.

Scarecrow Go away . . . please.

A muffled laugh from wardrobe. A deep-throated guffaw.

Yes, I understand this is all in a day's work for you. You find us amusing, but this is her wardrobe and she requests your departure from it.

An angry outburst of growls and glottals. Scarecrow backs away. Closes door timidly.

Woman Is he gone?

Scarecrow Of course he's not gone, and don't annoy him any more or he'll take you right now.

Woman But I'm not ready.

Scarecrow You think all the dead were ready? (*Whispers.*)
That thing will eat you alive. He doesn't care. I've seen
him in action. He's in there now making a bracelet out
of infant anklet bones.

Woman He has taken enough of mine before their time.
I thought my tribe were due a break.

Scarecrow It seems not. (*Looks out.*) The clouds are so
beautiful today. Why doesn't everyone just look at the
clouds? It should be a law like paying taxes, the clouds
passing, everything is there, every shape that can be
imagined, there's one going by, wings of a bird, torso of
a man, gaping mouth, triangle eyes, looking for all the
world like it could eat the world. You did not eat the
world.

Woman I barely tasted it.

Scarecrow And what did it taste of?

Woman Put on some music to drown that fella in the
wardrobe out.

Scarecrow What do you want to hear?

Woman Demis Roussos.

Scarecrow No way. Not again.

Woman Just do as I say.

Scarecrow All my life I've been doing as you say and
look where it's landed us.

Woman What about the twins' lunches? Did someone
buy bread? Cartons of juice? Who is making the
lunches?

Scarecrow We're beyond making lunches.

Woman I wonder did Toby bother bringing home his
lunchbox. I'm blue in the face telling him, and who is

washing the uniforms, I have to stay on top of the uniforms.

Scarecrow The time for washing uniforms is past.

Woman And Hal won't do his homework. Hal can't even read yet. I have to do his reading with him. I have no business lying here. Who is going to make the sandwiches? . . . This is all thanks to you . . . their little backs . . . their little necks . . . if you'd just put on Demis Roussos.

Scarecrow All your problems would be solved.

Woman And what exactly are your objections to Demis Roussos?

Scarecrow Where to start?

Woman He's sentimental I know, and the dentist on the twenty-eighth. Who will remember that? And Aoife, she's such a slob. She'll never get to university if I don't sit on her for the next six months. Who is studying with Aoife? And Tom is somewhere in Asia. Did Tom ring? Does he know I am going? Did anyone bother to tell him? Tom, oh Tom, my black-haired baby. No one congratulated me when you were born. No one. That's why he's trying to climb Everest. Can no one contact him? Put on the music. I'm asking you nicely . . . If you don't put him on, I'll . . . I'll . . . I'll . . .

Looks around desperately.

Scarecrow You'll what? . . . What'll you do?

Woman I'll stop breathing! This second!

Scarecrow Go on! Stop! Let me see you stop breathing! Remember him in there. Go on! Stop!

Woman I'm not playing with you. I'm going to count to three. If by three I don't hear 'My Friend the Wind' blasting off the CD. I'm going to put an end to it all. (*Counts ominously.*) One . . . two . . . three.

Scarecrow stands there defiantly.

Right! That's it! Goodbye, you vicious parasite that's led me a crazy dance. Barking orders to kingdom come. All that unnecessary guilt. All those sly commands. All that wrong advice! All that metaphysical claptrap. Goodbye and good riddance, you stinking old turkey box!

Woman refuses to breathe. Things are calm for a while as they eyeball one another. Then both start to go red in the face. Then woman starts thrashing around. Scarecrow clutches her throat, doubled over. They both fight it a while, both refusing to give in. Eventually Scarecrow reels towards CD player and struggles to put on Demis Roussos. Woman is now catatonic, oblivious until she hears 'My Friend the Wind' or 'Forever and Ever' blasting out. She inhales violently as soon as she hears music. Smiles triumphantly. Croons softly as Scarecrow falls on floor panting. Woman raises a fragile hand and conducts the music.

Now . . . that's all I wanted . . . I spoke to a chef once at a party . . . what's this his name was? . . . very boring . . . no, not boring . . . very calm . . . still . . . odd . . . like most away from the thing they know . . . anyway it turned out he had cooked for Demis Roussos once. The man ate nine lobsters in one sitting. That's what I call passion for living. A man who can eat nine lobsters, well there's no stopping him, is there?

Silence from Scarecrow, who lies on the floor, fuming.

Is there?

Silence.

Thick, are we? Thick as a brick? I warned you.

Scarecrow You nearly took us to the blue beyond is what you did.

Woman Now you know who's boss. I love this. This is great. Gets me churning. (*Shouts over the music.*) I was meant for someone of Demis Roussos' magnitude. Someone who can devour nine lobsters as an appetiser. You can hear the lobsters in his voice. Floor-of-the-sea stuff. Greek sea stuff. Written off by snobs like you.

Scarecrow This has been your problem all along.

Woman (*shouts*) What?

Scarecrow All this gush. All this hugeness.

Woman Speak up!

Scarecrow (*shouts*) All these passions and nothing, nothing back of them.

Woman So I'm not cold and articulate like you. I have no reserve. No restraint. No, what do they call it? . . . that awful quality they rate so highly these days?

Scarecrow Subtlety?

Woman Yes, that, I have none of that. What else do I lack?

Scarecrow An eternal sense.

Woman That's right. I can't even see tomorrow.

Scarecrow There'll hardly be one now.

Woman Oh the children, the children.

Scarecrow This is more of it. If you'd just shut up for five seconds about your children. All those pregnancies. How many was it? Several million the way you go on.

Woman It was eight! Eight. Nine if you count the one who didn't make it. My little half-moon baby with the livid face. Where are you now, my half-cooked morsel? Why couldn't you bear me? Why didn't you stay the course? Did something sift in the womb that appalled you? I should've had nine. There should've been nine in the photograph. Oh my God, I'm not over him yet . . . I'll never be over his . . . what . . . his what? You're the articulate one . . . his what?

Scarecrow That he came and went so quickly.

Woman Yes, gone before he was here.

Scarecrow Did it ever occur to you that he was a signal?

Woman A signal of what?

Scarecrow A pointer to this.

Woman Leave my children out of the witch turnings of your mind.

Scarecrow Numbers. You just wanted numbers. You just wanted to look and say, this one is mine and this one and this and him and her and those and that pair up there in the oak tree. Mine. All mine. That's what you wanted. Greedy for numbers. Insatiable for the head count. The leg count. I own sixteen pairs of legs and the two that didn't make it and eight noses and sixteen eyes and the two that didn't make it and sixteen ears and eighty fingers and eighty toes and reciting their names and ages to knock yourself out after another exhausting day of counting and coveting and even still wondering if you could squeeze another one in as you slide to your grave.

Woman I can't bear it. I can't bear leaving them. Turn him off! Turn him off!

Scarecrow (*turning Demis Roussos off*) Well, maybe you should've thought a bit harder about that before you decided to die.

Woman I didn't decide to die. How dare you!

Scarecrow You can lie to everyone except me.

Woman It's you who's the liar. I'm sick. The body has caved in. That's all.

Scarecrow Yes, that's all.

Woman My body has betrayed me or I have betrayed it or the betrayal was mutual. Who cares. I'm fatal. Terminal. Hopeless.

Scarecrow But admit it, you've always loved the idea of dying.

Woman You make it sound like a crime. Yes. In theory, death is magnificent but somehow I thought my own would be different.

Scarecrow It's not up to scratch?

Woman A bit prosaic, all said. It feels more like I'm drifting into a bad-tempered menstrual sleep. Ophelia now. She had a good death.

Scarecrow Ophelia died of love.

Woman And what am I dying of?

Scarecrow Spite.

Woman Spite is an honourable emotion. It's not right up there with love but it's better than dying by accident. Spite has been given bad press for too long now. Very well, I'm dying of spite. And since you're such an expert on these matters I'm sure you're going to tell me what it is I am most spiteful about.

Scarecrow I certainly am. I suppose you could say that your main artery of venom comes from one fact.

Woman Spare me your facts. Spare me your lethal mathematical precision. I want none of your facts. Your litany of crucifying facts. Facts are to be avoided.

Scarecrow Your main artery of venom comes from one fact and one fact only.

Woman Go on, spew the poison all over me . . . I dreamt the other night, when was the other night? Dreamt you were a rattlesnake with your mouth stapled shut and I got up on you and rode you down some boulevard. Go on, tell me about my main artery of venom.

Scarecrow The world has not yielded all you had hoped of it.

Woman Yes, there it is in a snake shell. The world has not yielded all I had hoped of it. That's as good a reason as any to die. Say it again. I should write that down if I wasn't unconscious.

Scarecrow The world has not surrendered to you. In fact the world has given you a bit of a battering, I think it's fair to say. But as I keep telling you it's a question of strategy. A question of how you deal with what's thrown in your lap.

Woman I didn't fight back enough? I wasn't brave?

Scarecrow You copped on too late.

Woman Did I? And what did I cop on to too late?

Scarecrow The first law.

Woman What first law?

Scarecrow You don't know the first law?

Woman Is there one?

Scarecrow I've told you! I've told you! You never listen!

Woman Tell me again.

Scarecrow You'll forget again. A waste of time now anyway.

Woman Then tell me because it's a waste of time.

Scarecrow The first law which should be nailed on every cot. The first law. This world's job is to take everything from you. Yours is not to let it.

Woman And how have I fared?

Scarecrow There is no describing what you have given away. Wilfully given away. You used up everything you had giving everyone what they wanted.

Woman Yes, you old gloom-eagle, peg it all at me now.

Scarecrow And hence your spite.

Woman Ah yes, my spite . . . I'd prefer to call it bitterness, if you've no objections.

Scarecrow You think bitterness sounds more important.

Woman Bitterness is the aristocracy of spite. Yes, it has a grander ring.

Scarecrow No matter how you dress it up, it's still nothing to be proud of. You're going into your grave out of bitterness, out of a sense of ruthless meanness. You who were given so much. You who I had such hopes for. I truly believed when I latched on to you before the weaver's throne, I truly believed that you and I would amount to something. I was wrong. Yes, your bitterness was a flaw in the weave, I noticed it, but I never thought it would bring us down. It looked such a small inconsequential thing, no more than a slipped stitch.

Woman I've surprised you then.

Scarecrow You've floored me.

Woman With my boundless capacity for bitterness. Actually boundless is a conservative estimate of my bitterness. Is there a bigger word than boundless?

Scarecrow Unboundable? Gargantuan rancour? I don't know. I give up.

Woman Do we have a dictionary handy?

Scarecrow You're too weak to turn the pages. You're almost blind.

Woman Never to read again.

Scarecrow Correct.

Woman Could we change our minds? Undie, as it were?

Scarecrow Not since Lazarus has someone undied.

Woman Am I still breathing?

Scarecrow Just about.

Woman Do you believe the Lazarus story?

Scarecrow Oh yes. Everything is possible.

Woman Except for me. I'm not important enough to be brought back.

Scarecrow Neither was Lazarus. Sure, who was he, only somebody's little brother. Mary Magdalene's, wasn't it?

Woman Martha and Mary's.

Scarecrow The two grannies who hung out with Our Lord. I'll wager they were great knitters like yourself or whatever the equivalent of knitting was back there, back

163

then. Maybe he raised Lazarus from the dead just to stop them knitting, to put a halt to their endless cups of tea and their wholesome gossip, give them something else to mull over besides the plain-purl.

Woman And what did he do after he was brought back?

Scarecrow What do you mean, what did he do?

Woman Well, how long did he live the second time? Did he drink coffee under the palm trees? Did he terrify the village? Did babies scream and dogs go silent when he walked down the street?

Scarecrow On that the great book is silent as it is on all the ordinary unbearable tragedies because the great miracle of Lazarus is not the pyrotechnics of Our Lord. No, the great miracle of Lazarus is that he didn't insist on getting back into the coffin.

Woman I take it you don't want to come back.

Scarecrow That's not what I said.

Woman You don't want to come back with me . . . you don't want to go on with me.

Scarecrow That possibility does not arise.

Woman Well, I wouldn't turn down another sojourn here with or without you.

Scarecrow I don't believe you.

Woman It's the encroaching annihilation is doing it . . . I've changed.

Scarecrow You haven't changed since your holy communion.

Woman You don't know the first thing about me.

Scarecrow I know when you're lying. I was there before you and I'll be there after. Lie away. I'm through with you. I'm just going through the motions. I'll find someone else.

Woman Who? Who will you find?

Scarecrow Someone with possibility this time. Someone who hasn't surrendered before they're out of nappies.

Woman Did I give up that early?

Scarecrow I'm exaggerating. I'm a little angry with you. I have loved you so long. You've never returned it. Threw me a few scraps from time to time. Kept me tagging along on whims and promises. Promises that were not kept.

Woman You asked too much. You're still asking it.

Scarecrow I only asked for a little happiness.

Woman A little happiness?

Scarecrow You make it sound like some obscure metal.

Woman And is it not?

Scarecrow No, it's easy to be happy. Happiness like most things is a decision, like going to the dentist or painting a wall. There's no great mystery.

Woman Well, it's a mystery to me and remains one. Maybe my destiny is to be baffled by happiness. You're right. Let's not go on like this. Let's end it all. Bring me the mirror please.

Scarecrow What do you want the mirror for?

Woman To watch myself die. I want to see how I am. I always look in mirrors to find out what's happening to me. Please bring it to me. I want to see if I'm still here.

Scarecrow You want to drool over the vestiges of your beauty.

Woman Yes. Let me drool. Thank God I still have my vanity.

Scarecrow (*brings Woman the mirror*) Not much left to feed your vanity now. Look at you. Your bones are pushing through your skin.

Woman Are they? Show? At last. That's wonderful. There's not much about this century I'd go on bended knee to, but to its ideal of beauty I will. Both of them. Bones, teeth, hair, the age adores. Well I always had good teeth and despite everything my hair is still magnificent. And now finally I have achieved bones. My dear, I have transformed myself into the ideal. Look at me! I am graveyard chic, angular, lupine, dangerous.

> *Woman raises an arm, turns it, runs mirror down a leg, admires it.*

Look at these arms, these legs, the contours of these limbs. I am slowly carving myself into a Greek statue. All those slices of bread and jam. All those pots of spuds and butter. All that apple tart and cream. All, all fallen away. Admire me for once in my skeletal queenality.

Scarecrow You're determined to provoke me.

Woman And yet some of my greatest memories are of food. Roast beef with gravy and mash, mackerel straight from the sea, so fresh you could taste the waves trapped in the meat . . . What else? Salmon sashimi with pickled ginger . . . oh . . . the foie gras that time . . . what was it served with again?

Scarecrow Melon I think, on a bed of lettuce.

Woman And I refused to share it. Devoured it. Who was it bought me the foie gras?

Scarecrow The one that wanted you to parade naked around the room.

Woman And did I?

Scarecrow You did.

Woman Pity I don't remember it then. Was I happy? Parading naked around the room?

Scarecrow Too much of the convent psyche in you to enjoy parading naked anywhere.

Woman It's wonderful to have such a critical spectator on all one's most intimate journeys. Was he the one used to watch this video of a shark before he made love?

Scarecrow That was the German in the cowboy boots.

Woman That's right. The German. He was a magnificent specimen of a man, wasn't he?

Scarecrow Yes, he had big bones.

Woman Six-foot-four with the cowboy boots off. And he kept rewinding to this shot of the shark erupting out of the water, the big maw of him and his hundreds of razor teeth. And then he'd freeze-frame the close-up of the shark's mouth and just lie there looking at it. Good God, I know what he was doing! He was fantasising that I was the shark!

Scarecrow That only dawning on you now?

Woman And when we'd part he'd always say, 'Ciao bella,' just like that, and he'd drive off never saying when we'd meet again. And when I wouldn't any more, couldn't any more, I think I was pregnant again, yes that was it, he kept calling for ages.

Scarecrow An act of revenge, that's all he was. That's what they all were, just acts of revenge. Your heart wasn't involved. I wasn't allowed a look in.

Woman They were more than that. In the beginning maybe. But they were more than that. They were more than revenge.

Scarecrow And I'm telling you they weren't. Your backward twisted little heart was tied, always tied to him who made little of you every opportunity he could.

Woman He wasn't always like that.

Scarecrow Remember what Auntie Ah said.

Woman Yes, I remember.

Scarecrow Tell me what she said.

Woman If you know why are you asking me?

Scarecrow Just tell me.

Woman No.

Scarecrow Then I'll tell you. 'I'd rather see your white body floating down the Shannon than for you to marry that man.'

Woman Well, I'm glad you've got that off your chest.

Scarecrow And several decades on would you agree with Auntie Ah's pronouncement?

Woman Oh yes.

Scarecrow You admit she was right?

Woman I've always known it. From the start I knew this man is no good for me.

Scarecrow And you went ahead.

Woman Yes I did.

Scarecrow Why?

Woman Because my dress was made and everyone was invited. Maybe I felt sorry for him.

Scarecrow Because you felt sorry for him you had eight children.

Woman I'd have had twenty if he wanted.

Scarecrow But he didn't want.

Woman That's not true. He's fond of them in a distracted sort of way.

Scarecrow I can't make head nor tail of you.

Woman It's all confusion, Scarecrow.

Scarecrow Can I just ask you one thing?

Woman One can always ask.

Scarecrow After all he's done . . .

Woman Don't start in on him again.

Scarecrow Let me finish!

Woman All right.

Scarecrow Do you love him still?

Woman Of course not.

Scarecrow I don't believe you.

Woman If I say, yes I still love him, you'll throttle me.

Scarecrow I won't.

Woman I know you.

Scarecrow I promise I won't go near you. I just want to know the lie of the land. Do you love him still?

Woman I don't know . . . yes . . . I adore him.

Scarecrow Good God.

Woman It's terrible, is it?

Scarecrow You've no idea.

Woman Then tell me.

Scarecrow No, I want you to go peacefully, without fear.

Woman And how am I doing on the peaceful scale? On the fear gauge?

Scarecrow just looks at her.

You see terrors ahead. Well, I'll meet them when I meet them. At least the terrors of the earth are over. It can't be worse than here . . . can it?

Scarecrow doesn't answer.

Well, you can just take that smug eternal look off your face or look away. Look away. Don't look at me like that as if you know something. If you know something tell me.

Scarecrow You don't want to know.

Woman You can't wait to fly off, dump me in the grave. Fly off with him. (*Wardrobe.*)

Scarecrow I assure you I have no desire to fly off with that thing in the wardrobe. I promised you I'd settle you into your grave. I have never yet broken a promise to you. Can you say the same?

Woman Then why am I afraid to close my eyes?

Scarecrow Close them, I'll watch.

Woman You'll sneak away.

Scarecrow Trust me.

Woman I need to sleep. Promise me you'll stand guard.

Scarecrow I told you.

Woman Lie here beside me, hold my hand.

Scarecrow Don't be such a coward.

Woman And if I don't wake?

Scarecrow You'll wake.

Woman Swear it.

Scarecrow I swear.

Woman Okay so . . . (*Mumbles as she drifts off, fighting sleep.*) And the mountains . . . what can I say about the mountains except they were there . . . purple on brown on blue on molten grey . . . and the memory of ice in the light on the water and the water, glass . . . was that out west or did I just dream it, and the dwarf oaks shaped by storm, bent and rounded as old women's backs . . . hopeless . . . hopeless . . . or is there such a thing as light at all . . . and the whole landscape, the mountain, the tree, the water, poised, waiting, for something . . . what? Yes, now I know what the mountain was waiting for, waiting for us to depart . . . leave it alone with the sky . . . they don't need us . . . never have . . . never will.

> *And Woman drifts off, lying on the floor. Scarecrow watches her a minute, then goes to wardrobe, puts her ear to the door, listens. Enter Him.*

Him Wake up! Come on, wake up, my dear.

Woman How long have I been here?

Him Where? Here . . . since Thursday . . . we found you on Thursday.

Woman I want to go back to where I came from.

Him You don't want to be here with me, with the children?

Woman I was here for decades . . . too late now, I don't see too well any more. I wouldn't see the sea.

Him Can you see me?

Woman Yes, I can see you.

Him Are you in pain, my dear?

Woman and Scarecrow burst out laughing.

What is it? Let me in on the joke. You're high as a kite. Maybe I should take a slug of this too.

He pours medicine into a beaker, lifts Woman's head. She drinks. He lays her back on the pillow.

Woman Thank you.

Scarecrow turns her eyes up to heaven.

Him (*smoothes her hair*) My dear, I haven't always treated you as I should and now there isn't time.

Scarecrow You have had abundance of time.

Him Can you forgive my callous treatment of you?

Woman (*to Scarecrow*) Can I?

Scarecrow Since when have you considered my opinion?

Woman Your callous treatment of me? Did you rehearse that phrase?

Him Did I what?

Woman It was more than callous. Don't pretty it up for a deathbed.

Him Yes, but can you forgive me?

Woman What does it matter whether I forgive or don't forgive?

Him Oh it matters. And will matter more when you leave me.

Scarecrow He makes your death sound like an infidelity.

Woman And is it not?

Him What, my dear?

Scarecrow No forgiveness since it matters to him. Let him suffer a little. Ask him why he kept returning.

Woman Why did you keep returning?

Him Because you are my wife, because you are the mother of my children, because despite how it appears you have always and will always be the one.

Woman If only you lived how you speak. I don't believe it any more. You kept coming back because you knew I would never have the courage to leave you, to bar the door, to break my children's hearts. You are suffocating me.

Him You know I will remember what you are saying now when you're gone.

Woman Yes, remember it.

Him You have a duty to leave me softly as I have a duty to watch you go without rancour.

Woman I am drowning in duty.

Him And what am I?

Woman Just play something for me. I don't want to talk to you now.

173

Him My dear, talk to me . . . forgive me . . . I will have to carry you with me until the end.

Woman Play something.

Him All right . . . What would you like to hear?

Woman Something romantic. There has been too little romance in my life.

Him I'll leave the door open.

In a minute we hear piano music. They listen a while.

Scarecrow You played it better when you played.

Woman I never cared . . . (*Listens.*) Yes, I played it better when I played.

Scarecrow And then you stopped.

Woman And then I stopped.

Scarecrow He didn't like you playing.

Woman I played when he wasn't here. A bottle of champagne, the children asleep, just you and me. No, I suppose he never liked me to do anything better than him.

Scarecrow Deal with that at the door of the tomb.

Woman How should I deal with it?

Scarecrow You martyred yourself to a mediocrity.

Woman Ssh . . . listen . . . he does remorse very well. You have to give him that. Give him that at least.

Scarecrow He's the high priest of remorse. He's jealous of your death. He's determined to wring the most he can from it. If you're not careful he'll hijack your last breath.

Woman No, he's more fragile than that. I've carried him and his shattered ego for years. He's more exhausting than all the children put together . . . Tell me, you who have an answer for everything, tell me what it is about dying that's so sexy?

Scarecrow You think this is sexy?

Woman Well yes, I do. Is there a moon in the sky? The music, my extinction, what is it?

Scarecrow A chance to be epic, I suppose. Life withholds the epic until the end.

Woman Then let's enjoy it. We'll only get to do it once.

Scarecrow I'm not in an epic mood.

Woman Why not?

Scarecrow Too many things about you are small.

Woman Epicness is for the brave. The beautiful.

Scarecrow You had it once when you were a fat teenager with permed hair. You knew then what epic was and epic asked.

Woman And then what happened to me?

Scarecrow You turned chicken and fled the battlefield.

Woman I fought the good fight if you didn't. I have the scars to prove it.

Scarecrow Skirmishes. Merely skirmishes.

Woman Whatever. Open the wine. This orgy of sobriety is killing me. Open the wine.

Scarecrow Your throat is almost closed. You'll choke.

Woman Wine's as good as anything to choke on.

Scarecrow Okay, let's open the wine. (*Takes a bottle of wine from locker. Opens it.*) The wine from him.

Woman Which him?

Scarecrow Which him? The him that should've been *the him*.

Woman Oh. His parting gift. Okay, let's drink it. The wine and the diamond ring. The big rock. Where is it?

Scarecrow I'm wearing it.

Woman And the song and dance under the weeping willows, I couldn't wait to get away . . . a little wiry fella . . . of no consequence really.

Scarecrow He borrowed a fortune to buy you this ring.

Woman Yes, I had it valued . . . was going to sell it . . . I don't know why I didn't.

Scarecrow He loved you. More, he loved me. He saw past your tattered hide. He saw you as you should be seen. He saw me and he loved me. But you couldn't handle that, jealous surface bitch that you are. You'd sooner listen to that barbarian murder Chopin than live and let me live too.

Woman I didn't know you were so taken with him.

Scarecrow He would've kept us alive!

Woman I suppose I did use him a bit when things were desperate here, but my car broke down . . . I was never meant to even meet him . . . just one of those things . . . he was very kind but kindness can be a nuisance after a while . . . anyway, the children.

Scarecrow The excuse for everything. Here.

Woman can barely hold the wine.

Drink his wine and just think you could be with him now. I could be with him now instead of this funeral parlour.

Drinks bitterly.

Woman Can you hold it for me . . . feed it to me?

Scarecrow does. Woman takes a sip.

Cheers.

Scarecrow Cheer me no cheers.

Woman Beautiful wine. The planet's last connection to the gods.

Scarecrow Might I ask what we're celebrating?

Woman It'll come to us eventually.

Scarecrow Will we chance a fag?

Woman Cigarettes are your fault.

Scarecrow Cigarettes were the only time I ever got you on your own. Yes, let's chance a fag. Where are they?

Woman There was a packet in my dressing gown, oh, a hundred years ago.

Scarecrow I'll smoke for both of us.

Woman No, if there are cigarettes on the table I want in on them.

Scarecrow In a minute.

Woman Now!

Scarecrow Ask me nicely.

Woman I'm sick of you! I'm so sick of you!

Scarecrow You have wine. You have cigarettes or the memory of them. Just imagine you could be sitting with him. Alive! By a big fire, your children roaming the house. You were meant for a long life. Okay, have a puff.

Woman Get away, I don't want one now!

Scarecrow I thought we were having a party. Your mood has changed.

Woman That's what moods are for. For changing. You'd have me on an even keel twelve months of the year. Yes, my mood has changed. Sometimes wine does that. Sobers you.

Scarecrow Come on, drink up.

Holds glass to Woman's lips.

Woman Who was it recommended three glasses of wine a day?

Scarecrow That was Keats. Three glasses. No more, no less.

Woman I wonder what size the glasses were in the romantic era.

Scarecrow The romantic era wasn't very romantic for Keats.

Woman At least he left something after him.

Scarecrow Aren't you leaving a brood of them? Maybe they'll amount to something.

Woman When did it all turn to tragedy, Scarecrow? When did I stop lampooning the world? And why?

Scarecrow What's your greatest regret?

Woman That I didn't study the *Kama Sutra* in depth. That wine is no good. Death should be intoxicating.

Scarecrow Have another sip. It may lift the fog. We mustn't meet the darkness with the dark.

Woman I look over the years and all I see is one wrong turn leading to another wrong turn. I cannot remember a moment when it was right.

Scarecrow Your mind is a swill.

Woman A sewer. Let it not erupt. Can I just go now?

Scarecrow Slip away mid-sentence, is it?

Woman Before we're interrupted again. They're all out there lining up for a gawk. I heard an argument over brass handles, must be for my coffin. Can I just go?

Scarecrow If that's what you really want.

Woman I'll stop breathing so.

Puts covers over her head.

It'll be easier this way.

From under the covers.

Right, on the count of three.

Scarecrow No final soliloquies?

Woman (*head out*) What?

Scarecrow No farewell speech?

Woman None. (*Back under covers.*) Okay. One. Two. Three. Goodbye, Scarecrow.

Scarecrow Yeah.

Hold a minute. Scarecrow begins to suffer. Doesn't fall this time. Enter Auntie Ah.

Auntie Ah (*takes covers off Woman's head*) So it has come to this.

Woman So it has.

Auntie Ah I put your mother in the ground too.

Woman Where is she buried?

Auntie Ah You don't know where your own mother is buried?

Woman No, where exactly in the graveyard?

Auntie Ah It was in the south corner, but graveyards grow all the time.

Woman There were the elms. And the sun slanting through. Came away empty-handed . . . a butterfly chased me to the gate. Never had the wherewithal to face it again. I left the children fighting in the car, was afraid to take them to her grave. I thought somehow she would suck them in. I needn't have worried. Not a trace of her. Did you even put up a tombstone?

Auntie Ah Why didn't you go to a doctor sooner? There's no call for this nonsense. I could have laid down too more times than I care to recount, but it wasn't for nothing I grew up on the western seaboard, a grey land of rock and thistle where little or nothing thrives. And it wasn't for nothing you were born there too. But the eastern blood of your father diluted the limestone and softened you to this. Would you ever sit up and have a bowl of soup and put an end to this contrariness and whim? And what's in store for your chickens now? You think to fling them on the walls of the world and have the rest of us pick up the broken bones. Your mother was the same. No finishing power. Anyone can get through the first half. You start a life. You finish it. You don't bail out at the crossroads because you don't like the scenery. It's weak. I despise it. And I'll tell you something, my niece of a girl, there'll be no ecstasies at the finish. I've handed many back to their maker and not a one of them sang as the curtain fell. They went confused, they went jabbering, they went silent, they went howling, but not a one of them went with the beatified light in their eye as if they'd seen a vision of something pleasing. All I ever saw was the light draining from the basalt of the eyeball. The light draining. And the light gone . . . I'm leaving five thousand under the pillow, sure you can't even afford to die.

Woman It's not many would offer you the price of your own funeral and you still breathing.

Auntie Ah Delicate sentiments. Delicate sentiments. And what do they weigh against a bag of gold? You've them all destroyed back west with this, this . . . I will not forgive this . . . I will not . . . this wilful jaunt to your doom.

And exit Auntie Ah.

Scarecrow Were those tears? Auntie Ah in tears. Could she possibly miss us?

Woman She only loves hanging out of the dying, laid out half of Connemara. She's looking forward to the whole catastrophe.

Scarecrow Alas poor Yorick.

Woman Alas indeed. Only if we're lucky will it end in the grave.

Scarecrow You're afraid of that, aren't you?

Woman Waking in the coffin with the serpent at my breast . . . yes, I'm afraid of that.

Scarecrow Or the rats boring through the plywood, their paws on your face.

Woman My belly a pudding of worms.

Scarecrow And you awake the whole time. Watching the serpent and the rat and the worms have their smelly feast.

Woman They will start with the softest parts . . . the eyes.

Scarecrow Then with their claws will scoop out the meat of your brain.

Woman Then the ears.

Scarecrow The lips.

Woman The tongue.

Scarecrow They will part your stomach like wet paper and reach for the heart, the breasts, the intestine.

Woman The kidneys, the womb, the ovaries, they will wrap themselves around my lungs and suck out the tripe of my spine.

Scarecrow And so on.

Woman And so on. How long will this ordeal last?

Scarecrow Hamlet's gravedigger says . . . is it eight years? Seems overlong to me.

Woman Let's trust the Bard. Eight years till we're clean as Yorick. And then?

Scarecrow Perhaps the real torture will begin.

Woman That has always been a possibility. All my life I've been afraid of rats. At last I know why.

Scarecrow Some poet or other said 'rats' backwards is 'star'.

Woman And poets backwards is stop.

Scarecrow Stop backwards is pots.

Woman Pots is even better.

Scarecrow Yeats was a great pot.

Woman A wonderful pot.

Scarecrow A pot born.

Woman With stupendous collections of potties to his name.

Scarecrow He overflew with potties.

Woman He even carried potties around in his head, there is nothing star-like about rats. Filthy creatures, and no wonder when we are their staple diet. I'll ask him to cremate me. Better the conflagration of hair and nails and crackling gristle than a banquet for rats. I read somewhere they have an intricate tunnel system from grave to grave. No. The roar of the furnace and then it's over. Scatter me on the wind and who's to say I won't become a particle of some new galaxy trying to be born.

Enter Him.

Him Is there anything I can do? Turn you? Will I turn you?

Woman Please. (*to Scarecrow*) Don't look at me, you.

Scarecrow I can look.

Him Let me raise the pillows too. What are you mumbling about, my dear? What are you thinking?

Woman Always the same, about my happiness and my unhappiness.

Him Are you?

Woman No. That's what Anna Karenina said. I've always wanted to say it . . . I was thinking of the house I grew up in.

Scarecrow You were not.

Him You grew up in many houses.

Woman The first one. My mother's house. From upstairs you could see right across the bay. Why did we never make it back to the sea?

Him I've missed the sea too.

Woman Maybe we would have been better people there.

Him Maybe we would.

Woman At the very least the sea would've added some sort of grandeur to this . . . The day my mother died . . . her infant son dead beside her . . . they were going to call him Michael . . . I never saw him . . . and I always meant to find out which of them died first.

Scarecrow What does it matter which of them went first?

Woman I'm sure it mattered a great deal to my mother.

Scarecrow They went. They went. You hold on too long. You always hold on. They went. What more is there to know?

Woman There is much, much more to know.

Him What, my dear? What is it you want me to know?

Woman Grief can be measured! Grief can be calibrated!

Him Yes, it can.

Woman (*to Scarecrow*) Ten pints of grief I can swallow but not a drop more! I'm not talking to you! Stop butting in. I want to tell him something.

Scarecrow You think this man is interested in the heartbreaking details of your life?

Woman You give him credit for nothing.

Scarecrow And you never consider how he has thwarted me!

Him What is it? You're all agitated. What is it you want to tell me?

Woman I forget . . . she drives me mad . . . oh yes . . .
that day, the day she died. Daddy and I went in on the
bus. A scorcher of a day but still I insisted on wearing
my red coat and red hat. I wanted to wear them because
a couple of days before my mother and I had spent a
whole day trying on coats for me. We went from shop to
shop but no coat satisfied her. She had in her mind this
red coat and red hat that failed to materialise. We went
to Lydon's for tea and buns. Her mood was sombre,
belligerent even. It was getting late. The shops would
soon be closed. She stared out the window and muttered
about it being a bloody miracle if we found it now. Her
voice so low, defeated, the huge hump of her belly
wedged against the table, her shoes kicked off because
they pained her . . . I can't remember where we found
the coat. Her hands shook as she did up the black velvet
buttons. She led me to a mirror. Now look at yourself,
she said, just look at you. But it is her I see now, her
girth disappearing in dusty shadow, old before her time
and still radiant, the white teeth flashing, the russet gold
of her hair and the expression in her eyes. I, in my new
red coat and hat, gave her pleasure, pleasure beyond
describing. For one brief moment, a mirror glance, I was
that thing she had yearned for and found.

Woman bursts into tears.

Him My dear. My dear.

Woman Do me the honour of not comforting me where
there can be no comfort.

Scarecrow Lies. Lies. Lies. You're unbelievable.

Woman And you are heartless! That coat, those buttons,
that coat has stalked me for years.

*He watches helplessly as Woman weeps and weeps,
a protracted grieving of sound and liquid. Scarecrow*

*looks on unmoved. This eventually subsides. He pours
some medicine into a beaker.*

Get away from me with that! It makes me crazy.

Him But the pains will return.

Woman It numbs me. I can't feel anything any more.

Him I can't have you suffering.

Woman For twenty-five years you've caused my
suffering. For once in your life speak the truth.

Him And what truth is that?

Woman You've wanted me dead for years.

Him This is crazy talk.

Woman But it's true.

Him It is not true!

Woman Then tell me one true thing. Just one. I don't
care how brutal it is.

Him Just stop this. You're upsetting yourself for no
reason.

Woman You've just been with her.

Him All right, you want the unvarnished truth. Yes, I've
just been with her. She's parked up the road. Now leave
it please. Leave it at that. It's no good going over and over
it.

Woman And after you pour that stuff into me, knock
me out, you'll go back out to her.

Him Yes, I'll go back out to her. She's taking me for a
quick dinner before I go mad here.

Woman Go then! Go! There are others who can provide
less venomous care.

Him Your relations. The house is falling down with them. A big coven of witches in bainin and black. They've eaten everything, drunk everything. I've had to borrow money from my mother. Right now they're devouring the stew I made for the children. Last night they got through eight bottles of whiskey. They hang out in the bathroom, smoking and shrieking. The children aren't talking to me because I won't let them go clubbing. They haven't been to school in weeks. We're all waiting! We're all waiting! Die if you're going to. If not. Get up!

Woman I don't want her at my funeral.

Him Don't worry, I'm finishing with her too. If she thinks I'm going to set up house when you're gone. I said it right out to her. What's the point in changing horses? Is that enough truth for you or will I go on?

Woman just stares at him.

You drive me to the limit every time so I say things that shouldn't be said . . . Look, take this stuff . . . it's revenge enough you're going. Must I watch you go howling?

Woman If that's what it takes. (*Pushes away beaker.*)

Him There are many ways to leave someone. Mine is a cliché. I lack your savagery.

Woman My savagery?

Him Yes, your savagery! You chose to leave me while staying to view the wreckage.

Woman I want you to know I've had my flings too.

Him You have not.

Woman You think I was just sitting here pining for you.

Him You're raving. You want to destroy me.

Woman It astonishes you anyone would want me?

Him I didn't say that.

Woman But you're thinking it. Believe it or not, you wanted me yourself once.

Him Right now that is hard to believe.

Woman Several sorties in fact.

Him You're just trying to make me jealous.

Woman I'm past trying to make you anything.

Him How dare you!

Woman How dare I what?

Him Lying like this. You want to leave me with nothing. I have to live. I have to look after those children. How dare you sully us like this?

Woman You don't believe me.

Him It can't be true.

Woman Do you want names? Telephone numbers?

Him You are capable of that?

Woman Yes, I am capable of that . . . of afternoons in other men's houses . . . of showering and perfuming for a stranger's arms . . . You think I survived this long on the scraps you threw me?

Him All the time acting the weeping virgin, the bleeding martyr, the woman abandoned . . . how dare you deceive me like that?

Woman Oh, I dared and I dared and you didn't even notice, and I'll tell you something else, if it wasn't for the children I'd have walked years ago. (*Takes off wedding ring and engagement ring.*) Take these. Sell them. Buy some more food and drink for my tribe. At least they know how to celebrate, ignorant old crones that they are. But they know this much. A person's passing is a sacred thing and merits some kind of overdose. So serve them well and let them drink and feast and sing me to my final place. Go! Look after them. You might learn something.

Him I have dirges aplenty too if you'd only listen.

Woman I've listened to you too long and all that listening has taught me nothing.

Him Nothing?

Woman Nothing save you were not worthy of my love.

Him So that's the way of it. Curse me on the lip of the grave.

Woman You drank the wine. Now drink the vinegar.

Him Just one thing you have never understood. You mistook, deliberately mistook my roving for rejection.

Woman Roving! It is annihilation! Annihilation of me! Roving!

Him I never withdrew from you. Never! You were the one slammed like a thousand doors as only a woman can.

And exit Him.

Scarecrow He's almost tolerable when he stands up for himself.

Woman I'm out of control. I won't be happy till I've ground him into the dirt.

Scarecrow Validation of oneself sometimes involves that.

Woman Right now nothing will satisfy but to bring him down with me. Oh Scarecrow, I'm so afraid.

Scarecrow Afraid is Disneyland.

Woman Terrified?

Scarecrow Horrified and every other ide.

Woman I am murderous with my own passing.

Scarecrow Close, you're getting close.

Woman I see tombs in shadow, mossy, weather-scarred tombs and all the dead squashed in and me with them wondering if there is starlight above. I'm being buried alive. I am my own ghost.

Scarecrow Shush for a while till we try and articulate it right.

> *The wardrobe door creaks open. Woman and Scarecrow turn to look. A wing droops from the wardrobe, then a clawed foot hovers, then lights down.*

Act Two

Woman lies in bed with blood trickling down her chin. She clasps a bunch of black feathers in her hand. Sounds of a battle from wardrobe.

Woman (*weakly*) Scarecrow! . . . Scarecrow . . . are you all right?

> *Battle increases in frenzy from wardrobe: grunts, cries of pain, growls, pants, howls.*

What is that thing doing to you?

> *Enter Auntie Ah.*

Auntie Ah There's blood streaming from your lips.

Woman He came at me with his beak. I pulled at his feathers.

Auntie Ah Where did you get those?

Woman I just told you.

Auntie Ah Let me swab your mouth.

> *Cleans Woman up, straightens bed, sheets, pillows.*

Woman It's going to kill her.

Auntie Ah The state of the room, swear there was a wrestling match here.

Woman Get her! Get her! Help her! Scarecrow's still in the wardrobe.

Auntie Ah Ah there's always someone in the wardrobe.

Woman His claws. I've never seen anything . . .

Auntie Ah Come on and we'll say a decade of the rosary.

Woman (*calls*) Scarecrow, would a rosary help?

Auntie Ah (*heads out*) Oh Lord open my lips so my tongue shall announce thy praise. The five sorrowful mysteries. The agony in the garden. Our Father who art in . . .

Woman Desist in your crazy orisons.

Auntie Ah You're above the old prayers, is that it? Above dust and ashes? Above God? Above the blue virgin and her entourage of bird men? What'll you say when you alight above and this sacrilege is played before you like a newsreel?

Woman And what of his sacrilege against me?

Auntie Ah What sacrilege?

Woman Well, how about you for starters?

Auntie Ah No call for taking your bad temper out on God and on me.

Woman God is for the living.

Auntie Ah God is for all time.

Woman In the Louvre there is a painting . . . the Italian section . . . saw it last summer . . . Imagine last summer I was strolling Paris. I drank glass after glass of Sancerre. I flirted. I smoked. I ate raw steak till the blood dribbled down my chin . . . and I looked beautiful. Paris is the correct backdrop for me. I was set free. A woman with eight children roaming Paris . . . alone . . . Why did I bother coming back? . . . Scarecrow, are you still alive? . . . What are you doing?

Auntie Ah Stop blathering, you're dying, not going mad. Focus your mind, girl, you were telling me about smoking and flirting in Paris.

Woman Many lifetimes ago and I went every day across the Seine to see the Caravaggio. *The Death of the Virgin.* Her feet were blue. Her dress was red. Everyone has their head bowed. Oh the grief . . . terrible to look at . . . frightening . . . and do you know why, Auntie Ah?

Auntie Ah Why what?

Woman Because the miracle is over. Yes it is. She's going down into the clay. Not up to the blue beyond. The apostles know it. Caravaggio knows it and we know it.

Auntie Ah Her feet were blue? What sort of a painter is that? You mean her dress was blue. The Virgin's dress is always blue because blue is for eternity.

Woman Yes, blue is too kind. Her feet were more a putrid greeny black. Bad circulation maybe, varicose veins, or maybe he was just faithfully recording the rot. She looks about fifty . . . and still there is something sacred going on. Not with her. She's just another of those invisible women past their prime. But the mourners are appalling . . . put the heart crossways in you, Auntie Ah.

Auntie Ah Would it, girl?

Woman She was the last mortal loved by a god. And with her end came the end of God's desire for any truck with us. The funeral bier of the last mortal some god briefly and casually loved . . . But do you know what amazes me, Auntie Ah?

Auntie Ah What?

Woman That he was here so recently.

Auntie Ah And won't you be lying in his arms before this night descends?

Woman That is just too much to hope for from here.

Auntie Ah He'll swaddle you to him. You wait and see, and us all left here one arm longer than the other.

Woman Something I've always been meaning to ask you, Auntie Ah?

Auntie Ah Ask away, girl.

Woman Why do they always have graveyards on the beaches in Connemara?

Auntie Ah For fear we'd enjoy the sun and sand too much, I suppose.

Woman We should all live beside graveyards otherwise we're likely to forget.

Auntie Ah Forget what?

Woman That the whole point of living is preparing to die. Why did no one ever teach me that?

Auntie Ah I did.

Woman You did not. You were all simper and gush about Heaven. Had to figure it out for myself. Too late of course. And now to be cut off in the blossom of my sins.

Auntie Ah Now you're talking. Father Gant is in the kitchen waiting on your confession.

Woman He'll be waiting.

Auntie Ah It's the height of bad manners. Confess for my sake. Sure, what could you be guilty of except ignorance and greed and vanity and cruelty to your relations, all that ordinary run-of-the-mill venality, oh and a bit of robbery from time to time. You used to rob from my handbag. Did you ever confess that? You think I didn't notice? I noticed and thought to store it up for the future. Confess now and confess all and you'll be able to look your maker in the eye instead of hanging back slyly among the ghouls, hoping he'll have forgotten your transgressions. He won't, you know. Good girl. Confess.

Woman It's a terrible state of affairs to arrive at the close of your life and realise you've nothing to confess . . . though looked at the proper way, I suppose I committed the greatest sin of all.

Auntie Ah What sin are you talking about?

Woman I wasn't good to myself . . . I refused to be happy.

Auntie Ah I remember you happy. Your holy communion, the day you left on the train to go up to university. Wild horses wouldn't stop you.

Woman That wasn't happiness. That was relief getting away from you.

Auntie Ah It was happiness. I have the snapshots to prove it. Happiness! Everyone thinks they have a God-given right to it. Sure, it's only a recent invention of the Sunday newspapers. It'll wither and pass in time and we'll go back to the way we were.

Woman Scarecrow . . . Scarecrow . . . come back . . . I need you. What are you still hovering for?

Auntie Ah I have earned the right to hover. It is not my fault you never allowed me to be your mother.

Woman You want to ogle me off the planet.

Auntie Ah I admit I'm curious. I like to see the finish of a life. How we die says it all about how we have lived. I'll lay you out. I won't let strangers near you. And I'll do what I can for your children.

Woman Oh Auntie Ah, don't make me savage you. I don't have the energy. Please, just keep away from my children.

Auntie Ah The times have softened and me with them. The terrible rages are gone, woke one morning, just flown.

Woman What's flown, what's fleeing, is the one you inflicted them upon.

The door of the wardrobe creaks open. Scarecrow steps out, covered in blood and bruises. Nightdress torn. Shaken from encounter.

Scarecrow (*in the door of the wardrobe*) Yes . . . yes . . . I am very grateful . . . thank you.

She bows shakily. A muffled sentence from wardrobe.

I never thought you were.

Woman What did it do to you?

Auntie Ah Rest now. Rest. (*Takes out rosary beads, prays quietly.*)

Scarecrow Don't you ever accuse me again of not loving you . . . I bartered myself for more time.

Woman How much time?

Scarecrow Half an hour.

Woman Half an hour.

Scarecrow You should have seen what it wanted for an hour. I couldn't do it. I'm sorry.

Woman Should I go in? What can anyone do with half an hour?

Scarecrow Or a century for that matter. What can be done with a paltry hundred years?

Woman He can stuff his half-hour. I refuse to enjoy it.

Scarecrow Who's talking about enjoyment?

Woman You told me that's what time was for.

Scarecrow That was when you had time.

Woman And now I don't?

Scarecrow That's right.

Woman After half an hour there will be no more half-hours?

Scarecrow What in the name of God did I ever see in you?

Woman One could make love in half an hour.

Scarecrow One could if one had a lover.

Woman Why didn't I have more sex when I could have?

Scarecrow You were too busy hoovering.

Woman These hands will not touch again. These battered old hands have not touched enough.

Scarecrow No, none of that will happen again.

Woman You needn't sound so final about it. And my dreams were all of infidelity. Strange that, and I thought I loved him but my dreams, all of escape, flying, bedding strangers. Why was that, Miss Know-All?

Scarecrow I was trying to prod you on; hoick you from this half-existence.

Woman What else must I acknowledge?

Scarecrow That you're a liar.

Woman What do we have? Minutes? Seconds? The twins aren't even six till February. Auntie Ah, I think I'm pregnant. Three months. It'll go to the grave with me.

Auntie Ah Aren't you too old to be pregnant?

Woman Either that or the menopause, but it feels like a baby . . . that exhilarating surge I get each time . . . life . . . life . . . overwhelming, unstoppable life.

Scarecrow Ask her did you ever have a red coat.

Woman You know well I had.

Scarecrow Ask her.

Woman All right, just to prove you wrong. I know what you're insinuating. You look like some Siberian convict out of Dostoevsky. Auntie Ah, did I ever have a red coat?

Auntie Ah (*smoothes Woman's hair*) Calm. Calm. Calm, girl. You'll need the vestiges of your mind to orient beyond.

Woman A red coat and a red hat to match? When I came to you?

Auntie Ah You came with only the clothes on your back.

Scarecrow I knew you made it up. That baloney about the red coat. It never happened.

Woman Now you're going to hijack my memories. Don't you start!

Scarecrow Why would you lie like that?

Woman Are you telling me there was no moment with my mother on the day she died?

Scarecrow There was a moment all right, but that wasn't it.

Woman That was a defining moment and now you want to take it from me.

Scarecrow Why not tell it as it was? You did visit the hospital that day.

Woman It wasn't a hospital. It was a private nursing home.

Auntie Ah (*from her beads*) Above the midwife she was. I laid her out too.

Woman And I was wearing my new red coat and my new red hat.

Scarecrow (*shakes Woman*) You were not.

Woman Okay. Okay. Let me think. I wasn't wearing my new red coat and new red hat. I'd left them in the wardrobe on account of the heat.

Scarecrow No wardrobe. No coat. No hat.

Woman Then what was I wearing?

Scarecrow It's not important.

Woman Details are all I have. The larger canvas has eluded me. Leave me the details.

Scarecrow I'll leave you details that are true.

Woman Then tell me what I'm wearing. What did I look like? I can't see myself.

Scarecrow Can you see her?

A pause . . . a long pause.

199

Woman Yes . . . I can see her.

Scarecrow And what is she doing?

Woman She's sleeping.

Scarecrow What else?

Woman Nothing else. She's sleeping. Her mouth is open. Her tongue is moving as if she's sucking on something.

Scarecrow And then?

Woman I go to her.

Scarecrow (*whispers*) No. No. No.

Woman I'm standing at the door. I'm just standing there, looking at her. I've never seen her asleep before. She's on her side. The sheets are hard and white. Her mouth is open, her tongue is moving. Her hair is flat across the pillow as if someone had ironed it and nailed it there . . . And that's all . . . surely that can't be all.

Scarecrow There's more.

Woman The basin. The daffodils.

Scarecrow Yes, but something else too.

Woman Yes . . . else . . . as I stand there . . . a terrible realisation comes flashing through . . . a picture from the future . . . as I stand there I see myself here. Now. I see my own death day . . . and now she wakes and looks at me. I swim in her eye, she in mine, we're spellbound, unsmiling, conspirators too wise to fight what has been decreed on high, long, long ago.

Auntie Ah The old people at home used to say when a person was mortally fading, if they could hold on till the tide turns they'll surely make it, because there's a moment of grace when the ocean pauses and in that moment of grace anything can happen.

Woman And did my mother go as the tide turned?

Auntie Ah I don't know, but the day she died I saw her walking across the sand. I can't explain it. I can't prove it and I still don't believe it, but there she suddenly was, walking up to me, arms swinging, and we had words. Or rather I spoke to her, something like, I thought you were beyond in Galway. But she touched my head and whatever way she laid out her hand and touched my head silenced me and then she continued walking. A farewell, I suppose, if you believe in that sort of thing. Yes, that's what it was. She married your father on the rebound, but sure you know all that.

Woman No, I don't know all that. I don't know anything about her.

Auntie Ah Oh, she was wild about this other fella who let her down badly. I never heard the whys and hows of it but I do know it nearly killed her. She only married your father because he asked her. Well, she wasn't the first and won't be the last.

Woman And who was he? The one she was wild for?

Auntie Ah Never mind. That's as much as I'm telling.

Woman So there's more to tell.

Auntie Ah (*smugly*) Oh there is, there is, indeed there is, much, much more to tell.

Woman Then don't withhold from me now.

Auntie Ah You have parcelled yourself from me your whole life and now you want information.

Woman Don't make me beg . . . I'm on my deathbed.

Auntie Ah And that excuses everything?

Woman You're a vicious old woman . . . It's not your information to keep.

Auntie Ah Oh but it is.

Woman May you choke on it.

Auntie Ah And me all the time thinking I'd nothing you wanted.

Woman It would mean the world to me . . . to hear about her . . . you know that.

Auntie Ah And what was I? Your servant? No . . . we're quits now. Nurse my scald, girl, as I've nursed yours.

And exit Auntie Ah.

Scarecrow She was saving that. Poison. Always poison. Since you were knee-high, cups of poison. I can tell you about her if you want.

Woman You remember her.

Scarecrow Of course.

Woman All this time you said nothing.

Scarecrow You never asked me. You never asked enough of me at all.

Woman I'm asking now.

Scarecrow Well, first of all there's no mystery about her. The only heroic thing she did was die young.

Woman Your cruelty has no bounds.

Scarecrow What have I said?

Woman I want to know how she drank her tea and you're rattling on about heroism. Christ, all I'm asking you is to tell me how she lived!

Scarecrow She lived bitterly. I remember her battering the spuds into a venomous pulp for the dinner. I remember her vagueness on the beach, her refusal to play. I remember the weeping in darkened rooms, the obsession with Mass and fawning over the priest, I remember her belief that she was somehow inferior and her living out of that belief with such conviction, such passion, such energy invested in taking second place. All of which you have inherited. And underneath it all I remember this volcanic rage that erupted given any opportunity on the small, the weak, the helpless. Hardship was all she knew. Hardship was all she understood. Hardship was her prayer in the morning and her evening song. A woman of rock, carved out of the rocks around her. Immovable. Devastating to behold from the cradle.

Woman That wasn't her at all.

Scarecrow Why would I lie? I loved her too.

Woman So is that where my coldness comes from?

Scarecrow Your conservatism. Your inability to function either the right or the wrong side of the sheets.

Woman All of that.

Scarecrow You never learnt there are two doors in and out of every house. Always to insist on the correct one, the narrow one, the one that has led you here. I'd like to write that letter now before we run out of time.

Woman I told you there'll be no letter.

Scarecrow You owe it to yourself.

Woman No, leave him be.

Scarecrow Someone has to tell him he can't wreak havoc in people's lives the way he has done with yours, with mine.

Woman You're smothering with revenge.

Scarecrow Yes I am. If I was you I'd have killed him long ago. You still think this man is worth dying for?

Woman I'm not answering that question! Don't keep asking me that question.

Scarecrow Well, I've got news for you. You're not dying for him. You're leaving this earth because I have given up.

Woman You have given up? . . . So if you decided I could live?

Scarecrow But I have decided. Look, I'll see you out. That's more than most of my kind does. I'll see you to the last breath, but only if you write that letter.

Woman And if I don't?

Scarecrow I'll walk away now.

Woman looks at Scarecrow . . . a long time.

Woman Okay . . . I'll write the letter.

Scarecrow And you'll take dictation from me?

Woman Do I have a choice?

Scarecrow gives her pen and paper. Woman starts writing.

Scarecrow What are you doing? (*Takes paper, reads.*) 'My darling, it's late, and there are a few things I want to say.' Well, for starters cut out darling.

Woman What's wrong with darling?

Scarecrow Just cross it out. 'It's late and there are things that must be said.'

Woman So hard. (*Writing.*) . . . First I want to give instructions . . . about my funeral.

Scarecrow You can do that on a separate sheet after.

Woman No, we'll do it first or he mightn't read it after your diatribe.

Scarecrow He'll read it. As long as it's about him he'll read it. The ego of the man is unbelievable.

Woman Will I write that down?

Scarecrow Okay . . . do your funeral first.

Woman (*writing*) The funeral. I'll underline it so he doesn't forget.

Scarecrow You think he might forget to bury you?

Woman (*writing*) I've already spoken to you about the baby's coffin. It will have disintegrated but tell the gravediggers what's left of it is to be placed on top of mine. Eventually he will sink back into me and maybe in time one glorious asphodel will spring from the manure of our bones. Don't forget to do this now. And don't let them carry me through the village in my coffin. I am not a hurler. Just from the hearse which should be opposite the church door. If possible hire four black horses with black plumes, they passed me by on the street, the coachman tipped his hat and Demis Roussos playing as I'm carried up the aisle, 'My Friend the Wind' or 'Ever and Ever You'll Be the One'. Let my sons carry me as once I carried them. Oh, and get someone else to say the Mass, not Father Gant, he has no way with words.

Scarecrow Okay, are you done?

Woman (*writing*) Funeral clothes. (*Underlines it.*) On a hanger on my side of the wardrobe are the clothes I want to wear. My black velvet dress with the V-neckline. My silk slip, my grey tights and my new black high heels, the ones I meant to wear on Christmas Day. They're in a box under the dress.

Scarecrow Do corpses wear shoes?

Woman (*still writing*) Around my shoulders put the green lace cape. Don't join my hands and no rosary beads. It's too smug. Just put them out straight with the palms facing upwards. Leave my hair down and a trace of lipstick. No other make-up. Read these instructions to whoever lays me out. No prayer books, no holy medals, no scapulars. What else? Kissing. I don't want anyone kissing me except the children and yourself if you care to. I have a horror of being kissed when dead. I will taste of iron. My lips will be frozen. It will repel. Better they just have a look and move on. And don't leave me in the church overnight. I never liked churches at night. Driving by in the dark I've always felt some fierce battle is going on in there. I don't want to be in the middle of it. Don't leave me in the church overnight. I'll underline that three times. If you have ever felt anything for me don't leave me there on my own.

Scarecrow Right, the purpose of this letter. New paragraph.

Woman (*writing furiously*) Just a sec.

Scarecrow If you'd put as much thought into your life.

Woman I'm just telling him to get everyone drunk after the funeral. I've always loved funerals, especially the afters, the excitement, the food, the drink, the relief on everyone's faces, even the best behaved can't hide their glee, there's something in us that loves the harmony of seeing someone out. The pure animal delight as if every cell in our bodies is shrieking, it wasn't me, it isn't me yet. (*Writing again.*) Drink up, dance, flirt, tell them to have sex on my grave. Have trays of champagne and mulled wine, pass them across the flowers and the wreaths, fall over me, I'll be listening, I'll be having my own spectral glass beneath.

Scarecrow Are you through?

Woman Yes, I'm through. It's your turn now. Now we're going to get a lecture on the meaning of life. Go on, do your worst, you seething superior sow. (*Begins writing.*)

Scarecrow I haven't said anything yet.

Woman I'm putting a disclaimer before this bit. This is not me but the other one, the filthy old scarecrow who has hounded me down the years. Okay shoot.

Scarecrow On the brink of extinction I have a few things to say.

Woman (*mockingly*) On the brink of extinction . . .

Scarecrow Heading into the dark I want to leave a trail of darkness after me. I want you to wake at three in the morning and think of me packed into the cold hard clay and when you think of me down there I want you to realise that you have killed me as surely as if you had taken an ice pick and plunged it to the hilt.

Woman I got sick, I died, that's all there is to it.

Scarecrow And what about me?

Woman You can't lay all this at his door.

Scarecrow Just write it down. I want to talk about your cowardice. Write it down. I want to talk about your parsimony. I said write it down. I want to talk about what you have withheld from me and from your children. Let's start with your cowardice. Before the second child was born you had gone. Question. Why didn't you stay gone? Why all the returns? Why all the whingeing and whining confessions and promises of change? Why all the ridiculous attempts to appear complicated? I never hated you more than when you returned after another sleazy transgression. Leave out the brazen lies of it, leave out my heart in shreds, even leave out the children for a minute. Leave all of that out and consider for one moment what you have done to yourself. You are without pride, without dignity, without any sense of who you are or where your place is in this world or what you are here for.

Woman And you know what I'm here for? What you're here for?

Scarecrow Don't interrupt me! Write it down! You have reeled through my life wreaking havoc at every turn. Well, I am crying out at last, Enough! You will go no further with me. And I want you to know I am going to my grave with my heart broken, yes, broken, but not for you, my heart broken for myself and my children, that I allowed your puling, whining need ensnare me so.

Woman (*writing, softly*) Yes.

Scarecrow And finally I want to talk to you about what we were and what we have become.

Woman What have the years done to us? Where did we go to when we weren't looking?

Scarecrow It was the first betrayal. The ones after were nothing compared with the first.

Woman The others I've become cynical about as if they happened to someone else. In a way they did. I even tried to play you at your own game for a while, which only took me further from myself. You told me I was the one, the only one, and I believed you.

Scarecrow And thought it would be so for all of time apportioned to us here. And then you denied me. And how? For a very long time I thought I had done something.

Woman And then I thought you had just stopped loving me.

Scarecrow I realise now I was mistaken in my generous estimation of your capacity to love.

Woman For it is clear as day that you are and have always been and I presume will continue to be incapable of loving anyone.

Scarecrow That is anyone except yourself.

Woman And your insatiable ego. And what drives my hatred now is my . . . my . . . my . . .

Scarecrow . . . blindness to what you have . . .

Both . . . slowly taken from me down the years, that is, my capacity to love, which was boundless in the beginning, long ago, when we walked by the river too poor to buy a cup of coffee. Be aware I go to my grave bewildered by your cruelty. I go angry, I go unforgiving and I wonder when the time comes how you will go to yours.

Pause.

Woman Look after the children, my unwanted gifts to you, my consolation prizes to myself.

Pause.

Scarecrow Put it somewhere he'll find it.

Woman does.

Enter Him.

Woman Tell Auntie Ah to leave this house.

Him What has she done now?

Woman She's not to lay me out. I dreamt she did something to my stomach with a sort of revolving cheese knife. I don't want her near me again. Dead or alive.

Him I'll put a bounty on her head.

Woman I'm serious.

Him I won't let her near you.

Woman Has the post come?

Him Yes.

Woman Anything for me? Anything interesting?

Him What are you waiting for? A love letter?

Woman I wouldn't say no to a love letter right now.

Him Your Visa bill came.

Woman My Visa bill has always interested you.

Him Nearly two grand in a shoe shop.

Woman Imagine, a Visa bill ago I was flinging credit cards at shop assistants.

Him Where are all those shoes? Can I bring them back?

Woman No you cannot.

Him So who's going to pay for them?

Woman I enjoyed buying those shoes. That's what you've driven me to. Shoe shops. There was a pair of crocodile-skin boots, mad heels, real don't-mess-with-me boots.

Him On your deathbed and still talking about material possessions, rattling on about shoes.

Woman And what should I be rattling on about? You think I should be calm and resigned and philosophical. You think the dying mull over eternity. They don't. They don't. They think about shoes and how they'll never get a chance to wear them. And when I land in eternity I'll still be praising those boots. I'll describe them to him till he aches to have a human foot the size of mine that he can encase in crocodile-skin boots. If I had another fifty years I'd put them on every day. I'd wear them to bed. You savage! How dare you accost me with Visa bills as I draw my last breath.

Him Well forgive me if I mention a small detail. There are eight of them to be fed and dressed and educated.

Woman That small detail never bothered you until now. And if I know you as well as I do you won't feed or educate them if you can get away with it. I'm leaving orphans! Orphans! You'll begrudge them a bowl of Weetabix. God help them with you at the helm, forever turning off the hot water and the lights and the heat. Tell me what it is you hate about light and heat? What is it about hot water that drives you crazy? I dreamt last night you were locking up potatoes. Yes, I said to myself. That's it. I married a man who locks up potatoes. Christ, get me out of here quick. You'll have my pension, my life insurance. I won't cost you a penny. Here. I'll even pay for my own funeral.

She rips open the envelope left by Auntie Ah and flings wads of money around.

Him Stop! Please stop this . . . I'll pay for your funeral.

Woman You don't deserve to pay for my funeral. Take it. Auntie Ah gave it to me.

Him We don't need Auntie Ah's charity. I'll give it back to her.

Woman Why are you here? What is it you want? I have nothing left to give.

Him Do you want me to go?

Woman Don't you have a date?

Him Of course I don't.

Woman You cancelled. You'll see her at the weekend.

Him This is the weekend.

Woman Are you looking forward to your freedom?

Him Are you looking forward to yours?

Woman I'm going to have a very long sleep. I'm looking forward to that. I haven't slept a night since I met you.

Him Another blot on my copybook.

Woman And you have fantasised about my death.

Him I have not.

Woman I know a little about fantasies of escape. I wasn't born yesterday.

Him I thought to relegate you to the background. That's all . . . my most vicious daydreams assumed you'd be living, healthy and, if not happy, then at least bearing up . . . but living . . . always living . . . you have no right to leave me like this.

He is close to tears. Woman looks at him standing there.

Take your fill of me. I am guilty, yes . . . I have no defence. Whatever you think I have done to you I have done and worse but, Christ, don't leave me like this.

Woman I'm sorry . . . I didn't mean to . . . come and lie beside me . . . come under the covers . . .

He gets into bed beside her. He wraps himself around her.

Him Am I hurting you?

Woman No . . . I've missed you in bed beside me.

Him I've missed you too.

Woman (*kisses him*) Ah . . . old friend . . . old battle-
weary foe.

Him Is that what I am?

He kisses her face, neck, hands, arms.

Scarecrow You never invited me into the bed.

Him Your feet are cold.

Woman Is it snowing?

Him Yes. Would you like to look out the window?

Woman How much snow? Inches?

Him More.

Woman What does it mean if I go with the snow?

Him If you have to go, winter is the time.

Woman What do you mean?

Him You're following the seasons.

Woman I was born in winter too. The symmetry is
appalling. And I remember something else about snow.
A woman gave me a lift once because it was snowing.
We drove and drove through all that whiteness until
finally she pulled in at the courtyard of an old house
with a wooden balcony going round it. And on the
wooden balcony painted scenes in that old red and gold.
We sit looking at these painted scenes, the snow
whirling, the darkening road, the courtyard and then
Christ passes by in a cart. He's a painting and not a
painting, and the woman and I stare, transfixed, as he
glides past, quizzical, peaceful, and his passing is such we
don't want to share it, speak of it, we refuse to look at
one another, refuse to acknowledge what we have just
seen, are seeing in the snow, in the courtyard.

Him Where was this?

Woman I don't think it has happened yet . . . Are you drinking . . . these days? These nights?

Him Like a fish.

Woman The wine will see you through.

Him I'll go off it soon . . . Did you really have lovers?

Woman Yes I did.

Him So sly.

Woman Does it bother you?

Him Yes, it bothers me.

Woman Good.

Him And why did you wait till the end to tell me?

Woman I think because it never occurred to you to ask.

Him So what were the last three decades about?

Woman You and I? They were exile of course. Exile from the best of ourselves . . . beasts in a cave with night coming on . . . no way to live at all.

Him You have some nerve. The one thing I was always sure of . . . thought I was sure of, was you, you here no matter what, you here for me and me only.

Woman For a long time I was.

Him How long?

Woman Too long.

Him I want dates.

Woman Leave out the prose. It's enough to realise we were nothing but a façade for procreation.

Him No, I want to know when you turned. I want to know how many? Who? Do I know them?

Woman I'm not telling you. Grim conquests most of them.

Him Most of them?

Woman There was one I almost . . . He gave me this.

He takes the diamond ring off her finger. Looks at it. Takes wedding ring and engagement ring from his pocket and puts them on her finger.

Him You will wear my rings to your grave.

Woman The rings go to the girls.

Him The rings go where I say they go.

Woman Not this time. (*Takes them off.*)

Him (*takes them from her*) I'll put them on when you're dead.

Woman You do and I'll put a curse on you.

Him You already have. My whole life with you has been one long curse. If I have to solder them to your fingers you'll wear these rings to your tomb. You think to escape me now at the end, to slip away having spewed the devious details all over me. My life was meant to be various. Huge.

Woman And mine?

Him Yours is over. It's over. And I'm meant to pick up after you. The mess you're leaving me with. And to top it all it was just a game, a game of charades for you. All the time deceiving me.

Woman So subterfuge is your domain?

Him Yes. Mine. Women are not allowed that. The whole point of a woman is not so much wanting her, that waxes and wanes, but that no one else can go near her.

Woman There have been a few small advances since that Neanderthal theory first did the rounds.

Him Like hell there have. You know our wedding day was the end of the whole thing.

Woman Yes, most marry at the end. Yes, our wedding day was the last door closing. The click has taken us until now to hear. Well, we were always slow learners. Each child a blind hope, for what?

Him What have they got to do with anything? They're just there. Strangers. I have problems remembering their names.

Woman You seem very proud of the fact. Well, they'll survive you whether you remember their names or not as I survived my parents or lack of, as you survived yours. We don't really figure except as gargoyles to bitch about to their lovers. They'll have the last word on you as you'll have the last word on me. And if you dare make a sentimental speech at my funeral I'll rise from my coffin and rip your tongue out.

Him I'll herd you to your grave like a cow to the byre.

Woman You'll come up with some whingeing panegyric. I know you.

Him You know nothing.

Woman Could you put me in the car and we drive out west? See the Atlantic. I'd like to finish up back west.

Him You can't be moved.

Woman You just want to be near her.

Him And if I do?

Woman I want to drive.west. I need expanse now, the open sea, the wolfish mountains. That's what's been missing. Don't let me die here.

Him I can't. The snow. The doctors said . . . it was a huge achievement to get you home.

Woman You've been talking to her.

Him Yes. Briefly.

Woman And what did you talk about briefly?

Him We talked about you.

Woman How my death is coming on. Will she never go? You said that to her.

Him I said no such thing.

Woman And you were whispering to her on the phone last night. I heard you in the hall.

Him . . . Yes, she rang last night. I asked her not to call the house.

Woman So virtuous. So honest. So truth-loving. What a lucky girl I am.

Him She wanted me to tell you something.

Woman There's nothing she can tell me.

Him She just asked me to tell you.

Woman I don't want to hear it.

Him Just that she's sorry the way she treated you that night you turned up in the rain.

Woman I don't want to discuss it.

Him That's why she rang. She can't sleep over you. She has never behaved like that before.

Woman And you believe her. You have no taste, no judgement. How can you stay with a woman who treats your wife with such contempt? How can you bear to be around someone who looks on her fellow creatures with such unbridled scorn?

Him You've had your scornful moments too.

Woman No I have not. I have raged, howled, wheedled, blundered, but I have not scorned. My abiding feeling for my fellow journeyers has been one of pity, yes, pity, and a gushing unasked-for love. Misguided I know but genuine. And never scorn. Maybe scorn would've kept me alive . . . Why do we always end up talking about her? She's ugly. She's boring. She doesn't even have the redeeming vice of witchery. She's a hag without the warts. If it's a hag you want there are uglier and more dangerous around. Or if it is my jealousy you crave then pick someone worthy of my jealousy. And keep that one away from my children.

Him She has no interest in your children.

Woman And that is meant to console me?

Him It's a fact, my dear, just a fact.

Woman Talk to them about me from time to time, will you?

Him Yes, I will talk to them about you.

Woman Try to keep me alive for them, for lately I have begun to suspect if there is such a thing as eternity it resides in the hearts and minds of those who have loved us, for time, memory, eternity are merely constructs of this fallen world and it is here among the fallen we will be remembered and forgotten.

Scarecrow Then what do you call that thing in the wardrobe?

Woman That thing with the cobalt beak? That thing is the opposite of time.

Scarecrow Then what am I?

Him What is it, my dear?

Woman I'm talking to Scarecrow. What are you? I'll tell you what you are. You are the parasite who has thwarted my every joy. Without you I would've been happy with him. Without you I would've wanted nothing.

Scarecrow If that's how you feel I can go right now.

Woman Then go! Go! Go! I'm sick of your threats.

Scarecrow And leave you with him?

Woman Yes, leave me with him.

Scarecrow There was another way to live.

Woman Yes, there was, and I didn't find it.

Scarecrow You didn't even look.

And exit Scarecrow.

Him Your feet are ice.

Woman (*looking after Scarecrow*) Then it must be nearly over.

Him Will I bring in the children?

Woman They're gone. They're gone. They're mostly gone.

Him It's all right . . . It's all right . . . Is there anything . . .

Woman Scarecrow . . . go after Scarecrow . . . bring her back.

Him Some champagne . . . you said once you'd like to drink champagne at the end.

Woman Did I?

Him I have a bottle in the fridge.

Woman Am I capable of a glass, do you think?

Him Yes, let's have champagne.

Woman And bring the dish-glasses . . . not the fluted.

Him Where would they be?

Woman I don't know . . . they used to be . . . Oh Scarecrow . . . I can't remember my own kitchen.

Him I'll find them . . . Wait now . . . wait easy . . . I'll be back in a sec.

And exit Him. Woman lies there. Hold a minute. Wardrobe door creaks open. Enter Death from the wardrobe, regal, terrifying, one black wing, cobalt beak, clawed feet, taloned fingers. Stands looking at Woman, shakes itself down. Woman stares at him.

Woman (*calls weakly*) Scarecrow . . . I'm begging you . . . he's here . . . I can't do this on my own.

Scarecrow You don't have to, my dear.

Woman Scarecrow . . . is that you . . . But I thought . . .

Scarecrow That I was your slave . . . that you were in charge? Not so. Not so. I've a few forms to fill out, so just bear with me a second.

Plucks a feather from her wing. Takes out parchment, unrolls it.

So you're nearly there? Exciting, isn't it?

Woman You swore you would see me out.

Scarecrow And I will. Now I need ink.

Scarecrow takes Woman's hand, pierces vein in her wrist, a fountain of blood shoots out. Scarecrow dips quill into Woman's wrist. A cry of pain from Woman.

I know, my chicken, I know, it is never easy becoming the past tense. Okay. It says here you had brains to burn?

Woman Then I must have burnt them.

Scarecrow writes, dipping quill in and out of Woman's wrist.

Scarecrow, don't do this to me.

Scarecrow I have no choice. You think I want to do this? It's out of my control. (*Reads.*) Next question. Why did you stop seeking?

Woman That's the big one, isn't it?

Scarecrow No time now except for the big ones.

Waits with quill poised.

You'll answer the question, please. The paperwork must be in order.

Woman Why did I stop seeking? . . . I didn't know what to look for and I was afraid what I would find.

Scarecrow (*writing*) Yeah, that's the usual excuse we get. And love? Why did you not flee when love had flown?

Woman But it hasn't flown.

Scarecrow It says here it has flown.

Woman It hasn't. He's here.

Scarecrow Where?

Woman He's getting me champagne. Anyway, how could I leave my children?

Scarecrow You're leaving them now.

Woman This is a different leaving.

Scarecrow It certainly is. We're not talking a few years here. We're talking never. Never. We're talking the five nevers and the four howls.

Woman So are you saying I could have turned up at the lover's door with the eight of them?

Scarecrow I'm saying exactly that.

Woman With what? How? For starters it would have taken two car journeys. I would've had to arrive twice. And to arrive twice at the lover's door is worse than not arriving at all. Give me some credit for timing. These are stupid questions. Who designed this questionnaire?

Scarecrow You did.

Woman Will all of this be used against me?

Scarecrow It will be used. (*Reads.*) And the children, admit it, they were your shield to beat the world away?

Woman Yes, they were.

Scarecrow (*reads*) You hid behind the nappies and the bottles?

Woman The mountainous bellies and the cut knees, the broken arms, the temperatures, the uniforms, the football, the music, the washing machine, the three square meals, yes I hid behind it all. Yes, I used them. They were my little soldiers. I was the fortress. And how they protected me from terrors imagined and terrors real, my soothers, my buffers to fortune. And I'm sure I've damaged them in some vital, irreparable way, but I have also loved them with a hopeless, enchanted love.

Scarecrow (*dipping quill into Woman's wrist*) This well is dry. I'm sorry, I have to do this.

Pierces Woman's neck. A fountain of blood, a wail from Woman.

Woman Scarecrow, don't . . . please don't.

Scarecrow We can't go back now. (*Reads.*) And if you could take a thought with you, what would it be?

Woman What would it be . . . that I have never felt at home . . . here.

Scarecrow (*writing*) Very few do.

Fade in Rusalka *at some point to end as play ends.*

Woman We don't belong here. There must be another Earth. And yet there was a moment when I thought it might be possible here. A moment so elusive it's hardly worth mentioning . . . an ordinary day with the ordinary sun of a late Indian summer shining on the grass as I sat in the car waiting to collect the children from school. Rusalka on the radio, her song to the moon, Rusalka pouring her heart out to the moon, her love for the prince, make me human, she sings, make me human so I can have him. And something about the alignment of sun and wind and song on this most ordinary of afternoons stays with me, though what it means is beyond me and what I felt is forgotten now, but the bare facts, me, the sun, the shivering grass, Rusalka singing to the moon. And I wonder is this not the prayer each of us whispers when we pause to consider. Make me human. Make me human. And then divine. And I wonder is it for these elusive prayers we are here, these half-sentences that vanish into the ether almost before we can utter them. Living is almost nothing and we brave little mortals investing so much in it.

Scarecrow You're determined to go with romance on your lips.

Woman I know as well as the next that the arc of our time here bends to tragedy. How can it be otherwise when we think where we are going. But we must mark those moments, those passionate moments, however small. I looked up 'passionate' in the dictionary once because I thought I had never known it. And do you know what passion means?

Scarecrow It comes from the Latin, *patior*, to suffer.

Woman Well, I said to myself, if that's the definition of passion then I have known passion. More. I have lived a passionate life. Yes, I have lived passionately unbeknownst to myself. Here it lay on my doorstep and I all the time looking out for it.

> *Scarecrow finishes writing, rolls up parchment. Puts it into a bag of scrolls hanging from her waist.*

Scarecrow That's that out of the way . . . I'm afraid it's time.

Woman But I'm not ready.

Scarecrow It's time to go.

Woman Scarecrow, please . . . my children . . .

Scarecrow I know, I know, but don't fight me . . . you won't win this time.

Woman Just hold on till he comes back.

Scarecrow You want him to watch you die?

Woman Yes . . . He was the closest I came to the thing . . . itself . . . I think I've stopped breathing.

Scarecrow Yes, it's over.

Woman (*throws herself on Scarecrow*) Oh Scarecrow . . . the next breath isn't coming.

Scarecrow And won't ever.

And she dies in Scarecrow's arms.

Hold a minute and fade lights and music.

End.

THE CORDELIA DREAM

The Cordelia Dream was first performed by the Royal Shakespeare Company at Wilton's Music Hall, London, on 11 December 2008. The cast was as follows:

Woman Michelle Gomez
Man David Hargreaves

Director Selina Cartmell
Designer Giles Cadle
Lighting Designer Matthew Richardson
Music Conor Linehan
Sound Fergus O'Hare
Music Director Eloise Prouse
Musicians Ben Davies, Eloise Prouse, Amy Wein

Characters

An Old Man
A Woman

Setting
A space with a piano

Time
The present

Act One

The Old Man sits at the grand piano playing a beautiful melody.
   The buzzer goes.
   He stops playing.
   He sits quietly, hands raised.
   He resumes playing.
   The buzzer goes again.
   He stops again.
   He resumes again.
   The buzzer goes again.
   The Old Man goes to the door.
   Opens it.

Man You.

Woman Yes. Me.

Man Well.

Woman It wasn't easy . . . seeking you out.

Man Wasn't it?

Woman I stayed away as long as I could.

Man You think I'm going to die soon?

Woman Maybe.

Man You want to kiss and make up before that event?

Woman Some people visit each other all the time.

Man I'm not some people. You of all people should
know that.

Woman Can I come in or not?

Man stands back for Woman to enter.

Thank you. This is where you live now?

Man Yes.

Woman No trees. No grass. No birds. No sea.

Man Old men don't need scenery.

Woman What do they need?

Man Just a piano and a stool, a few pens, paper.

Woman Where do you sleep, eat?

Man I manage. Sit down.

Woman Where?

Man Here. (*Piano stool.*) Or there's the floor, the window. Let me take your coat.

Woman (*takes off her coat, hands it to him*) I brought wine, cheese.

Man I've no bottle-opener.

Woman I brought that too.

Man I don't drink now.

Woman You don't drink?

Man Not since my false teeth fell into the toilet. I drink water obviously and one cup of black coffee every morning.

Woman (*looking around*) Coffee. Where do you get that?

Man From women mostly.

Woman Women. Not one woman but women.

Man Does that annoy you?

Woman Yes, it does.

Man You want to be my coffee maker?

Woman One time I was.

Man I get coffee as a reward. Black. Steaming. I gulp it down. Scald on the throat, then a mad dash for the door before I'm asked to fix the washing machine or worse, speak the language of love and loss in the morning.

Woman What's wrong with the language of love and loss in the morning?

Man Love needs a streak of darkness. The day is for solitude. Morning especially. Morning is for death.

Woman And afternoons?

Man At your age they're for transgressions, at mine they're for remorse.

Woman You know about remorse?

Man I'm an expert on it. That's why I don't have an armchair. If I had an armchair I would sink into it and never get out of it again. Remorse is fine in its place. Whatever feeds the flame, as they say. And then there's the night, the arms of women.

Woman I wish you'd stop talking about them in the plural.

Man Women? Women are plural.

Woman And men?

Man We don't exist. We have pianos and stools. We part with semen to procreate. We are remorseful in the afternoon. At night we disappear into women. If we're lucky. That's men for you. Sometimes we read a book or two and have really strong opinions. We make grand statements on art, music, poetry, the state of the country, you name it, we can pronounce on anything. And what never ceases to amaze me is, people believe us – worse, take us seriously. And somehow that's enough, that sustains us for eighty years.

Woman You're not fooled?

Man Will I open that wine for you or are you just going to look at it?

Woman Only if you have a glass.

Man I couldn't. But I could drink water out of a wine glass if that helps.

Woman That would help.

Man I don't know why women are so afraid of drinking alone. When I was drinking I enjoyed others' company, but it was nothing to the marvels of myself I unlocked when drinking alone.

Woman Yeah.

Man You're not going to ask me what marvels?

Woman You're going to tell me anyway.

Man I discovered one thing. My soul –

Woman You're not the first to uncover his soul in his cups.

Man Let me finish. I discovered my soul stands appalled.

Woman Appalled. Why?

Man Appalled that it is attached to me. Trapped in time, stitched to me.

Woman Isn't every soul appalled with its mortal frame?

Man Some souls are smug. They can't believe their luck. Some fall in love with the earth. Imagine that.

Woman I have known moments when I'm in love with the earth.

Man You in love is one thing. Your soul is another. Your soul to be seduced by all of this. It's pathetic. Cars, houses, the rising sun, children romping in the garden come evening. To think it doesn't get better than this.

Woman I have five children now.

Man Yes, I heard you had another one.

Woman You're not curious?

Man About what?

Woman If it's a boy or a girl.

Man I'm not curious.

Woman If it's called after you?

Man That I think is unlikely.

Woman You're right there. It's not called after you. None of them are called after you. None of them ever will be.

Man Well, I'm glad we've sorted that out.

He hands her a glass, sniffs the bottle, pours.

Just as well I don't drink. I couldn't drink this.

Woman But it'll do for me.

Man You bought it. You decided you and I were not worth a good bottle of wine. No, we're worth an almost good bottle of wine. Though this wine is expensive, it's

237

plonk. Let me give you some advice, my dear. Things are never what they seem. Never. Cheers.

Woman You're not going to congratulate me?

Man On what?

Woman On the new baby.

Man Why?

Woman It would be a normal response from someone in your position.

Man Congratulations.

Woman You take no joy in new life?

Man Why should I when mine is coming to a close?

Woman You're not sick, are you?

Man Why should I delight in birth after birth? What have your obsessions with maternity to do with me?

Woman Not even a card.

Man You don't want my cards!

Woman No, I don't.

Man My baby presents. I sent those baby things, those outfits to the others. What were they? Boys? Girls? I've forgotten. I sent or rather my women sent those baby rags. Did you reply?

Woman You really want me to reply?

Man Look, I've left you alone!

Woman Only after you lost. Only after there was nothing else you could do. You haven't left me alone. You've retreated to this sulphurous corner to gather venom for the next assault. You? Leave me alone? You haunt me.

Man I? Haunt you?

Woman I know what you're planning. I know it.

Man What am I planning?

Woman Your death. You're going to die and I'm going to be left with the fallout. I refuse to deal with your ghost. That's why I'm here. I want to sort you out while you're alive. While there's breath in my body.

Man Are you dying?

Woman Can I smoke?

Man Yes. Yes. Smoke. Smoke.

Woman What'll I use as an ashtray?

Man Flick it out the window.

He opens the window. White curtain blows in and out. Woman goes to the window. Stands there smoking. He looks at her.

You're very like her.

Woman Am I?

Man Standing there by the window, always at the window.

Woman I remember long ago when I loved you. A funeral and she was weeping, and I said, 'You look lovely,' and she did. I'd never seen her weep before. It suited her, tears suited her. For once she was open and real. And she caught me by the arm and hissed, growled, whatever that elemental throat sound is. 'Well, I feel far from lovely.' And suddenly you were there, between us, freeing my arm. 'Leave her,' you said, 'leave her alone, she's only trying to comfort you.'

Man Who would've thought I'd have it in me?

Woman To stand up for me?

Man To respond humanely. What did you have?

Woman What?

Man The baby?

Woman Another boy. I almost called him after you.

Man I understand.

Woman No, you don't.

Man Does he have long fingers?

Woman He does.

Man Musician's hands?

Woman Big and capable anyway for such a little fellow.

Man That's good. I hate small hands in a man, a boy, a male child. Women are so unwieldy. Without big hands they're impossible. And is your husband the father of all your children?

Woman What sort of a question is that?

Man Why not move around a little?

Woman There are things like fidelity. Stability. Love, even. I know they don't rate highly in your book but they exist nevertheless.

Man If I was a woman I'd have a different father for each child. Think of the variety, the expanding gene pool, the colour spectrum, from snow-white to blue-black. Really women are terribly conservative when it comes down to it.

Woman And who would feed this colour spectrum? Who would bind them together?

Man The world, of course. Don't tell me you've been seduced by the middle-class jaunt. The stable childhood, the good schools, the extracurricular activities. All death for the child. The only thing children need to learn is passion.

Woman They need to learn a lot of things.

Man No, only passion. Find the child's passion. Feed it. And you have an extraordinary individual. The rest are dodos. You see them up and down the streets of the cities and the kingdoms. The walking dead, and they're not seven. The walking dead nursing Mommy and Daddy's darkness.

Woman What about Mommy and Daddy's light? There's that too.

Man I've not come across it.

Woman You don't want to see it.

Man I'm telling you, just put them in a field. Leave them alone. That's my advice. Feed them, wash them occasionally. The rest will take care of itself. Only leave them alone. Leave them to their enchantments. They'll stumble across them if left alone. I did.

Woman Well, I didn't.

Man I don't know how you can say that in the light of what you have achieved.

Woman I have achieved nothing.

Man I know that. But the world thinks you have. There must be a golden shimmer off you. I could never see it.

Woman No, you couldn't.

Man The gods have favoured you.

Woman Is that what you think?

Man That is what I think and I ask myself why, because really, my dear, you are very mediocre.

Woman Does mediocre need 'very' in front of it?

Man When talking about you, yes, it does. A very mediocre gift I would say.

Woman I do the best with what I've been given.

Man And I don't?

Woman No, you don't. You haven't. It's too late now.

Man You're wrong, you know. Why do you think I've chained myself to this room, this piano? Why do you think I've given up kitchens and dining rooms and wine and champagne and cigars? I want the channels clear for all incoming signals.

Woman And are the signals incoming?

Man They're getting closer.

Woman This will be your great opus?

Man I'm listening. I'm waiting . . . Yes, it will.

Woman Not since Beethoven, they will say. Not since Mozart. Wagner. If you had the gift to match your ego.

Man I do, my dear, I do.

Woman Old men are always writing their magnificent opus. Their farewell to the earth. Their swan song. Most die in the middle of it.

Man At least I'll have attempted it.

Woman And I'm disturbing you. I'm botching the signals?

Man Yes, you are.

Woman I'll go so.

Man Finish your wine.

Woman Play me some of this magnificent swan song.

Man No.

Woman Why?

Man Because you'll steal it.

Woman I? Steal from you? You're too much.

Man You stole my gift!

Woman You had the field for fifty years before I came along. And what did you do in those fifty years? What did you do with that half-century?

Man I was limbering up. I was living.

Woman You were destroying all round you.

Man I was living. If I destroyed, then destruction is part of living. An artist will watch his mother die and wonder how he'll record it.

Woman Yes. Yes. Your poisoned anthem.

Man Isn't that why you're here? To record me. To put me into one of your mediocre compositions?

Woman Maybe. Yes. That's certainly part of it.

Man And the other part?

Woman I should've told you the minute I came in. It seems stupid now.

Man I contradict your idea of me?

Woman You talk too much.

Man Then let me listen a while to your pearls of wisdom.

Woman I came here because I had a dream.

Man You had a dream, so you came.

Woman That's all.

Man So what was the dream?

Woman About my life and my death. About your life and your death. We are horribly meshed. I dreamt of the four howls in *King Lear*.

Man When he carries the dead Cordelia on?

Woman Yes.

Man How is anyone meant to deliver those four howls? I've seen *Lear* more times than I can remember. Not one of them, and they were good, but not one of them could deliver those four howls to my satisfaction. It is four howls, isn't it?

Woman Yes. Four.

Man Not five?

Woman There's five nevers. Four howls. Some argue for three, that they're stolen from Hecuba.

Man The brazen genius of it. The four and the five. The proximity. It shouldn't work. It's wizardry. *Lear* is impossible.

Woman Yes, he is.

Man And his hanging daughter is risible. You think you're Cordelia to my Lear. No, my dear. You're more Regan and Goneril spun.

Woman And you're no Lear.

Man So that's what brought you here? A dream of Lear?

Woman A dream of Lear and Cordelia. Immediately you delete the woman.

Man So the woman is deleted. Can I tell you something about Cordelia?

Woman Please do.

Man Cordelia wanted to be hung.

Woman She did not.

Man Her death was necessary for her father's salvation.

Woman I won't be dying over you.

Man Won't you?

Woman You'll have to find your salvation elsewhere.

Man It was you sought me out. I've left you alone.

Woman You call writing to newspapers leaving me alone? Interviews! Photographs of you! Smiling! Your sordid jealousies spewed over my life, my children, my husband, my home! You call screaming at me in public leaving me alone! Your purple-faced obscenities, your paranoid speeches at my concerts, bullying and shrivelling me to a quaking ghost. You haven't left me alone! I've been hiding! You haven't been able to find me! Given one chance you'll annihilate me again. In the dream Lear comes on with the dead Cordelia and it's you and I. You have a cigar in your hand and a glass of champagne. You're wearing a tuxedo. I lie like a sack of drowned dogs at your feet and do you know what you say?

Man What do I say, Regan?

Woman You say, howl, howl, howl, howl, but it's the way you say it. Brazen. Cynical. Triumphant. And I'm dead. That'll be you at my funeral.

Man Perhaps it will. Perhaps it won't.

Woman All the clichés say hate is merely love twisted. I disagree. There is such a thing as pure hatred. Like you feel for me. It is very difficult to be so hated.

Man And what of your hatred for me?

245

Woman I am not capable of such hate. Such cold annihilation of the opponent.

Man You romanticise yourself.

Woman Do I? Women's hatred, at least mine, goes inward. It's directed at myself. Never underestimate how badly women feel about themselves. And how could we feel otherwise when you look around you? It's not a good time to be a woman right now. It hasn't been a good time to be a woman since the Bronze Age.

Man And that's my fault too?

Woman You take your superiority for granted. You think it is God-given. It isn't. This time will pass and with it all you dinosaurs. How dare you call me mediocre? You who haven't finished anything for years.

Man I am an old man who shouldn't have opened the door to you.

Woman Don't give me that helpless old man spiel. You're a vicious piece of work.

Man I don't want you dead. I just want you to go silent. Leave me the field for a while. I don't have much longer.

Woman You want me alive and silent? What is that but a sentimental form of murder? Why not have the courage to nail the lid on?

Man All I know is, for me to flourish you must be quiet. I would give anything for you to be quiet.

Woman People who know you, when you were part of the music scene –

Man I was never part of any scene, always the outsider. I never needed the herd like you and their ignorant approval. I was always beyond them.

Woman Well, I meet them from time to time, these people you were always above. They're still there, these elderly men valiantly working and finishing things despite their great age, and they always ask for you. Are you well? And are you proud of me? And for years I would smile and say yes, yes, of course he is. But recently I've stopped lying. It is very difficult to tell the truth. And when they ask now, I say, no, he's not proud. He's not one bit proud. And I watch the shock on their faces. It's a great conversation-stopper. I stand there with my cocktail sausage and my glass of Prosecco, I stand there and say, we're in competition. I say, the only thing that would make my father happy right now is to be putting flowers on my grave. At this point they excuse themselves and vanish into the crowd.

Man Because I put your mother into an early grave you think I'll do the same with you?

Woman Isn't that what you're trying to do? Isn't that where all your energies have gone this twenty years?

Man And what about your energies?

Woman All my energies go in staving you off. I have erected a force field around myself so you cannot get through.

Man But I do get through, my dear, don't I? I do get through.

Woman Three in the morning I wake from another nightmare of you, you're beating the door down, you come meaning harm. I get –

Man I am not responsible for your nightmares!

Woman I get up and wander the sleeping house. I check the doors, the children, fearful your black rays will invade their infant souls. The baby stirs. I hold his hand till he settles again. I go to the window, look out at the sea, light a cigarette. (*Whispers.*) My father, my father, I must cut him out of me. I must drain every last drop of his blood from mine. This silence of mine you crave. Well, you have it. I've done nothing for years.

Man You had two dreadful symphonies last spring.

Woman So you listened to them?

Man I listened! The better parts robbed from me! The weaker sections your own little attempt to strike out.

Woman They were made a long time ago.

Man And nothing since?

Woman A song cycle, a few sonatas, nothing to write home about.

Man It'll come back.

Woman I'm afraid it's gone.

Man And its going is connected with me?

Woman Have you listened to a word I said?

Man Now we're talking.

Woman This is not blame. This is beyond blame. This is tectonic plates, this is living, dying. This is cartilage, marrow, blood stuff.

Man Difficult to believe my blood runs through you. Difficult. And more difficult to accept this savage I see before me I had some part in making.

Woman You think I like looking in the mirror and seeing your tracks there?

Man If I could I would remove them. What star decreed we should be related?

Woman A malignant star from some awful furnace. One of us has to capitulate.

Man To go back to your Cordelia dream. When Cordelia dies, Lear does too.

Woman Meaning?

Man We won't survive each other.

Woman Don't say that.

Man But isn't it so?

Woman I know I'm more Regan and Goneril than Cordelia, but in the dream world, in the dream world we are shown our untrammelled selves before living mucks it all up. And you, though I would never equate you with Lear, for I have always loved Lear, I have to accept that somewhere buried inside you, deeply it must be, irretrievably buried, lies Lear, that arrogant foolish wise old man.

Man Your point?

Woman My point . . . I don't know what my point is. What the point of this black pilgrimage to your door is, except to tell you I had a dream about Lear and Cordelia. Just a dream, not even a recurring one, just one fleeting image of you and I and what we have come to. I wanted to tell you that. I probably shouldn't have bothered. And now I'll go.

Man But what is it you want?

Woman I want us both to live and flourish.

Man You want your gift back!

Woman Yes! Give it back!

Man You want me to come for Sunday lunch! You want me bridled! In awe of you? You want me to be proud of

249

your petty achievements? You want me to marvel at my grandchildren? Grandchildren I have never seen!

Woman And whose fault is that?

Man Haven't you learnt anything? I am not the paternal kind.

Woman And why do you sound so proud, so wilfully proud that you are not the paternal kind?

Man I'm not. It's just a fact. The jaunt bores me. It bored me beyond belief with my own children. I'm not about to get into it again.

Woman There is no room for anyone in your world except you. And I don't think I could bear you at my table. No, I'm not talking about Sunday lunch or any of those common civilities that you despise. I'm talking about something different, older, something ancient, something civilisation is founded on.

Man And what is that, pray?

Woman The blood bond of parent and child.

Man You stopped being my daughter a long time ago.

Woman Yes, I stopped when I felt your claws around my throat, strangling all fledgling aspirations. Yes, I removed myself for protection, protection of this gift you spit on. I watched you. I gave you chances – too many! – to redeem yourself. I let you hold my firstborn. But I watched and I saw you wanted me to be a failure like you.

Man I am a great artist.

Woman I'm glad you think so, for no one else does.

Man I am a genius. A genius! And you are a charlatan! A charlatan who stole my gift when I wasn't looking. You are a charlatan who has plagiarised from everyone.

Woman That's what art is. Plagiarism and cunning disguise, a snapping up of unconsidered trifles. And coursing through it all, good faith, begging from above and underneath the throb of creation, that you are the first to do this, the last to do this, that you will surely die if you don't put something down. Right now! This minute! You think it's loose living, bad behaviour and the jottings of your hungover soul. It isn't. Artists are the most disciplined people on the planet. And I hope some day to call myself one.

Man That won't happen.

Woman No, not with you on my back it won't. Your pretensions are appalling. Your treatment of me is appalling. Of my mother, my siblings. Who gave you the licence to treat everyone so badly?

Man I am jealous of you.

Woman Jealous? Of me?

Man Yes. Jealous. It's hard not to be. You have a quarter of my gift, if even, but the gods have favoured you. They've put you on a list, some list I am excluded from. I walk down the street and they say your daughter this and your daughter that and how great it must be to have such a daughter and I say, yes, yes, it's great, great altogether, I pretend we are friends. Pretend I love you. Don't ask me why. It's not easy watch your own outstrip you. You wait, the clock moves, you wait till one of yours leaves you in the ha'penny place. And let me tell you something, I hope you never have the misfortune to have a child the likes of you.

Woman I think the only thing would make you happy is me removed from the Earth.

Man Yes. Yes. Remove yourself. Go. Do it now. Do it here if you wish. You vicious ingrate! When you were a newborn your mother and I couldn't bear to have you in the room. All the others slept in the cot beside us. You, we put away. Screaming the house down till we thought we'd go mad. We put you downstairs and let you scream. You'd scream for hours and one night I went down and stared at this screaming thing, blue with an untraceable rage, sweating and stinking. I tried to calm you. Nothing doing. I remember thinking I can do one of two things. I can pick her up or I can kill her.

Woman Hard to imagine you picking up a child.

Man Is it? Yes, I picked you up and walked you till you calmed and fell asleep. And that's as close as it gets to love, my dear. One night I refrained from smothering you in your blanket because you were small and pathetic. You're a bad egg. Well, there's one in every dozen.

Woman Yes, I'm a bad egg, but I was hatched in a dark place too.

Man You bet you were. All these unlovable children from that loveless bed. You're a horror, a nightmare. The old laws had it right. Foster them out. Let them like strangers be for strangers they are. Please go away. I have work to do.

Woman We can't part like this.

Man Oh yes, we can! You have come into my lair and savaged me again. You have come sauntering in with Lear on your lips and the pretence of reconciliation, when really you have come like the cuckoo to foul my nest, to clock and make sure I have not risen above the place you have allotted me. Well, you can see I have not, though I am trying.

Woman I wish you great success in your work. I know you don't believe that. But I do. I wish for them all to throw flowers at your feet. Maybe then you'll be happy. Maybe then you'll leave me alone.

Man No. I don't believe that.

Woman Well, believe it for this reason if no other. Every child wants a parent of note. I am no different. You flourishing would strengthen me. You articulating beautifully would give me great happiness.

Man Go! Go! Go! Before I hit you.

Woman You dare and I'll knock you to the ground.

Man Will you come to my funeral?

Woman Will you come to mine?

Man I'll be there.

Woman With your speech prepared.

Man With my speech prepared.

Woman So be it.

> *And exit Woman.*
> *Old Man stands there looking after her.*
> *Goes to window. Leans out.*
> *Hold.*
> *Music.*
> *Lights down.*

Act Two

Five years later.

The same room.

The Old Man reclines on divan, a cigar in his hand, ash wafting to the floor. A glass of champagne in the other hand. He conducts imaginary music. We hear it. Piano and strings. He allows music to wash over him. He is sublimely happy.

Enter Woman.

Woman The door was open.

Man Oh . . . hello, my dear.

Woman Do we kiss or what?

Man I'm always partial to kisses from women.

Woman kisses him.

Man Are you a nurse?

Woman You don't know me?

Man (*looks at her*) Give me time. Give me time . . . You're not my mother?

Woman No.

Man And you're certainly not a lover because all the women have disappeared, even Mozart's.

Woman Mozart's?

Man Did you know when Mozart died his widow sold his manuscripts? What was her name again?

Woman Constanza, wasn't it?

Man Constanza. That's the correct name for a
composer's wife. But poor Constanza found it difficult to
figure out how much her husband's manuscripts were
actually worth. Then she had a brainwave. I'll sell them
for the cost of the ink, she said. Don't you just love it?
That's women for you. The cost of the ink. You're not
the dog-hearted one are you?

Woman Who is the dog-hearted one?

Man The dog-hearted one that lives under the piano.
You're not the vicious ingrate, are you? The vicious
snake-eyed ingrate?

Woman I think maybe I am.

Man Then I'll get some twine and stitch your lips. I'll
crucify your feet with wooden pegs. Oh my mother, my
mother. Forgive me, my dear, all the long day I've been
fighting off my mother.

Woman Have you?

Man She flies around the room on her broomstick,
her grey hair spinning. She tries to haul me onto the
broomstick and I spatter her to the wall. She's asleep
now. Even witches have to sleep. Did you know that?

Woman I never thought about it.

Man Oh, they sleep in spite of themselves. They curl up
on people's chests and sleep their malign suffocating
snoozes. It's hard to breathe. Light my cigar, my dear.

Woman (*lighting it*) Don't you have an ashtray?

Man Champagne. Champagne. My glass is empty. She
must have drunk it when I wasn't looking.

Woman (*pours for him*) Who brought you this?

Man One of my minions. He wants to be a great artist.
Like me. He wants all my secrets. I say, bring champagne

and you shall have them. All my tricks, all my wizardry. He plays for me. Badly. I think he's a bit gone. I tell him, you have to be born with it. Born with it, do you see? You have to be disturbed, eternally dissatisfied, always watching, listening, waiting. I tried to explain this to him. He doesn't understand. He wasn't born with it. He believes in happiness. I say to him, good. It's a fine thing to believe in happiness, but you mustn't let it rule your life. We mustn't slide into happiness. The dog-hearted one also believes in happiness. She believes it is her God-given due. She believes I should adore her. And I do. Oh, how I love the dog-hearted one who has fouled my life.

Woman I heard your concerto for piano and strings.

Man And what did you think?

Woman A good first draft. A bit busy for me. It lacked beauty. You weren't in it.

Man Was I not?

Woman Why do you never finish anything?

Man A great artist never finishes a work, he merely abandons it.

Woman That's not true. Artists finish things. They finish things. Unless they die and maybe then they finish them properly in eternal time.

Man What would you know about eternity?

Woman You called it 'The Cordelia Dream'?

Man Yes. Why did I call it that?

Woman Yes, why did you?

Man I don't know where it came from. A snatch of something someone threw my way a long time ago. I wrote it when I was a young man before I knew anything.

Woman I was very proud to hear your name announced. Proud and moved.

Man Yes, it's nice to have one's name announced every now and then. As a child I loved gold stars, couldn't get enough of them from my teacher, used to buy packets of them in the shop and give myself gold star after gold star. Paste them on my legs. And what do you do if you're not a nurse?

Woman I don't do anything.

Man Then you're nothing.

Woman That's right. I'm nothing.

Man Do you even have children?

Woman Oh yes, there are children.

Man Well, that's something, isn't it? I had the most beautiful children once, sons, daughters romping in the garden. I forget how many, blond-haired, dark-haired, blue-eyed, brown, and some in between. The girls had long hair and giggled every time they saw me. Yes, I had beautiful children and then they were gone. What's the point of that?

Woman They don't come to see you?

Man They died. It was in the papers. They died eating cream buns, choked or something. Somebody said I did it.

Woman Well, one of them is here now.

Man Where? Oh, you mean the dog-hearted one, the vicious ingrate. Yes, she lives in the piano. Between her and the witch on the broomstick I have no peace. I even bought a gun and shot them. Still they whisper together in the dark. If you listen you'll hear them. Give me my hat.

She finds his hat, a woman's straw bonnet with flowers. He puts it on.

This hat frightens them. See. They're quiet now. They look at this hat with their mouths open. (*Opens his mouth.*) This was my wife's hat.

Woman I recognise it.

Man Throwing black shoes is no good. You need this hat and wooden pegs to crucify their feet. I have asked for wooden pegs. Repeatedly!

Woman I'm finding it difficult to get through.

Man To get through what?

Woman Oh . . . everything.

Man But that's the world, my dear. It is not easy for anyone. Anyone. Here, have a puff of my cigar.

She has a puff.

Can I offer you some champagne?

Woman Is there another glass?

Man Have mine. Have mine. Don't upset me. I can't be upset. What's the matter? No tears. I can't bear women's tears.

He takes out a handkerchief, dries her eyes.

No tears. Now, what is wrong?

Woman You'll go to your grave thinking I'm dog-hearted.

Man Are you?

Woman I never thought so, but you seem so certain.

Man No, I'm talking about one I brought forth. I'm not talking about you. You dog-hearted? You're a kind woman. I can tell. Look at me.

They lock eyes. Hold.

(*Whispers.*) Oh my God. It's you. It's you.

Woman Yes. It's me.

Man The dog-hearted ingrate.

Woman I'm not.

Man Disguised as a woman.

He leaps up, runs behind the piano.

No. No. No. Keep away from me. Keep away. I thought I killed you.

He waves his hat.

My hat. My hat. Doesn't my hat frighten you?

Woman No, it doesn't.

Man (*runs to the window, shouts out*) Help! Help! Help! She's here. She came! She's here! Someone please help me. She's here with her army.

Woman Stop. Stop. Stop this.

Man (*terrified*) Now look what you've done. I've wet my trousers and my mother will go mad.

He looks up at the ceiling.

Now look what you made me do. Someone come and save me from this dog-hearted, snake-eyed, vicious ingrate.

Woman I just came to see you . . . I miss you.

Man Miss me. Well, miss me and be gone. Croak not, dark angel, I have no food for thee. The Prince of Darkness is a daughter.

He makes the sign of the cross with his arms to ward her off.

Woman Please, please, just listen for a minute. Give me one minute and then I'll go. I have left you alone for five years because you asked me to. I have stopped working because you asked me to. I have given you back your gift you said I stole. I have given you the field. Why have you not flourished?

Man Flourished?

Woman Yes, why have you not flourished? Why not one composition after another, one more beautiful than the next?

Man So I made something beautiful after all?

Woman No, you did not. Nothing beautiful. Nothing worth talking about.

Man Beauty takes time . . . it takes aeons and still there is no guarantee it will not all collapse down around your ears . . . My trousers are wet.

Woman Where do you keep your clothes?

Man My what?

Woman Your clothes?

Man My pyjamas are in the piano. Don't touch them! Don't you dare touch anything of mine.

He goes to the piano, opens it, takes out a pair of trousers, a pair of pyjamas, a toothbrush.

Keep off! Keep off, witch crab! Keep off.

He puts on pyjamas over his trousers, takes off his shirt, puts on the top of his pyjamas, brushes his teeth with toothbrush.

Woman Is it night?

Man When I put on my pyjamas it's night. Now where's the champagne? Devils should always be wrestled with

champagne. The dog-hearted one doesn't like me
drinking champagne. The dog-hearted one doesn't like
me to enjoy myself. She would rather die than watch me
swoon with pleasure. Well, look. (*Downs the glass.*)
Now. What do you think of that? Where's my hat?

Woman On your head.

Man You are terrorising an old man. Who will forgive
you for that? Who?

Woman I have no wish to terrorise you.

Man My wife and I had a goat-faced child. Goat-faced,
dog-hearted with the soul of a snake. We buried her
under the blue swing in the field of beech trees. But out
she came, ate the coffin, clay in her eyes, and we took
her in. My wife said, we'll pay for this. I said no, I had
such faith in the heart of God. This is what she sounded
like.

He plays a few notes on the piano.

And we loved this goat-faced, dog-hearted one as if she
was our own. I even taught her the violin.

Woman Yes, you did.

Man I said, name your instrument as I said to all my
children. Them all, she said for the dog-hearted one is
insatiable. Them all. But being mediocre she settled for
the violin, screeching 'Air on a G String' till we thought
we'd go mad. My mother warned me about women like
these. They come in on the night tide and bite the legs off
lambs and suckle infant monsters, these mermadonnas
with their thousand breasts and their slithering eel-like
tails. Jewelled serpents with the appetites of wild dogs.
And I promised Mother I would avoid such creatures
and I did till I gave birth to you. They will carry you
away, she said, away to their nightmare palaces of obsidian

and painted coral, they will carry you away, and I fear you will.

Woman It seems I have already. Sit. Sit for a minute.

Man No, one can only kneel or stand in front of the dog-people. If I knelt would you forgive me my transgressions, though I don't know what they are?

Woman You know. Now sit. The dog-hearted one is asking you to sit.

Man Commanding me.

Woman OK, commanding you. Sit. Please . . .

Man If I sit will I be allowed up ever again?

Woman Of course.

Man Very well, I'll sit. See, I'm not trembling. This sweat is old age, not fear.

Woman Don't be afraid.

Man No, listen, what women don't understand is . . .

Woman What is it women don't understand?

Man What women don't know is all a man gets from the moment he's born is rejection.

Woman No, women don't understand that.

Man It's true. Forget the fat cats. Forget the unfeeling achievers. They're not men. I'm talking about the men who love music, who dream, who weep, they are lower than women.

Woman That low?

Man There is no place for them in this world. Anyone who would tolerate them is sick.

Woman I heard you had a great eightieth birthday party.

Man Did I?

Woman In Jimmy's house.

Man Jimmy?

Woman You gave a concert.

Man No, that was Schubert.

Woman It was you.

Man Me? No, no, no. I've finished nothing in twenty-five years. The dog-hearted one silenced me.

Woman No, you played, beautifully.

Man Did I? What did I play?

Woman You played me.

Man And who are you again?

Woman You couldn't be stopped. You had it all by heart. You knew all my scores.

Man One must always have the enemy by heart. You were there?

Woman No.

Man Why not?

Woman I wasn't invited. You couldn't be upset so I wasn't invited.

Man That's a pity. You're a good-looking woman. That's what concerts are for . . . good-looking women.

Woman And there was a party afterwards.

Man Was there? Why wasn't I asked? I love parties.

Woman The party was for you.

Man Really? You're being presumptuous.

Woman Jimmy comes to see you every day. He wants you to live with him.

Man No, my sons were drowned on a white ship, oh, a thousand years ago. All of them. And my daughters . . . To neglect an old man like this is inexcusable.

Woman They all still want you.

Man I know you do.

Woman No, I don't want you any more. I have no use for you now.

Man Because I'm old and weak?

Woman Because it's too late. The party, you enjoyed the party.

Man Well that's good. I enjoyed myself even if I don't remember. You were there watching me from outside the window. In the dark. I could feel you there.

Woman Seems I am always there.

Man You're mocking me. I haven't left this room since the dog-hearted one gave her express instructions for me not to move. Move left or right, buster, and I'll flay you alive like Marsyas was flayed by . . . by . . . what god was it flayed Marsyas? The one with the lyre and the garland in his hair. That's the one. You budge, mister, and that's what'll happen to you. I came up from the mountains of the south, at seventeen, to this city. My gift was prodigious. A genius, they said. I'd been schooled by an old fiddler back in the hills. He'd come into the kitchen every night and we'd play for hours. I learnt more from him than the so-called elite of this capital. Alcoholics. Mediocrities. All. They never heard dangerous music on the wind the way this old fiddler heard and caught it in his hand like he was cupping

butterflies and gave it to me as if it were nothing.
Scattering gold everywhere he went. I at least had the wit
to stoop and collect. Is my hat there? (*Feels his head.*) I
know you. You pretend you don't fear it, but you do.
You want me to take it off. Then you'll get me. Why
aren't you snarling and baying for my blood?

Woman I'm taking a rest.

Man Oh, the dog-hearted one is tired. Do you want a
bone? I have bones in the piano, elephant bones. Would
you like a tusk to slobber on or is it me you're waiting
for?

Woman It's you I'm waiting for.

Man How do the dog-hearted get through the day when
they're not ransacking graves?

Woman With great difficulty.

Man Oh, they have their moments, have they? Their
moments of remorse in armchairs?

Woman They certainly do.

Man And what have they to be remorseful for? I swear
I've never seen a regretful wolf unless it's to regret there
wasn't more in the carcass to devour.

Woman I regret my cruelty.

Man An apology?

Woman I regret my cruelty, but you were heartless too.

Man Never. Never. Never.

Woman You are wrong about me.

Man I am never wrong. That's what living intensely
means. To be never wrong.

Woman I had to do what I did to protect myself.

Man Cordelia is blue when Lear carries her on. Blue from the neck up. Her tongue is four times its normal size. Her eyes bulge. I remembered all this when I wrote my Cordelia suite. Not a pretty sight. I said to myself, the colour of Cordelia is blue.

Woman And what colour is Lear?

Man Oh, Lear is the rainbow. He must go through all the colours till he is bleached to wizard. You know Lear's abiding feeling when he carries on the dead Cordelia?

Woman No, I don't.

Man Relief. Finally it's over. Lear is an old cynic. You can't teach Lear anything. Nothing moves Lear except Lear.

Woman That's nonsense. Lear changes and grows till the last second. Something you refused to do. Something I no longer have the courage for.

Man No, you just don't have it, do you?

Woman And you do?

Man You still dispute this?

Woman I don't dispute you were given something. What I dispute is what you have done with it.

Man Every time I turn on the radio they're playing you. You know why?

Woman Because I'm good?

Man Because you're easy, because you have a facility for jingles I could write in my sleep and often do and toss in the bin first thing in the morning. I have more pride. I am

a great composer, yes, I am complex, erudite, difficult.
I set trends. I am the winged horse to your braying mule.

Woman Your self-delusion is complete.

Man You have hounded me down the days of my life,
down this one and down others I cannot clearly recall.

Woman Yes, it's bigger, isn't it? This battle between us?
Ancient. Eternal.

Man You want my adoration?

Woman Once I did.

Man Men should not have daughters.

Woman When I meet my siblings we do not speak about
you. Or rather I do not speak about you. That's the
unspoken agreement, the condition of their company.
I am only permitted to listen. I am permitted to hear
first-hand, second-hand, third-hand how I have
destroyed you. They quote your blubbering tirades. I
don't always play by the rules. Sometimes I erupt, once I
even dared to say the destruction is both ways. A
shocking concept, you for once not genius martyr with a
monstrous offspring but ordinary, flawed man. And
another time I hissed what has destroyed you is that I do
what you do only better. Marginally. I'm not proud any
more but I think it is fair to say I do it better. Of course
that cannot be acknowledged, not to mind spoken of.
They lie across your altar like dead flowers, my siblings,
you have cut them down. My playmates of long ago.

Man And have I cut you down? The tallest flower in the
field?

Woman What do you think?

Man I think it is hard to believe you have siblings. I
dread the thought of seeing them.

Woman You see them every other day. They're the ones bring you champagne and stack your ironed clothes in the piano.

Man And do they look like you?

Woman I'd say they look kinder, more dutiful.

Man Who cares about dutiful?

Woman You do, obviously.

Man They want me to die in an orderly fashion.

Woman Well, the country is full of orderly deaths.

Man The old man from back in the hills. The fiddler. My first and best teacher. Did you ever meet him?

Woman No.

Man No, of course he wouldn't have any time for you. He'd have banished you with some fairy tune he heard on the cliff. I went to his funeral. To his wake. He lay like a little hen. They'd decorated him with leaves and twigs. He looked like a new-hatched wren, lashless eyes staring out from this nest. His children were all mad. On the wall over this nest his fiddle hung, and when I entered the room to pay my respects the fiddle exploded. I have wondered since was that a good or a bad omen?

Woman An omen, to be sure.

Man I gathered up the pieces and I asked his demented children could I have them, the remains of his fiddle, could I buy it? No. It was going into the grave with him. Was that an orderly death?

Woman I would say that's the death of an artist. They die differently. Reminds me of Shelley. You know how they identified the drowned Shelley? He'd been in the water a couple of weeks.

Man They identified the drowned Shelley by a volume of Keats' poems which was found in his breast pocket, with the spine bent back. He must have been reading Keats when the squall came up. I think I've had this conversation before.

Woman Yes, you have.

Man With you?

Woman It was the first beautiful thing you ever told me.

Man And the second?

Woman You told me what a phoenix was.

Man The third?

Woman There was no third. You saw my hunger so you locked those beautiful morsels away from me. You locked your library away. You locked your piano.

Man I locked the piano for sure.

Woman From my mother.

Man Absolutely.

Woman She was good.

Man She wasn't bad.

Woman As good as you.

Man Don't be ridiculous. Far too heavy-handed. Her fingers were too short. Her ear was scattered. Too many things whirling in her to hear or be heard.

Woman Still, to lock the piano.

Man Couldn't she buy her own?

Woman She loved you.

Man I know. I took advantage. There can only be one winner in that situation. I was determined it would be me . . . and yet . . .

Woman And yet?

Man She took me too seriously. Look. I try very hard not to see people, see women as meat on legs. I try very hard.

Woman And do you see yourself that way?

Man What way?

Woman Meat on legs?

Man How dare you! How dare you! I was flung to earth with my gift perfected.

Woman And how were the rest of us flung?

Man My gift perfected! Not many are. Most come with half a gift, or a longing for the gift, or a smidgeen of a longing. I came with the gold. All I had to do was scatter it.

Woman Then why didn't you?

Man Did I not?

Woman You locked it up with the piano for fear anyone would get their hands on it.

Man Was that what I did? Then that was a mistake.

Woman Yes, it was.

Man Is that why you're here? To tell me my mistakes?

Woman I'm here because you are my father and you're going to die soon.

Man You want a clear conscience?

Woman Too late for that.

Man Decades too late, I would think. Have I succeeded in putting a curse on you?

Woman You have succeeded.

Man I've stopped you working.

Woman You have.

Man I've managed to do that?

Woman For ever.

Man For ever. That's an achievement.

Woman It makes you happy?

Man No, it doesn't make me happy.

Woman I don't believe you.

Man I am always humble in victory. I will try not to appear ecstatic.

Woman You have silenced me.

Man I have found the dog-hearted one's Achilles heel. I can take off my hat now.

Woman Yes, you can.

He takes off his hat.

Man Do you mind if I celebrate with a new cigar and a glass of the good champagne? This (*glass*) is everyday stuff.

Woman Celebrate away.

Man goes to piano, takes out a dusty bottle of champagne. Blows on it.

Man I've been saving this up for an occasion.

Woman And this is it?

Man This is it, baby. This is it. Your silence, my garrulity. I have the field again, my gift soaring, you a fledgling in the ditch. Will you join me?

Woman Drink to my own demise? Why not?

Man opens champagne.

Man There are two glasses in that box. Could you get them for me, please?

Woman does so, dusts them off, holds them out for champagne.

I thought you looked a little woebegone when you came in. I never dreamt of this. Are you sure I can dispense with the hat?

Woman Make up your own mind.

Man I have on a wooden cross under my pyjamas, so don't get any ideas.

Woman I have no ideas, no designs.

Man Good . . . good. (*Raises glass.*) To . . . to . . .

Woman To my death.

Man Yes.

They drink.

I'm curious. When did this silencing occur?

Woman Oh, it was gradual. It stole upon me so quietly, so softly, till one morning I woke and I knew the magic was gone, gone as quietly as it had come.

Man Yes, that's the way magic goes and comes, comes and goes. I'm glad you escaped with your life. I'm glad you're alive. You are my daughter, after all.

Woman Oh, but I'm not alive.

Man What are you saying?

Woman I thought you knew. I'm dead.

Man What?

Woman Didn't the siblings tell you? I imagine you were at my funeral.

Man I was at a gathering recently. Was that your funeral?

Woman It may have been.

Man There was lots of wine after and familiar faces and people kept shaking my hand. I thought I was at a concert. I think I may have made a speech. I'm sorry, I didn't realise it was you.

Woman That's all right.

Man Why do I suddenly feel afraid?

Woman Are you afraid?

Man (*puts on his hat*) Just a precaution.

Woman Don't you want to know how I died?

Man You hung yourself.

Woman How do you know that?

Man I'm guessing.

Woman An accurate guess.

Man Cordelia hung herself.

Woman Cordelia was hung.

Man Same thing. It was what I always wished for you.

Woman Death by hanging?

Man Just a fantasy. Not in my wildest dreams did I ever imagine.

Woman Is it hung or hanged?

Man I think the correct usage is hanged. You say I hung a picture. I hanged a daughter. Personally I prefer hung.

Woman So do I . . . And how will you die?

Man I will die bravely, smug as a bridegroom.

Woman Lear again.

Man But all those children? To leave them like that.

Woman To leave them like that. If the truth be told, we leave long before we depart. For a long time now I have been the ghost in that innocent group.

Man Well . . . my dear . . . well . . . always knew that savage note in you. Was there like a rope burn in all your music. The dominant note, I think it is reasonable to say now you've proved it.

Woman The rope note. No, I can't argue with that verdict now. You want to see the weals on my neck?

Man (*touches rope marks on her neck*) You always went too far, always had to go further than the next even if it meant taking yourself out. Your face is blue.

Woman Is it?

Man I was wondering why. You're too much, my dear. You're too much.

Woman Nine days ago.

Man Nine days ago? Let me check my diary. Nine days ago was when?

Woman The seventeenth.

Man The seventeenth . . . let me see . . . there's no mention of you dying here.

Woman No?

Man No. The seventeenth. Are you sure?

Woman Yes.

Man Why are you so sure?

Woman I chose that day. I like that number.

Man Well there's nothing. All I have for the seventeenth is . . . (*Reads.*) 'A cold bright winter's morning. I've spent the last hour looking out the window and thinking about act three of *Lear*. What a sublime act, act three is. When I was a boy the master used to stand me on the chair to declaim, yes, declaim *Lear*. My clothes were always wrong, my feet were bare but up I would climb onto the table and declaim *Lear*. "Oh fool, I will go mad, let me not go mad." Or the great four howls at the end of act five or the five nevers. Those lines were written for me. I would howl and never with a passion I could not have possessed but somehow seemed to possess me, howling and nevering for what was, for what had never been and for what has yet to be . . .' That's all that's there for the seventeenth.

Woman Do you have an entry for the eighteenth?

Man Yes, I do.

Woman Read it.

Man Just a couple of lines.

Woman Read it for me . . . please.

Man (*reads*) 'It's late. I've just opened the champagne and lit a cigar. Spent the whole day sketching out "Lear's Lullaby". Had a bit of a breakthrough towards dusk. What can Lear sing about after Cordelia?' (*Pause.*) 'He can only follow her. Something momentous is about to happen.'

Woman And has it?

Man Of course not. If you write something like that down it usually vanishes in the fog of wine and dawn. The gods hate pride and reserve their severest punishments for the proud.

Woman My passing doesn't merit an entry in your diary.

Man It seems not.

Woman Maybe they didn't tell you.

Man Did you enjoy your death?

Woman It was so-so. A bit quick.

Man That's all?

Woman No, that's not all. The youngest found me.

Man Found you?

Woman Yeah. Escaped from the housekeeper. They were meant to be on the beach. Rain . . . then home, I suppose. And he runs into my studio. I thought I'd locked the door, but there he was with his bucket and spade. Last image from this blue, blue globe, a child, my child, a bucket, a spade poised, small sand-covered toes.

Man Oh my dear. My dear. What can one say?

Woman I know. Forty-five thousand years will not wash that one clean.

Man And is it very different there?

Woman I'm still getting accustomed. It's strange, the colours, the light is different. The symmetry is dizzying. There's no champagne, though the air sometimes feels like a light golden wine, and the evenings are endless, and swarming, teeming, you can hardly move with the stream. But I'm heading up country soon, where they say it's quieter.

Man And do you miss the Earth?

Woman I miss it. I know how to live now.

Man I'd like you to leave.

Woman I'm here to give you a gift.

Man A gift?

Woman Yes. A parting gift. Sit at the piano. Please.

She takes his hand, leads him to the piano.

Man You won't harm me?

Woman Why would I harm you?

Man Because I have harmed you.

Woman If only you had admitted that when I was here.

Man It was too soon.

Woman And now?

Man Yes, too late.

Woman Come, sit and play for me.

Man Am I dying?

Woman Yes, you are.

Man You're going to take me out?

Woman It was you who said once that we won't survive each other.

Man That was just talk for dramatic effect.

Woman And this is real?

Man With you gone the space is immense. I feel I could do anything now.

Woman Come and play for me. I want to give you a few notes.

277

Man I don't want your notes. I have never needed your notes.

Woman You'd like to die at the piano, wouldn't you? Mid-composition?

Man I don't want to die at all.

Woman Suit yourself. But let me tell you something before I begin the long gallop ahead. I was the most beautiful thing in your life. I was. And you didn't know it.

Man I did and I didn't.

Woman No, you didn't know it. You wanted the most beautiful thing to be you. Even still you fight me, I who have come from beyond the grave to tell you otherwise. I am dust now and before this hour is over you will be dust too. Dust. The winds here won't even bother to blow us away.

Man That is your parting gift?

Woman I was hauled before them, and you know what they told me? That the way I have lived is unforgivable, and I reckon they will tell you the same. Be afraid, they are savage here. The indisputable savagery of the wise and the true.

She lays her hands on his hands.

This is my gift. Close your eyes and play. This is what eternity sounds like.

Man plays a beautiful, haunting sonata.
  Lights fade.

End.

MARBLE

Marble was first performed at the Abbey Theatre,
Dublin, on 10 February 2009. The cast was as follows:

Art Stuart McQuarrie
Ben Peter Hanly
Catherine Aisling O'Sullivan
Anne Derbhle Crotty

Director Jeremy Herrin
Designer Robert Innes Hopkins
Lighting Designer Paul Keogan
Sound Designer Fergus O'Hare
Composer Conor Linehan

Characters

Art
Ben
Catherine
Anne

Setting

One space. One couch. One table. Two chairs.
One drinks cabinet. One lamp.
All use this space as if it is their own.

A backdrop that can be flooded with light
and indigo sky for the marble passages.
There should be an emptiness to the set
which can take on great beauty at times.
De Chirico's painting *Melancholy and Mystery
of a Street* is the mood and landscape I would like
to catch: the near absence of people, the dream
shadows, yet full of vibrant colour and intrigue.

Music

To underscore the marble passages and to create
mood during scene crossovers. Possibly clarinet and
strings, chant and strings. Haunting.

Time

Now.

Act One

SCENE ONE

*Art and Ben sit outside a restaurant puffing on cigars
and drinking brandies.*

Art And what age is she now?

Ben She'll be forty-five in December. Why?

Art No reason, I dreamt about her last night.

Ben Was it a good dream?

Art It was fantastic.

Ben How so?

Art I was making love to her.

Ben Were you?

Art I never dream or I never remember them but this
was so vivid. The sheets were gleaming, her legs perfect
against the dazzling white.

Ben Was it in your bed or mine?

Art I've never seen your bed. It was just a bed, a room,
marble somewhere, yeah marble, the floor, the windows.

Ben Marble windows?

Art Well, it was a dream.

Ben Why can't you dream about your own wife?

Art She was beside me. Why should I dream about her?
Are you going fishing this weekend?

Ben I don't know. Catherine has booked tickets for the theatre.

Art What are you seeing?

Ben I forgot to ask her, she sorts all of that out. She has good taste. Generally I enjoy her choices.

Art Yeah, I read somewhere ninety per cent of theatre tickets are booked by women.

Ben Yeah, they seem to do everything. Are you planning a fishing trip?

Art I was, but the young fellah's communion is on this Saturday. But it was an amazing dream. Tell Catherine. It'll amuse her. It was so real, that's the extraordinary thing. I don't believe I've ever spoken to Catherine for more than three minutes together. But there we were as happy as . . . Oh God . . . She's a good-looking woman.

Ben She is.

Art But I've never fancied her.

Ben I would hope not.

Art Do you not like other men fancying your wife?

Ben I don't mind them looking, but any conversation on the topic I find distasteful, I suppose.

Art I love when men give Anne the once-over, feel I've made the right choice.

Ben A bit late now if you haven't. What are you? Twenty years married?

Art Eighteen. We were very young. Men now are starting off at my age, older.

Ben Are you going to leave Anne?

Art Why would I do that?

Ben Well, you're dreaming about it.

Art But that's nothing. Do you mind me saying I dreamt I made love to your wife last night?

Ben I'm not sure you shouldn't have kept it to yourself.

Art You're very old-fashioned.

Ben Am I?

Art I didn't realise you were so repressed. Have you never dreamt about Anne?

Ben Would you like me to?

Art Why not? As long as it's just a dream, what do I care?

Ben I never dream about sex.

Art Come off it. It was fantastic, the light was beautiful. I couldn't stop looking at her. It'll never happen again. Why do I suddenly feel guilty?

Ben Are you going to have an affair with Catherine?

Art I can't help what I dream . . . I was such a powerful man in that marble room.

Ben Were you?

Art It was so male and female, so clear, that was the thing about it, not like when I'm awake . . . Does Catherine have affairs?

Ben Not that I'm aware of.

Art Are you telling me you're not sure?

Ben I'm not sure about anything.

Art But you love her?

Ben And Anne? What do you feel about Anne?

Art What do I feel about Anne? That's an odd question. She's one moody wagon, I'll tell you that much.

Ben Have you told her about your dream?

Art God no, it would only upset her. Why should I upset her like that for no reason?

Ben You don't mind upsetting me.

Art Have I? Ah! Forget it. I should've kept it to myself. I thought we could say anything to one another.

Ben There is no one you can just say anything to.

Art Is there not?

Ben No, there isn't.

Art Then I've blundered.

Ben Ah, it doesn't matter.

Art No, I'm out of line. If you'd dreamt about Anne like that I'd probably never speak to you again.

Ben What exactly were you doing to her?

Art Nothing, I swear. There was a beautiful room . . . The door is open and I walk along this grey-panelled hallway and come to this door, and the light and the smell and the sound from it is intoxicating. I walk into the room holding my breath, afraid I will sully this beautiful space, that it's not for me, but someone far more deserving. And the marble glistens all around her as she lies there on the bed. I'm sorry, Ben . . . but just thinking about her. All of this for me? Her hair was a star-shot, splintered gold. Does Catherine dye her hair?

Ben Yes, she does her roots. Sometimes I do them for her. She hates hairdressers, they waste her time.

Art So her time is precious. I love that about women, they sit around doing nothing, complaining about never having a minute. But in the dream her hair was natural, a waterfall of spun gold, I was climbing all over it, I had to resist the urge to eat it.

Ben Maybe it was someone else.

Art No, it was Catherine. And her hair was golden.

Ben She's never been golden. Catherine is dark. I don't think she'd like us talking about her like this.

Art Why not?

Ben Look, we're very happy.

Art I'm not disputing that for a minute.

Ben You are. I am a good husband and father. You have no right to speak about her like that.

Art I was just telling you a dream I had.

Ben I am the one should be dreaming about Catherine.

Art But you're not. It was my dream.

Ben About my wife.

Art What's wrong, Ben?

Ben I need to go home and see her. Make sure she's still there. Will you take care of the bill?

Art Of course . . . I'm sorry if I . . .

Ben (*exiting*) It's nothing . . . nothing . . . It's nothing.

Art looks after him, takes last puff of cigar, exits.

SCENE TWO

Catherine enters in a bathrobe with a towel on her head.
She drinks from a large glass of red wine. Music in the
background. Enter Ben.

Ben They're all asleep?

Catherine You say that every evening. Yeah, they were
very good, no one shouting. How was dinner?

Ben It was fine.

Catherine You had a salad, then arrabiata with
artichokes, or maybe you went crazy and had arrabiata
without artichokes.

Ben I had steak.

Catherine Very adventurous.

Ben It was good . . . I'm tired.

Catherine Who isn't, my darling?

Ben Show me your hair . . . take the towel off.

Catherine (*flings off the towel*) My hair!

Ben examines her hair, a close inspection of strands.

What?

Ben Nothing.

He fingers her hair dreamily, lazily.

It smells lovely. It's so dark.

Catherine It's always been dark.

Ben I dreamt last night it was blond.

Catherine I've never been blond. Would you like me blond?

Ben I don't think so.

Catherine And what was I doing in the dream?

Ben You were making love.

Catherine To you?

Ben Of course to me. Why would you ask a thing like that?

Catherine No reason.

Ben Did you dream last night?

Catherine As a matter of fact I did.

Ben About me?

Catherine No, about Art.

Ben Art?

Catherine I dreamt I was making love to him. Isn't that ridiculous? I don't know when I last saw him and there he was beaming at me, so intense, on a white, white bed . . . Marble windows, was it? Or was it a marble door? Anyway marble, lots of marble.

Ben What's so important about marble?

Catherine I just remember it, the gleam off it. I shouldn't have told you. I wish it was you I dreamt about.

She kisses him.

Ben I wish it too.

Catherine How is Art?

Ben You know old Art, easy company, Art is the same, he's getting on.

Catherine We're all getting on, none of us boys and girls any more and yet I still don't feel ready to be a woman . . . What age is he now?

Ben The same age he always was . . . a year younger than me.

Catherine I thought he was younger.

Ben He's aged. He drinks too much.

Catherine Well.

She drinks, finishes glass, pours.

Ben Talks about dying a lot.

Catherine Only recently have I started noticing graveyards, hearses, churches, I always thought they were some kind of decoration that had nothing to do with me, but now they follow me everywhere.

Ben Graveyards follow you?

Catherine You know what I mean, and dead butterflies seem to be stalking me, they appear at my feet, on the doorstep, in the bathroom, under my pillow.

Ben Yes, I know what you mean.

Catherine I'll be walking along or making the kids' lunches and it creeps over me, you're going to die soon, all of this will be taken from you. Impossible, but there it is.

Ben Art should stop smoking cigars. He's too old for that sort of indulgence.

Catherine And you?

Ben I only smoke when I'm with him. If I get cancer it'll be his fault.

Catherine Has he done something on you?

Ben No, why?

Catherine You're very grumpy about him.

Ben Art is great. He's great.

Catherine And how is Anne?

Ben I think they're going through a bit of a crisis.

Catherine Like us?

Ben Us?

Catherine What sort of crisis?

Ben He's dreaming about other women.

Catherine What's wrong with that?

Ben He's dreaming about you.

Catherine About me?

Ben Last night he dreamt he was making love to you in a room full of marble.

Catherine Last night?

Ben Yes. Last night. While you were dreaming about him, he was dreaming about you. What crisis are we going through?

Catherine That's fantastic. I love it.

Ben You love it?

Catherine Adds a bit of fizz to my life.

Ben Is your life so boring?

Catherine I believe it is.

Ben Do I give you such a terrible time?

Catherine I've no one to compare you with, have I?

Ben I'd like to know what's so fantastic about dreaming you were making love to Art?

Catherine We snared something in our sleep, Art and I.

Ben Art and you?

Catherine Yes, that's all. Darling, there is always regret for the life you didn't lead.

Ben Is there?

Catherine I think so, yes, the life not lived is what kills. I bet Art and Anne are very happy. They always struck me as a model couple.

Ben 'A model couple', what does that mean?

Catherine Well, all those dogs on the furniture, all those dirty children, Anne doesn't give a damn, just cooks and drinks red wine. I bet she forgets to collect them from school and they all make their way home safe and sound. I'm too conscientious and you're looking for a row and you lied to me.

Ben When did I lie to you?

Catherine You didn't dream about me last night.

Ben Oh, that. No, that was Art. I borrowed his dream, that's all.

Catherine Maybe you should dream about Anne, even it all out.

Ben Anne is not my type.

Catherine So now you have a type?

Ben I do. I certainly do.

Catherine And what is your type?

Ben You are my type.

Catherine I'm what life threw at you.

Ben That too.

Catherine Don't forget it was I who asked you to marry me.

Ben Did you?

Catherine You don't remember?

Ben No, I don't. Come to think of it, I don't seem to remember making any decisions at all . . . ever. Things just have the habit of happening to me.

Catherine So if I hadn't asked you to marry me, we wouldn't be married?

Ben But you did ask me. Did I say yes?

Catherine I don't remember – did you mean to say no?

Ben I organised everything. I must've said yes or meant to. I even had to buy you a slip on the way to the church, that's what I remember most about our wedding, buying you a slip in a shop because your dress was see-through.

Catherine You should tell Art I dreamt about him tomorrow. And tell him there was marble in the dream, lots of marble, that's all I remember – and wild pleasure.

Ben Wild pleasure?

Catherine It was a good dream.

Ben Maybe the pair of you should run off together.

Catherine In a way we have, we seem to have managed an escape of sorts, a co-ordinated escape while staying put. What colour was my hair in the dream?

Ben Blond. A star-seared, gold-shot blond.

Catherine Yes, in my dream I was blond too. Should I dye my hair before it's too late?

Ben Too late for what?

Catherine Before I go completely grey?

Ben I like your hair dark.

Catherine Then dark it stays . . . but just for a week, a month, imagine a decade of blond licence before I'm filed for the tomb. It might be interesting to do something interesting with myself for a change.

Ben I want your hair dark.

Catherine It's that important to you?

Ben Yes, it is. You must remain dark.

Catherine And if I don't?

Ben Well, that's as good as betrayal.

Catherine Is it?

Ben Yes, it is . . . What play are we going to see on Friday?

Catherine Why?

Ben No reason.

Catherine You've never asked before.

Ben I trust your judgement.

Catherine And now you don't?

Ben Art was asking me.

Catherine I forget the name of it, about the auld one dying.

Ben Auld ones dying don't interest me. Women who've stopped ovulating should die offstage. Who cares?

Catherine You don't have to come.

Ben Of course I'll come. I'll probably love it.

Catherine Someday I'll be old if I'm lucky.

Ben (*examining her hair*) You need to do your roots again.

Catherine Why can't you bear me getting old?

Ben Women aren't allowed to get old. I mean, of course you're allowed, but it's not mannerly. It's somehow not appropriate. Old women interfere with my sense of myself.

Catherine And what about old men?

Ben Ah, men don't matter. Can't stand them. It's never about men.

Catherine You're wrong as usual. It's all about men, always has been, we're not even allowed to grow old without your disdain.

Ben Just don't turn into one of those gangs of hags who go to flower shows.

Catherine Those gangs of hags look happy. They've buried their men. I could do worse than end up going to flower shows.

Ben Well, at least wait till you've trampled my grave.

Catherine We're talking rubbish now. It's late. I'm going to bed.

She kisses him.

See you in a while.

Ben Don't dream about Art tonight.

Catherine But darling, not even you can control that.

And exit Catherine.

SCENE THREE

Ben sits there a minute, dials on his mobile. Enter Art with cigar and brandy.

Art Ben.

Ben Why aren't you in bed?

Art How do you know I'm not? I'm too tired to go to bed. Are you up?

Ben Catherine's just gone up.

Art How is she?

Ben She dreamt about you last night.

Art Oh?

Ben There was loads of marble in it.

Art Was there? Wow! Was it a good dream?

Ben It was wild and her hair was blond.

Art She's dyed her hair?

Ben No, in the dream. It was the same as yours, marble, sex, blondness.

Art Ben, you're exhausted.

Ben Are you going to bed now?

Art I'm having a brandy.

Ben Are you having a cigar?

Art Far too late for a cigar. (*Puffs, laughs to himself.*) Are you all right?

Ben I'm fine . . . I just . . . I don't know, I was ringing to ask you something.

Art What is it, Ben?

Ben Don't dream about Catherine again.

Art Sure I never dream. That was a once-off.

Ben Where's Anne?

Art She's asleep.

Ben Are you going to wake her up?

Art No, it's too late, she always wakes when I get into bed.

Ben Talk to Anne, you'll feel better about it.

Art I feel fine . . . Is Catherine asleep?

Ben Why do you want to know?

Art Is she dreaming about me?

Ben I doubt it, she's just gone up, she always reads herself to sleep.

Art What's she reading?

Ben Some travel book . . . by your man who was drowned . . . a torpedo.

Art Did he drown?

Ben I believe he did. It's on the blurb, anyway. Someone drowned at the end of some war.

Art Is it a good book?

Ben Well, Catherine's reading it.

Art Ages since I read a good book . . . Well, goodnight, Ben.

Ben Just don't dream. Or dream about Anne, me, anyone except Catherine.

Art It's a coincidence, though. I'm glad I was wild in her dream.

Ben Why?

Art I don't know, out there I'm someone's fantasy man.

Ben You're not, you know.

Art Yeah, well, goodnight.

Ben And put out that cigar, I can smell it over the phone.

Art It's nearly finished.

Ben Are you going to pour another brandy?

Art I haven't thought that far ahead.

Ben I might have one too, don't feel like sleeping tonight. Isn't it ridiculous the way people go to bed every night? We're far too trusting, anything might happen.

Art Have a brandy, Ben, relax. Night.

Ben Night, Art.

He sits there a minute, takes a cigar from a drawer, clippers, lights it, puffs, pours a drink. Art does the same in his space. They look at one another without seeing. And exit both.

SCENE FOUR

Anne comes on in coat and nightdress with takeaway coffee, paper and bag of croissants, which she eats during this scene. Enter Art in suit, with briefcase, drinks her coffee, eats some of her croissant.

Anne What time did you come to bed last night?

Art Don't know, I sat in the garden. I saw the hare.

Anne Yeah, she's back with two leverets.

Art I know, raised my glass to them. 'Welcome to the world, little creatures,' I said.

Anne Did you? . . . You were talking in your sleep.

Art Did I wake you?

Anne You were mourning with pleasure.

Art 'Mourning with pleasure'?

Anne Leave my croissants alone, you can get your own in town. Moaning . . . whatever it's called.

Art Did I say anything I should be ashamed of?

Anne Lots.

Art I did not. I'm always on my best behaviour when asleep.

Anne You look extremely guilty standing there in your suit.

Art I was born guilty . . . Kids are all fine?

Anne Yeah, they're fine.

Art Are we all set for the confirmation?

Anne Communion.

Art That's right.

Anne I'm getting caterers in. I can't be bothered any more.

Art Well, don't look so sad about it. Are we inviting the world and its mother or just our own ghastly shower?

Anne Just our own ghouls.

Art All the crones?

Anne Every last one of them.

Art Remind me to start on the wine early. Could we have a few friends? A few people we actually like?

Anne Like who?

Art Is there no one you like?

Anne Now that you ask, no, no one I like enough to put up with all day.

Art What else was I saying in my sleep?

Anne I can't remember . . . sable or scrabble or . . . Did you have a dream or something?

Art I never dream.

Anne But last night?

Art No . . . definitely no.

Anne I dreamt I was French-kissing a dog. He was forcing my mouth open with his paws. He had my tongue clamped between his teeth.

Art Was it good?

Anne And then you woke me up.

Art With my mourning with pleasure.

Anne No, after that.

Art What happened after that?

Anne You don't remember?

Art No, what did I do?

Anne Don't look so frightened. You just made love to me.

Art Last night?

Anne Towards morning.

Art But that's impossible.

Anne What are you saying?

Art I have no memory of it.

Anne Maybe you drank too much.

Art I had two bottles of wine with dinner and four brandies. I don't think that's excessive. You must have been dreaming.

Anne I know when I'm being made love to.

Art Maybe it was the dog. Well, I'm glad one of us had a good time.

Anne You enjoyed it too.

Art Did I?

Anne Your back was a river of sweat.

Art And that equals enjoyment?

She kisses him.

Anne Darling, try and remember when you make love to me.

Art I do. I usually do. This is bizarre.

Anne Maybe you thought I was someone else . . . Look, if you ever need to have an affair, just go ahead, only don't tell me.

Art Why would I have an affair?

Anne I'm just saying.

Art I'm not that kind of man. Why would I do a thing like that?

Anne People do the strangest things.

Art In their thoughts, maybe, but the waking world is different.

Anne I don't find it so different. Recently I find the daylight strange, distorted, shadowy, where all was clear before.

Art Are you going to have an affair?

Anne Not that I'm aware of.

Art Then why are you telling me to have one?

Anne Just if you need to.

Art Are you tired of me?

Anne I'm just tired, I'm tired of living, of course I'm not tired of you.

Art Are you having an affair?

Anne God, you're so literal. Just forget it. Forget it, Art. You're late.

Art I don't care if I'm late. I get no credit for being on time. What are you talking about?

Anne Just breakfast conversation. I was so happy with you last night. Look, if you need to destroy us, do it without my knowing, that's all. I don't want honesty. I don't have the energy for honesty any more.

Art What?

Anne Go to work. We have lots of bills. Go to work.

Art I'll go in a minute.

Anne Will I make a pot of coffee?

Art I don't want coffee . . . (*Drinking Anne's coffee.*) What are you doing today?

Anne What I always do?

Art What do you always do?

Anne You know what I always do.

Art And what's in it for you?

Anne You come home, the children are healthy, I'm alive.

Art That doesn't seem like much.

Anne Lots survive on less. My life is full.

Art Have I been neglecting you?

Anne Probably . . . Have you?

Art No, you have to tell me.

Anne Tell you what? It's just living, Art. Just waiting for it all to end like everyone else.

Art I'd better go.

Anne Do you want dinner or will I just eat with the children?

Art Can I call you later?

Anne Don't leave it too late.

Art I won't.

He kisses her. And exit Art. Anne sits there eating croissants. And exit.

SCENE FIVE

Enter Ben in a suit. Drinks from a bottle of water. He stands there looking out. Enter Art with a pile of papers, glasses, jacket over his arm.

Art I've been all over the building . . . What're you doing up here?

Ben I like looking down on the city.

Art We've a meeting in five minutes. I thought you were meant to have this sorted.

Ben Fractions and decimals. Nothing to do with anything.

Art This is not the time for philosophy.

Ben Do you ever look down on this city? God bless us all is all I can say. You'd need to be made of steel and concrete to survive this place.

Art We are, Ben, we are, steel and concrete, decimals and fractions, the square root of nothing. But so what? So is everyone else.

Ben In time this will all be ice again. You know we're actually living in the middle of an ice age? Always thought it was millions of years ago. The rising water is only the ice melting and when it's all melted it'll freeze again.

Art It's an ice-lolly world.

Ben Catherine dreamt about you again.

Art Did she?

Ben That's two dreams in forty-eight hours.

Art Was there marble in it?

Ben No, it was full of sand.

Art That's strange. I dreamt last night I was with Catherine on a beach, we were shipwrecked on this beach and I kept thinking, as I made love to her, I'm the one who's going to have to find water, build a hut, fight off natives, lions, scorpions, and night was coming on.

Ben Just what did you do to her?

Art I'm sorry, but I've done nothing . . . Did you dream?

Ben As a matter of fact I did have a dream last night.

Art About Anne?

Ben No, about you.

Art About me?

Ben You were prancing around in your underpants showing me the cherry blossom.

Art And was I a turn-on in my underpants?

Ben 'Smell the cherry blossom,' you kept shrieking, and there were two cherry blossoms shedding, miraculously shedding in my garden. I have oaks in my garden, oaks for Christ sakes, and there you are like some mad Cinderella waltzing round in your underpants, invading my lawn.

Art Suddenly I'm irresistible. Everyone's dreaming about me, even Anne, she said I made love to her last night.

Ben And didn't you?

Art I think she made it up.

Ben Maybe you thought Anne was Catherine and reached for her on your shipwrecked beach among the scorpions.

Art We're late. Let's get this meeting over with and take a long lunch.

Ben There's no time for lunch today . . . I hate my life.

Art (*papers*) What's the story on this shower?

Ben Up to their necks in gutter. We don't go near them.

Art You better have your reasons. I hope you're in the mood for a row.

Ben Oh God, I'm going to die in a boardroom looking up some fella's hairy nostrils.

And exit both.

SCENE SIX

Enter Catherine in nightdress with a glass of wine and a child's story book. A child cries offstage.

Catherine Go to sleep now . . . Good boy . . . I'll be up in a minute. (*Under her breath.*) Oh Christ, give me a break!

Enter Ben.

Ben What's wrong with him?

Catherine He just won't settle. I've read him three stories.

Ben I'll go up.

Catherine Give him a minute, he might drop off.

Ben Does he cry every night?

Catherine Most nights, yes.

Ben It's pitiful.

Catherine After seventeen years of crying children, you get pretty immune.

Ben Why is he crying?

Catherine Because he wants a chocolate bar and I wouldn't give him one, then he wanted me to cut my hair off and leave it on the pillow, which I cruelly refused to do, and then he wanted to paint his nails pink. But he's really crying because he can't make sense of this world and neither can his mother.

Ben goes to her, kisses her.

Did Art dream about me?

Ben On a tropical beach, no less.

Catherine What a cliché. I suppose we were happy.

Ben Ecstatic.

Catherine Is Art good-looking?

Ben I don't know.

Catherine Don't you have eyes?

Ben Not for men, no, I certainly don't.

Catherine Describe him.

Ben Art?

Catherine Yeah.

Ben He's an in-between man, I suppose. Not too bad despite his cigars and his brandy. Eyes wide-spaced, dark I think. Teeth are good, tans easily, veiny legs which he says he inherited from his mother, but his mouth is unfinished.

Catherine What do you mean?

Ben Foetal or something, like he's never been weaned.

Catherine And your mouth?

Ben I never got the breast. That's what's wrong with me. Rejection from day one. Were you thinking about him today?

Catherine Yeah . . . can't stop.

Ben It's really not on.

Catherine Why isn't it on?

Ben Well, there's me in the background.

Catherine I think about you too.

Ben A lot?

Catherine Enough.

Ben And what do you think about when you think about me?

Catherine What is this? The Inquisition?

Ben You're the one dreaming about people you shouldn't be.

Catherine There is no vocabulary for this.

Ben Do you want me to die?

Catherine You're not exactly burning with life. Widows have a great time, it has to be said.

Ben They do.

Catherine All that freedom, no big man stomping round the kitchen rattling the knife drawer . . . Yeah, I'd like to be a girl again, without the stupidity, yes, I long to be alone, all this clutter is too much for me.

Ben Have you dyed your hair?

Catherine I set out the dye. I put on the gloves and then I said, what's the point? I suppose what I'm no longer capable of is deep feeling – you know, when your breath stops – except when I dream about Art. It's fantastic. Don't be jealous, Ben. I can't wait to go to sleep tonight and dream about him.

Ben I wish you'd dream about me.

Catherine But I'm not. I'm dreaming about Art and he's dreaming about me. Just who is it hurting?

Ben Me.

Catherine It's not. You can't control my mind. I can't control it. You can't tell me to switch off a dream just because it's not about you.

Ben I don't have to like it.

Catherine I think you should if it makes me happy.

Ben I'm the one should make you happy.

Catherine Don't be ridiculous.

Ben So I'm just here taking up space?

Catherine Well, yes, but that's normal.

Ben What? Hovering with my hands in my pockets? Waiting for you to start the conversation? Sort out the day for me.

Catherine Is that what you do? I suppose that's the way we go on. I hope Art dreams about me tonight. Johnny got ninety-five in his reading. He told me to tell you, not to forget. Ring Art and tell him to dream about me tonight.

Ben You're mad. I never realised it before.

Catherine Well, I can't ring him.

Ben Why not? You've such a fantastic time together.

Catherine Anne might think I have designs on him.

Ben And don't you?

Catherine Only in bed, only in sleep.

Ben I have a premonition of an impending catastrophe.

Catherine A what?

Ben A sentence from my English teacher. She made us write it down, she was talking about Macbeth. That's what I have, a premonition of an impending catastrophe.

Catherine It's only a bit of distraction.

Ben So if he stops dreaming about you it won't matter?

Catherine He won't. We're too far in to just stop.

Ben Too far in?

Catherine I can't explain it. It's as if my real life is happening when I go to sleep and you and I are a dream, a fragment, difficult to remember on waking. Being awake is no longer important.

Ben But if he stops?

Catherine Don't say that to me.

Ben Why not?

Catherine You're tampering with the hard-wiring of my mind, my heart, my soul. Stop tampering with me.

Ben And you're playing with me. You like to see me jealous.

Catherine I didn't notice. Oh Ben, it's the prose of living I can't take much longer. I look around me and everything irregular, irrational, opaque is what seems beautiful to me now. What are these senseless rules we live by? Who decided them and why? And the minute I assert any personality, I'm rejected by you. Any whiff of the essential me is off. I'm so tired behaving myself.

Ben (*goes to her, kisses her*) I wish you'd stop this nonsense and go back to your dreamless sleeps.

Catherine You like me catatonic.

Ben I like you to think about me.

Catherine Night.

And exit Catherine. Ben wanders round, turning off lamp, tidying up. And exit Ben.

SCENE SEVEN

Enter Art with coffee in a takeaway cup, briefcase. He stands there a minute, staring off into the distance. Ben walks by, briefcase, coffee, newspaper. Passes Art without a word.

Art Ben.

Ben I see you.

Art Stop. Stop for a minute.

Ben You want to tell me about your fantastic dream?

Art No dream.

Ben You mean you're not going to tell me.

Art No, I didn't dream about Catherine last night. I didn't dream at all.

Ben Well, she dreamt about you.

Art It'll stop soon.

Ben She couldn't wait to wake and tell me.

Art What was I doing?

Ben The usual Romeo stuff under a marble statue – marble floor, white marble everywhere and the pair of you sprawled all over it.

Art If only it was real. I don't think I've ever been in a room with a white marble floor. You get all that fake

313

stuff in hotel lobbies . . . but a real marble room,
classical proportions, pillars, columns, statues that are
not copies . . .

Ben You dreamt it too?

Art Yeah, yeah, I dreamt it too.

Ben Then why did you lie?

Art Because you look awful. Look, I don't give a hoot
about Catherine. She's your wife so I want her to be
okay so you're okay, but that's all, Ben, that's all.

Ben Are you having an affair with Catherine?

Art That's crazy.

Ben No, listen, I've been thinking that all this dreaming
is just a front, hiding the real thing that's going on.

Art What real thing that's going on? Tell me. I'd love to
know something real.

Ben You can't continue playing with me like this. Look,
I've known you too long. If it's a big joke, you've had
your laugh, now come clean.

Art I'm not playing with you, Ben.

Ben Aren't you? Between the pair of you you've unhinged
me. Catherine said last night that she'd like me to die.

Art She didn't. I don't believe that.

Ben And what was terrible was she was being
philosophical about herself. She didn't mean to be cruel.

Art This is getting out of hand. Will I call Catherine?

Ben Don't you dare!

Art All right. Christ!

Ben You're just looking for an excuse to be near her.

Art I am not.

Ben She's the same. She's fascinated with you. She can't stop herself talking about you. She loves saying your name.

Art So, what's that to do with me? I can't remember the last time I saw Catherine, spoke to her, I can't visualise her – she's blond, right? Sandy blond, darker in winter, blue eyes is it? Or grey?

Ben I don't know.

Art You don't know the colour of your wife's eyes?

Ben They keep changing. Last night they were brown.

Art Has she dyed her hair yet?

Ben What's it to you? She's just a woman like any other. I can't see the individual in her, the space that defines her, that makes her who she is. I suppose I haven't thought about her in a long time, and now when I'm forced to look at her she's not there, she's so strange all of a sudden.

Art Is it that you and Catherine are not happy and I'm being blamed? Piggy in the middle, gooseberry, the scapegoat who'll take the rap for everything?

Ben No, we're happy, we're happy, no more miserable than anyone else. There are children, gardens, afternoons looking out on the bay. All of that. We're not miserable, Art, far from it, but something has to happen, you and Catherine have started something. I'm just the sleepwalker in the middle of it.

Art I refuse to take any responsibility if you and Catherine break up.

Ben What are you talking about?

Art I'm just saying it now. I want no part in it. It has nothing to do with me.

Ben You think you'll come out of this unscathed? We're all in this. All of us.

Art Is that a threat?

Ben You think you can spill your sleeping world all over me, all your hidden fantasies and passions, all over my house, my wife, and walk away scot-free?

Art I thought we were friends.

Ben This is way beyond the call of friendship.

And exit Ben.

SCENE EIGHT

Art looks after the departing Ben. Takes out his phone, clears his throat, dials. Enter Anne. Glass of wine, some crooner in the background.

Anne What is it, Art?

Art Can't I call you whenever I want?

Anne But you never do. Is everything okay? (*She takes a sip of wine.*)

Art Of course, a glorious morning. The sun is shining.

Anne Don't talk to me about the sun (*Looks out.*) It goes on all day.

Art I'm drinking coffee in the plaza before I head in to work.

Anne Isn't that great for you?

Art I just thought I'd ring to say hello.

Anne What is it, Art? I'm busy.

Art You're always saying I never call you and when I do you have a go at me.

Anne Has something happened?

Art No, nothing has happened. How are the kids?

Anne They're fine, about their day.

Art And what are your plans for the day?

Anne I'm going to the shop to buy digestive biscuits and washing-up liquid.

Art Have you noticed anything about me?

Anne The cat's iris has fallen out.

Art Fuck the cat, have I changed?

Anne She's staring at me through the window like it's my fault, with a hole in her eye. No, you haven't changed – do you want to change?

Art Of course not.

Anne What is it, Art? What's wrong?

Art I just wanted to hear your voice.

Anne Are you about to do something you shouldn't and you want me to say it's all right?

Art What would I be about to do?

Anne God knows. I don't know, Art, I like to hear you too.

Art But have you noticed anything odd in my behaviour this last while?

Anne You're the same old Art, a bit more passionate these nights, but that's you too.

Art Is it? Is that me?

Anne Look, I can't tell you who you are, darling, I'm saving all vital energy for defining Anne, the several Annes that seem to have taken up residence in this old carcass. Don't worry, sweetheart, I'll be here this evening, one of me will at any rate.

Art I never for a second suspected you wouldn't be there this evening. What in the name of God are you talking about?

Anne Oh Art, I'm just babbling on – enjoy the day, darling, don't work too hard.

Art But there's something you're not saying.

Anne Is there?

Art Yes, there is.

Anne What, what have I forgotten?

Art That you love me.

Anne Oh that, I suppose I'm out of the habit.

Art But do you?

Anne I don't like to be coerced into those three words. I'll tell you I love you if and when I feel like telling you.

Art It's impossible to have a romantic conversation with you! You think just because you have me in the bed you don't need to woo me out of it!

Anne Is that what I think?

Art Yes, that's what you think! I know you, woman. You always think you know better.

Anne Well, I'm glad you told me what I think. That's one thing off my list today. Thinking.

Art You're a contrary rip! Impossible to please, sitting on your fat arse, smug with sex.

Anne I'm going to hang up now.

She hangs up and exits.

Art That's right, hang up on me! Why can't you just say what you're supposed to say? I'll break you down yet. (*He flings the phone away.*) That's the last time you get a romantic call from me.

Picks up phone, straightens tie, preens himself. Cuffs, jacket, briefcase. And exit Art.

SCENE NINE

Enter Ben, the room is in shadow.

Ben Catherine? . . . Catherine, are you here?

Catherine (*a sigh*) Oh God . . . what?

Ben Why is the house in darkness?

Catherine I fell asleep . . . I was dreaming . . . I don't suppose you want to hear it.

Ben Art has stopped dreaming about you.

Catherine He hasn't?

Ben He told me this morning he dreamt about another woman.

Catherine Who?

Ben What does it matter who? It wasn't you, that's the important thing.

Catherine I don't believe it.

Ben Can I turn the light on?

Catherine No, I want shadow, candlelight, stars.

Ben There are no stars here any more . . . Just the lamp then.

Catherine Why must you always break the spell?

Ben Is that what I do?

Catherine You ruin every dusk. And when it's dark you ruin the dark. Why did you tell me Art dreamt about me in the first place only to take it from me?

Ben I'm sorry. I should never have told you.

Catherine You actually believe you're innocent, wronged, that Art and I are the deviants?

Ben And aren't you?

Catherine That was my lifeline!

Ben Art dreaming about you?

Catherine I didn't think I needed one, but now you've taken it I feel I'm being sucked up out of here. I live for sleeping, dreaming about Art, my waking life is just pretence.

Ben Well, of course it is, Catherine. It is for everyone.

Catherine I don't care about everyone. The same for everyone! What about me? Me? I am here now, in time, for a very, very short time, and I doubt I will ever be again, why this thing called me if every avenue of expression is closed off from me? And all I have to look forward to is dying?

Ben There are codes and rules and contracts we must live by, Catherine. And as for dying, we are dying all the time – look at this hand, the skin on it is dead, look at your face, the skin on your cheeks died yesterday. Ridiculous to think, monumentally stupid, to hope it all just happens at the end.

Catherine And love?

Ben An awful repetition of nights and days and days and nights.

Catherine Please, Ben, tell me – has he really stopped?

Ben No . . . I made it up . . . I just want . . . just want all of this to be over.

Catherine It is over. I've crossed some line or other without realising it. And it's fantastic, Ben, something is happening to me.

Lights down.

End of Act One.

Act Two

SCENE ONE

Art sits at table drinking glass of red wine and smoking a cigar. Enter Catherine with a glass of red wine.

Catherine Art?

Art My God! I was just thinking about you, was thinking how lovely it would be if I bumped into you.

Catherine You were not? . . . And here I am.

Art And here you are.

Catherine Ben's not here, is he?

Art No, he won't have a glass with me these days.

Catherine Well, I will.

She sits.

Cheers.

They clink glasses.

Art Why are you here?

Catherine I got a babysitter. I went to the art gallery. I thought I might run into Ben. No, I wanted to be on my own . . . I just wanted to have a look at you.

Art And how was the gallery?

Catherine A blur . . . a blur of relentless colour . . . drank it all in too quickly, feel dizzy now, like there are moths fluttering and banging around my brain. I stood in front of this painting, can't remember who it was, but a woman just staring out at me with dirty fingernails, one of the Dutch maybe, and I wished I could be her, fixed in a painting somewhere, trapped behind glass. And people could come and stare and think what they liked about me and it wouldn't matter. My expression wouldn't change, my dress would still be green, my hands filthy.

Art And what do you think of me? Do I disappoint?

Catherine Your neck is a bit . . . I don't know . . .

Art What's wrong with my neck?

Catherine Well, it's a bit . . . thought it was longer . . . It's hardly a neck at all. There's nothing wrong with your neck.

Art This is the real world, baby. Some people are neckless here. No marble around to glisten off.

Catherine I must be a fright to look at?

Art Let me tell you something, Catherine, you are exactly as I dream you. Ben said your hair was brown.

Catherine I dyed it.

Art For me?

Catherine For the dream. For me. Yes, for you. I want to be that dream. I want to live it. I want it to be my waking world.

Art And Ben?

Catherine Oh Ben, Ben, Ben. What is Ben at?

Art Ben loves you.

Catherine Ben loves the idea of me. He doesn't know the first thing about me.

Art And I do?

323

Catherine Describe to me the dream you had last night.

Art No.

Catherine Why not?

Art It seems ridiculous now.

Catherine You believe in the day too much?

Art The day is where we must live.

Catherine I disagree. Night is where it all happens.

Art In a million years perhaps, but not now. This is the age of ice, an era when men and women's hearts were frozen – that's how they'll describe us in the future. But we can't live in the future. It has been given to us now, this age of prose and flint, and it is here, just here, we must bide our time.

Catherine No, no, Art, you mustn't talk like that. You know, I've been looking around this last while, I've been looking at people a lot, and I see us all now as some fabulous species, and you know something, Art? It is we who are the beautiful thing, yes, us – not God, not mountains, oceans, rivers, architecture, none of that haphazard vastness, but us, wandering through this hostile landscape, so full of hope, for what? And despair, for why?

Art It's what we do, Catherine. It's called living. It happens to everyone.

Catherine This blinding joy?

Art Moments. Yes.

Catherine I know I don't seem like a great prospect right now, but that's because I've spent all these years cutting bits of myself off. With you . . . I would retrieve them.

Art Catherine . . . that is not possible.

Catherine You get enough just dreaming?

Art Well, no . . . but . . .

Catherine Anne . . . the children.

Art Yes . . . all of that.

Catherine You coward . . . You're using me.

Art How am I using you?

Catherine You deny me now? Last night I was sprawled under you.

Art You were not.

Catherine Ben told you to say the dreams have stopped.

Art They have.

Catherine You're afraid. Don't be. It's me, Art. I'm afraid too. But what awaits us if we would only . . .

Art I can't, Catherine.

Catherine Look, I have a whole show on the road too. You think I come to you on a whim? I know the fallout for Ben and the children will be terrible.

Art I have a wife I wouldn't hurt for the world. I have four children.

Catherine I know how many children you have.

Art I have a good life. You have too. Ben is a good man.

Catherine I am so sick of being told I have a good life. That I have a good man, that my children are beautiful. I'm not denying any of it and I'm not ungrateful, and may the gods not strike me down, but I want more. I want more than good. I want spectacular. I want marble, marble, marble.

Art Last night was spectacular.

Catherine So you don't deny it?

Art I don't deny it, but how do we get from here to there? It's the coldness of this world I can't take, the terrifying greyness that saturates my days and nights. Half the time I look up at the sky, when I remember to, and it's just not there, only a cloak of elephant iron weighing me down where that indigo should be, and you know, sometimes I think our dreaming is about dying, that I don't care to prolong the jaunt much further here.

Catherine Then let it be about dying. It's happening anyway.

Art You're dangerous.

Catherine Am I?

Art You want destruction, don't you?

Catherine Anything new seems to involve it. There can be no change without change.

Art Change is what I do not want.

Catherine You think I want it? It would be far easier for me to stay with my good life, my good man, my beautiful children.

Art Then stay.

Catherine And give up is it?

Art It's what everyone does.

Catherine So like sheep we should do the same?

Art Yes, exactly the same.

Catherine So what you're saying is, there is no place in this world for our dream of marble.

Art You assume too much. A handful of dreams. How can they possibly impact here? Where is the place for them?

Catherine In our hearts – there is nowhere else.

Art Just because you know me intimately in that marble room you shouldn't presume anything out of it. I am, or rather was, your husband's oldest friend.

Catherine Don't lecture me on loyalty. I know the cost of what we're talking about.

Art What you're talking about.

Catherine I know the price that will be extracted in blood. Your blood. Mine. I have thought this through. I don't sit here talking to you lightly. I don't ask you to come with me lightly.

Art I'm going nowhere with you.

He gets up.

I'm going home. If you're wise you'll say nothing to Ben about this.

Catherine I'm past protecting anyone, least of all myself. Don't go. Have another glass with me.

Art I have to go.

Catherine You're afraid of me.

Art Yes, I am.

Catherine I am too. Feel like a lone magpie on the wind, a bad omen, sorrow for everyone around me, so be it.

Art Goodnight, Catherine, and don't say anything to Ben. He'll read it all wrong.

Catherine You're more worried about Ben than anything.

Art I am. I just can't do this. It's not I'm not tempted, but there are laws . . . unwritten, but there nevertheless.

Catherine Your laws are crippling.

Art That may be so, but they're all that's between us and chaos. For the third time, goodnight.

And exit Art. Catherine sits there looking after him. Takes stub of his cigar from ashtray, smells it. Holds it. Sips from his unfinished wine . . . and exit.

SCENE TWO

Enter Ben with sandwich and coffee, sits, begins opening sandwich, forgets about it, stares out. After a minute, enter Art. Stops, looks at Ben.

Art Are you avoiding me?

Ben Damn right I am.

Art I was wondering if you'd care to go fishing on Saturday or Sunday?

Ben I work. I go home. That's it now.

Art Is she improving?

Ben Sleeps all day.

Art So who's looking after the kids?

Ben No one. She sits like a statue at the kitchen table and they tiptoe round her.

Art Dare I ask?

Ben Yes, the dreams keep coming and coming.

Art Yeah.

Ben You're still dreaming about her?

Art Yes, I suppose I am.

Ben You never stopped.

Art So? It's nothing, Ben.

Ben Why don't you just fuck her and be done with it?
Run away with her. It'd be over in a week.

Art You're blaming me for all of this.

Ben Just for your part in it.

Art Ever occur to you it's you wants everything to
change? It's you wants rid of Catherine?

Ben I am not the dreamer here.

Art And suppose I do go off with her, what then?

Ben I don't know – build your marble room, frolic in it
till ye suffocate, tear it down around ye. Puncture your
wild fantasies.

Art And what of your wild fantasies?

Ben There are none.

Art Everyone has them.

Ben Mine are darkness and silence.

Art I don't believe you.

Ben That's the official version. My private life is my
private life. I don't spew it over the first passer-by.

Art Well, if you believe I would walk into your house
and just steal your woman you don't know me.

Ben No, I don't know you. I begin to realise I don't
know anyone.

Art We're dealing with elusive territory, Ben, things imagined, without rhyme or reason. You and Catherine are confusing the two worlds, trying to apply there to here. And trying to hold me to ransom because of it. I am not responsible for my dreams. They're just visitors, uninvited, come and go as they please.

Ben She says your spirits meet in this marble room.

Art So? So what? So they meet?

Ben Easy for you to say. I have a woman at home who sleeps twenty-four hours a day, she gets up in the middle of the night, eats crackers and hard-boiled eggs from their shells which she scatters around the carpets, the stairs. She hovers around windows, doorways, leans against the fence for an hour at a time and then sinks back into her catatonic dream of you.

Art I can't help you, Ben. I can't help Catherine. I have my own circus, children in school, a wife I love. I'm not throwing that away for . . .

Ben Do you love Anne? You don't look to me like a man in love.

Art And you do?

Ben Nothing bears scrutiny, does it? I told you at the start how it would be. You laughed in my face, lit another cigar, sloshed down more brandy. You leather-skinned slobs who dribble and drool over other people's lives, smearing and sundering without even realising, all the time pleading innocence. Well, I'm sorry, but that sort of blundering innocence is a crime. She is pining for you. She's skin and bone, she is very fragile right now and you treated her so callously.

Art She told you then?

Ben How dare you treat my wife like that? You dare to get on your high moral horse with her when you started the whole thing.

Art I was very reasonable with her. What do you want from me, Ben? Are you asking me to have an affair with her?

Ben Yes . . . I believe I am.

Art Maybe it's you wants the affair with me?

Ben Is that what you think?

Art The whole thing is so out of control I don't know what to think any more.

Ben Well, be assured on one point. I have no desire to have anything to do with you. I want my wife back. Look, I'm feeding and dressing a woman who no longer loves me and now I wonder if she ever has. I want her back. And if I have to give her to you to get her back then that's what I have to do.

Art That is never going to happen.

Ben I'm afraid she's going to die on me! We're dealing with hearts and minds here, Art, mine and Catherine's, not some after-dinner titillation. I knew you'd run when the chips were down.

Art I'm protecting my own hearth is all.

Ben I should ring Anne, tell her the lie of the land.

Art Leave Anne out of this. I don't want her sullied with this. I don't want this near my house.

Ben This is what thirty years' friendship comes down to.

Art Don't threaten me with Anne.

Ben But Catherine is fair game?

Art I am so sorry, Ben, if I have been careless.

Ben Careless?

Art Yes, careless! That's all it was. I am sorry, but for you to attack my wife because of a lapse in me is despicable. That's what cowards do, go after the women and children.

Ben And what of my woman and my children?

Art Not in my house! This is your mess. Catherine's mess. Don't bring it near my lair.

Ben It's already there.

Art What have you done?

Ben I don't need to do anything. Look at you.

And exit Ben. Art stands there a minute, shaken, recovers his composure, then exits.

SCENE THREE

Sound of Anne off.

Anne Come in. Come in. Honestly. Once I answer the door I let people in.

Catherine What a lovely hall.

Anne Of course I never have visitors.

Catherine (*entering, followed by Anne*) I don't either. I hope you don't think it odd of me just dropping in without calling first.

Anne It's very odd. You're lucky I wasn't napping.

Catherine How are you?

Anne Keeping going, keeping going.

Catherine Yes, I can see you're keeping going with that bright smile on your face.

Anne Is it bright, my smile? Well, it was the smile I was given or maybe I learned it along the way. Will I make tea? Wine? Coffee?

Catherine I brought you these (*flowers*).

Anne No, keep them for yourself.

Catherine Well, they're dead. I certainly don't want them. Why do people bring dead things to one another?

Anne Look, I've enough rubbish in my life, it's a lovely thought though.

Catherine I don't suppose you heard I've been . . . I don't know . . . not myself, anyway.

Anne You look fine to me.

Catherine But I'm not, despite the lipstick and the new shawl and trousers . . . I'm very far from myself right now.

Anne Yes, Art told me, Ben is very worried about you.

Catherine Feel I've been peeled like an onion, I'm down to the core and there's nothing there.

Anne There's breathing.

Catherine Moss breathes. Cement breathes.

Anne As long as you're breathing there's something going on.

Catherine But the mind, the heart, the soul, whatever it is that's me, is just not there. Maybe it never was. I am far more than just breath.

Anne No you're not. None of us are. You're smoke. A light breeze will blow you away.

Catherine You're one of those old cynics.

Anne I just don't expect anything. I live by ritual, repetition. This old machine thrives on cappuccinos and emptying the dishwasher and polishing my white marble tiles in the hall. I'm in love with those tiles. I made Art import them.

Catherine Yes, I noticed them.

Anne I love the sheen, the light, the texture and grain.

Catherine And that's enough for you?

Anne I do have a few other things of course to disguise the journey.

Catherine Like what?

Anne Am I boring you?

Catherine No, tell me.

Anne Well, I have half a bottle of red wine in the evening. Every evening. I think I would murder someone if I couldn't have my three glasses of red wine in the evening. I measure them out. Generous measures. And I have a cigarette with each glass. I'm not a fascist about the cigarettes but I must have the wine. No one but no one can interfere with that.

Catherine It's very . . . I don't know what.

Anne Yes, I refuse to panic.

Catherine What else do you do?

Anne I read to the children.

Catherine Everyone does that. That's nothing to sustain you. Even I read to the children.

Anne And something a lot of people don't realise and forget to do and become depressed or psychopaths, but I figured out years ago . . .

Catherine What?

Anne I leave the lights on all day in winter, lamps, overhead lights, every light blazing in the house, all winter.

Catherine Your battle against the dark.

Anne Pathetic I know, but I need to. It keeps me . . . I suppose it keeps me here.

Catherine So you refuse darkness, you deny it. Do you sleep with the lights blazing?

Anne Until Art comes to bed. Then I don't mind if they're off.

Catherine He's like a lamp, is he?

Anne And every morning I decide what time I'll go to bed at. Before I get up I'll say to myself, okay, tonight bedtime is at ten for you, missus, or nine or eleven. It's a matter of light-policing of myself, not engaging, because I've long figured out there's nothing there to engage with. Just a simple police state. At the appointed hour I do this or that and so time does not encroach on me or weigh me down or disturb me in any way.

Catherine Is my visit disturbing you?

Anne There is room for the unplanned up to a point.

Catherine This is what Art is married to. What Art comes home to in the evening, kisses goodbye in the morning. This is what Art is so desperate to hold on to.

Anne I'm past caring how I appear. As long as it keeps me off window ledges.

Catherine You like window ledges?

Anne What woman doesn't? It's one of the big themes, isn't it?

Catherine So seductive to fly off one.

Anne The will I, won't I, thrill of it.

Catherine And do you dream?

Anne Why?

Catherine Because I do.

Anne Other people's dreams don't interest me.

Catherine Not even if they're about your husband?

Anne You dream about Art?

Catherine I can't stop.

Anne Oh.

Catherine Erotic dreams like a drug.

Anne You can't have him.

Catherine So you own him?

Anne I surely do.

Catherine He's part of your police state?

Anne The chief superintendent. I'd rather you didn't dream about him.

Catherine So would everyone.

Anne It's time for my wine. (*Pours.*) Do you want a glass?

Catherine Only if it doesn't interfere with your quota.

Anne I have cases of it.

Hands her a glass of wine. Catherine takes it, wanders around. Anne lights a cigarette, watches her.

It's messy. There are cobwebs and I don't wash windows or floors, gave that up a few years ago. I'm a housewife who does no housework.

Catherine There are a lot of us. (*Of the photo.*) Is that one of your sons?

Anne That's Art. That's what he looked like when I met him. I took it. He'd just caught his first salmon of the season.

Catherine He's so beautiful.

Anne (*looks at photo*) Yeah . . . he was.

Catherine Can I have it?

Anne Just because I give you a glass of wine doesn't mean you can bare your soul to me. I hate confessions. I can't stand them.

Catherine I would like this photograph. I could get a copy made and return it to you. And since I've lost all my pride asking you, I think you should give it to me.

Anne I don't like to see people without their pride . . . Take it then . . . as a loan.

Catherine Thank you.

She puts it in her bag.

Anne Would you like a cigarette?

Catherine I don't smoke.

Anne Is there anything else you want?

Catherine Your life. I'll just drink this and go.

Anne What is it?

Catherine Oh, you don't want to know.

Anne You came to tell me something.

Catherine Did I?

Anne I thought you were a missionary at the door before I recognised you. You want to convert me to something.

Catherine I had something to say, but it seems appalling now in front of your wholesome decency.

Anne My wholesome decency?

Catherine I don't mean it as an insult, or maybe I do. I don't know any more, but you've read the book on etiquette, you're too civilised for me.

Anne What else is there?

Catherine There's more, believe me, there's more.

Anne Like what?

Catherine No, you're too innocent, too decent, you've it all planned to your grave. I wish I had a grave plan, a scheme that would take me to the end without my noticing. I should congratulate you on the ingenious scaffolding you hang about yourself to evade time, which is really just another name for emptiness. Oh, the emptiness, the emptiness . . . To die of an empty heart must surely be a crime. Here, take this (*photo*) back. I don't know how I could've asked for it.

Anne Keep it. It's nothing.

Catherine It's not nothing. It's your husband.

Anne That's not him, he's as dead to me in that photo as someone from the eleventh century.

Catherine And is he alive for you now? As he is now?

Anne What an odd question.

Catherine He is dreaming about me.

Anne So that's what's wrong with him. That's all. Thank God. I thought he had cancer and wasn't telling me.

Catherine You don't believe in the finer things, do you? The subtle things that quicken the blood and quiver the knee?

Anne Oh, I believe in them, too much to ever mention them. My motto now is: keep the head down, stay out of trouble, hold fast to those you need and who need you.

Catherine I used to be like that too.

Anne I know it's not living on the edge but there isn't room on the edge for everyone. Countries have to be run, children fed, taxes paid, all the stuff the drones take care of while you lost little wisps have your crises. Art belongs here. You can't have him. He is necessary for my life and my children's lives to run smoothly, without event or upset.

Catherine So you decide everything for Art?

Anne Always have. Is it not that way for everyone else?

Catherine No, it's not.

Anne They just don't realise it yet.

Catherine No, there's a percentage – dwindling, yes, but a number nevertheless – who believe in the individual and the individual's rich and varied journey.

Anne The only individuals I know are in mental hospitals or remote rural parts of the country which are really just open asylums. Do you want to end up there? Drugged to the eyeballs, weeping for having crossed the line?

Catherine Is that what you're afraid of?

Anne Crossing the line? To be sure I am. And let me tell you something, Catherine, you can cross as many lines as you want, but I won't let you take Art with you. You'd probably survive. He won't. Just what do you expect? For me to hand him to you on a platter?

Catherine Not quite, but I didn't expect such fierce holding on to someone you no longer love.

Anne Leave love out of it. It's about deals, deals between strangers. There's your definition of love.

She pours wine.

You want another glass?

Catherine No, I'll go. Just one thing. Whatever I am, a blunderer, a fool, I am not heartless. You're the heartless one, talking about yourself and Art like that. You are people, you are here, you will never be again. How can you be so hard on him? How can you be so terrible to yourself?

Anne And Ben?

Catherine Ben is none of your business. This has nothing to do with Ben. This is between Art and me. It was stupid of me to come.

And exit Catherine.

SCENE FOUR

Ben wanders around the room, hands in his pockets. After a while enter Catherine in coat and scarf, handbag.

Catherine Oh, you're up.

Ben You were staying out until I'd gone to bed?

Catherine Something like that . . . yeah.

Ben I decided to sit up all night, wander the rooms like you, see would it throw light on anything.

Catherine We are not an equation to be solved.

Ben One thing has occurred to me, traipsing the house.

Catherine The wisdom of the night.

Ben For some time now I suppose we have passed the point where anything new can happen to us.

Catherine Long passed it.

Ben This city is grey and brown, not the colours of possibility. The odd patch of green in public spaces, usually locked, our garden perhaps, but really there is no refuge from the inevitable, no softening, no buffer any more.

Catherine No, there isn't.

Ben We must rear our young until they can survive without us. And that's it. The life pared back to the essentials. Sooner or later it comes down to this.

Catherine It's not enough.

Ben Is it not?

Catherine You know it isn't.

Ben There's travel.

Catherine I have lost the capacity to walk the pavements of other people's cities. I can't even walk my own any more.

Ben Come here.

Catherine No, you'll only kiss me.

Ben Then I'll come to you.

He does, takes her in his arms.

Catherine Don't kiss me.

He does, a long passionate kiss.

Ben Was that so terrible?

Catherine We've done this a million times, what does it alter? . . . There's nothing wrong with your kisses.

Ben Which means there's nothing right with them . . . 'With this body I thee worship' . . . Remember that?

Catherine I wanted to run down the aisle.

Ben You think I didn't?

Catherine I wish you'd find someone else.

Ben You don't.

Catherine I do. I swear. You need someone who believes in all of this. I need to be alone now with myself. I need to leave while I still love you, before it all turns ugly.

Ben What?

Catherine You heard me.

Ben Just like that?

Catherine Nothing happens just like that. It swells and swells inside until one day you make a decision, probably the wrong one, but just to decide something. Hopefully it will lead on to . . . somewhere else.

Ben To Art?

Catherine No, no . . . Art despises me.

Ben And I should comfort you because Art despises you?

Catherine I was so wrong about Art. I don't know why he is still such a huge presence inside me . . . Maybe he's just a signal, a beacon, not important in himself but a sign that has brought me to a different place . . . Strange that, and I thought he was the great magic thing that has been missing.

Ben And the children?

Catherine Don't mention the children. Please. I've done my time. I'm no good for them any more. You must keep them safe now.

Ben And what will you do?

Catherine I will sit in a chair or stand looking out a window until the end comes. I won't force it but neither will I stop it.

Ben What is happening to you? Why are you talking like this?

Catherine I'm about to take a dive, Ben, a dive down into the dark, the blue, blue dark. I know I won't return, but if I do I will be altered beyond recognition. If you're wise you'll let me remove myself from you and the children, let me just flounder down there.

Ben These dreams of marble that won't stop coming. I've been thinking about them and all I can think of are those marble beds we lie under when we die. Is that what you want? A marble bed? And to be under it, not over, because you won't in this world, and probably not in the next. A marble bed, all its weight fastening you down, glinting dimly under star and moon but mostly dull, weed-strangled, forgotten. Is that what you want, Catherine? Someone who cannot be brought back here? Never to be whole again?

Catherine Do you believe– actually believe – this sojourn here means something?

Ben Yes, I do. If it doesn't, then there is nothing, nothing to hold on to.

Catherine Houses, jobs, children, art galleries, theatres, stadiums, wine bars, trees, mountains, birds . . . For God's sake, who can possibly believe in the fact of a bird?

Ben Yes, I believe in all of those things, Catherine. We are surrounded by mystery, glutted with it, so much so we must deny it all to go on.

Catherine They believed it in Babylon too and there is no trace of them now. I walk this city and all I see is scaffolding, building, building, building, an avalanche of warrens and rat holes to stuff us in, and all I can think of is Troy. And when people ask me for directions in the street, I have to turn away quickly so I don't laugh in their faces. How can they possibly stand there with a map when everything is in such chaotic flux? But they point with their mortal fingers, insisting that such and such a place actually exists to be visited and admired or criticised. Turn left, I say, always left, when what I really want to tell them is, there will be no trace of you or I or that child you hold so lovingly by the hand, a hundred years from now there will be no trace of us, not a whisper, not a puff of ether, we're gone, we were never born.

Ben You're not well, really you're not.

Catherine I'm just talking, Ben, about my life. It's not pretty, but it's mine. This is what is happening to me.

Ben It is not yours. It is mine too. It's the children's. You cannot talk like this in our house. I won't permit it. This guffawing at innocent strangers whose only crime is to ask you directions. It's barbaric, Catherine. It is barbaric.

Catherine Yes, it is. My reptilian brain is on the ascent, and I'm on a descent, a descent away from some marble room that cannot be reached. Why are we given such images, such sublime yearnings for things that are never there? A dream was given to me, inside me from birth, a dream of marble, a woman in a marble room with her lover. And all the waking world can do is thwart it and deny it, and say, no, it cannot be, childish, impossible, you must walk the grey paths with the rest of us, go down into the wet muck at the close. That's your lot. That's what you have to look forward to. Well, I refuse it, Ben, I refuse it. I refuse this grey nightmare with its ridiculous rules and its lack of primary colours. And I despise you for lying down under it, worse, for embracing it, for being so smug, satisfied with so little.

Ben You think I'm satisfied?

Catherine You're not champing at the bit.

Ben If I'm not champing at the bit it's because I know the wilderness is out there, and that we are safe inside seems to me a great miracle. That we are run of the mill, escaping all the terrible things that living can bestow or withhold. Why court tragedy? Why bring it into our nest? Why speak with such disdain against those who love you most?

Catherine Because I need the wilderness now.

Ben You realise what you're saying cannot be unsaid?

Catherine I realise it.

Ben There will be no reconciliation if you walk out that door.

Catherine The price is high . . . ferocious.

Ben What'll I say to the children?

A long pause.

Catherine Whatever you need to.

Ben But where will you go?

Catherine God knows. I might disappear off the face of the earth tonight, that's how insubstantial I feel right now . . . I'm just going to get a few things together. I'll take some money too. Is that all right?

Ben I don't believe this is happening.

Catherine It seems to be . . . I don't want to talk to you any more, or I'll waver. I'll just look at the children and then . . . gone.

And exit Catherine. Ben stands there looking after her.

SCENE FIVE

Enter Art with brandy and cigar. Anne enters, sits reading and sipping wine. Art wanders the space, watching her.

Art Is it good?

Anne Riveting.

Art What's it about?

Anne This woman who is having an affair with her son.

Art Do people still do that?

Anne People do everything.

Art Except us.

Anne It's set in France, exotic, kind of high-class incest. It happens between the croissants and the boeuf bourguignon and the Veuve Clicquot. More palatable, I suppose.

Art You'd marvel at their energy, all that passion. I don't read any more but there was an article in the paper today –

Anne Don't tell me, something about what a happy little nation we are, a woman in a bikini telling us to invest so we'll be happier.

Art No, this was about the nuclear family. It's over.

Anne Of course it is. Too much has to be excluded for it to survive.

Art I suppose.

Anne It's a throwback, like believing in God.

Art Do you believe in God?

Anne No one asks that question any more, apparently.

Art I'm asking it.

Anne I saw a red sofa today.

Art Do we need another sofa?

Anne It's just something to do. Order it. Pay for it. It won't arrive for six months by which time we'll have forgotten about it. I'd like to put it in the hall instead of that table.

Art Then do.

Anne But where will I put the table?

Art You know what, Anne? I don't give a damn where you put the table.

Anne And what do you give a damn about?

Art Right now, another brandy.

Anne You should eat out more. I see far too much of you.

Art I've no one to eat out with.

Anne What's wrong with Ben?

Art Ben is having a breakdown.

Anne Catherine was here today.

Art What was she doing here?

Anne Haven't a clue. She looked fantastic . . . hollowed out, on fire with something. Whatever's wrong with her, it suits her.

Art She has no business here.

Anne Are you afraid of her or something?

Art I hardly know the woman.

Anne Yeah, well, ferocity coming off her in waves, felt helpless in front of her, that she would take my life and trample on it if let. She was admiring your photograph.

Art Was she?

Anne She wanted it.

Art And you said no.

Anne No, I gave it to her.

Art Don't give my photograph to people.

Anne Why not?

Art Just don't. It's dangerous.

Anne What's wrong with you these days?

Art Why don't you have some more wine, a brandy, knock yourself out?

Anne Is that what you're doing?

Art I don't like to be too sober in the evening.

Anne Thank God for that.

Art I wish something would happen to us . . . to me.

Anne Something good?

Art Of course something good. No one seems to know who they are in this house.

Anne That's why I want that sofa.

Art So you can concentrate on the sofa's faults.

Anne It's not even beautiful. I'm sick of it already.
I bought it anyway.

Art Then why ask my opinion?

Anne I want you to believe you are considered in the matter of sofas in your hall.

Art So we can leave all the visitors in the hall?

Anne What visitors?

Art Is it that bad?

Anne We're under siege. Haven't you noticed? My God, you're so dim.

Art Am I?

Anne Say something interesting or I'll have to go to bed. Just write the day off like all the yesterdays and all the tomorrows. Tell me a story.

Art I have no stories.

Anne Make one up.

Art About what? . . . Okay, here's a story for you. Once there was a man, happily married, big house, good-looking wife, healthy children. He made enough not to have to worry.

Anne About sofas.

Art His wife bought five sofas every day. There wasn't room to move with all the sofas. Then one night it struck this man that all these sofas were a trap, a banal trap. His wife sat opposite him on her new sofa. He sat opposite her on his new sofa. We're death sitting opposite one another on designer sofas, the man said.

Anne To himself.

Art Of course to himself. He was a businessman, he didn't deal in metaphors. He didn't read, didn't listen to music, go to the theatre, the opera, he was past all of that and grown coarse with its passing, though in his youth he had loved distraction, more than distraction, to fill himself up with all the good and necessary things. All that was left was fishing. So he went fishing, but the salmon he caught was seeping green and cancerous because the river was over and the ocean was silted up. So he threw the salmon back into the filthy water and never went fishing again. Now what's left, the man wondered as he sank into another new sofa and drank a brandy from another new brandy glass and smoked an ever more expensive cigar. There is nothing left, he said to himself as he watched his good-looking wife read a story about tasteful incest. He went to bed thinking he could die that night and it wouldn't matter. But instead of dying he had a dream. He dreamt he was in a room full of marble and on the marble bed was a beautiful woman, her hair was spun gold, her eyes were a turquoise grey, her throat was smooth and white as the marble pillar she leaned upon. He lay beside her on the gleaming bed, the veins in her arms running like the crystal blue rivers of Eden. How have I come from nothing to this, the man marvelled, from nothing to this awesome soul breathing beside me? She leaned on one marble elbow and ran a finger across his lips. You have come to this place of marble, the woman said, because you have asked. And then he woke.

Anne And then what happened?

Art Then the man got up and left the room, left his sleeping wife, his children, his sofas, his brandy, his expensive cigars, and he went and found the marble woman who lived not far. He went into her marble room and they lay down together and wept. That they should be so happy. That they should cause such suffering to the good-looking wife and the good husband and the healthy children and all the sofas. But even so they vowed to one another that they would stay in the marble room together forever.

Anne So.

Art (*phone, laptop, briefcase, puts on jacket*) Do you know where my overcoat would be?

Anne What do you want an overcoat for in this weather?

Art It'll be winter soon.

Anne It won't work out like that, Art.

Art I have to leave because you won't.

Anne Why should I?

Art You want to be the martyr, the abandoned one.

Anne You're not leaving me for a mere dream of marble. Did you even dream it?

Art I certainly did.

Anne Who is she?

Art I have no idea.

Anne That Catherine.

Art I've hardly spoken three words to her in as many years. But yes, I'm going to ask her to come with me.

Anne You would do that to Ben?

Art I'm beyond loyalty.

Anne To me? To your children?

Art Yes, I would do that.

Anne I should shout and scream, hit you across the face. I can't muster up the wherewithal. Go. Go. Go. You're braver than me. And don't come back. You'll end up under an archway.

Art I may.

Anne The other won't happen.

Art You don't know what'll happen when I walk out that door. Sure as hell nothing happening here.

Anne That at least is true. Go on then. Let me see you walk out that door.

Art Can't we part amicably? This is so predictable.

Anne You must be joking.

Art Right so. Take me to the cleaners. Use the children as weapons.

Anne I aim to.

Art This is our love in a nutshell. This is what it comes down to at the toss of a coin. The great happy marriage.

Anne It surprises you? That it's a fiction? An empty fiction? The dogs on the street know that much. Step out of line and the sky falls in, glance sideways for a second and it's gone. Don't look so hurt. Go. Go on. Go to your brilliant future, your marble fantasy.

Art I will. I'll head in that general direction.

Anne You're a fool.

Art Then let me be foolish.

And exit Art. Anne watches him. And music and fade.
End.